Integrative Counselling and Psychotherapy

Integrative Counselling and Psychotherapy: A Textbook is an engaging and comprehensive guide to integrative counselling, providing an explanation of the theoretical ideas underpinning person-centred, interpersonal, cognitive-behavioural (CBT) and hypnotherapeutic modalities.

Divided into two major sections, this book first provides a detailed exploration of the key integrative concepts – presence, emotional and psychological processing, attachment, thinking, and the unconscious – and then practically applies these concepts to the issues commonly brought by clients to therapy.

With the help of case studies, exercises and chapter questions, *Integrative Counselling and Psychotherapy* will be essential reading for students on integrative counselling and psychotherapy courses and for integrative practitioners.

Basia Spalek is a Visiting Professor in Conflict Transformation at the University of Derby. She is also a BACP accredited counsellor, working within the student counselling services at the University of Leicester, and has her own private practice.

Mark Spalek is a Clinical Hypnotherapist, NLP Practitioner and Brief Solution Focussed Therapist. He is also a Lecturer in Music Technology at Leicester College and De Montfort University.

Integrative Counselling and Psychotherapy

A Textbook

Basia Spalek and Mark Spalek

Routledge
Taylor & Francis Group

LONDON AND NEW YORK

First published 2019
by Routledge
2 Park Square, Milton Park, Abingdon, Oxon OX14 4RN

and by Routledge
52 Vanderbilt Avenue, New York, NY 10017

Routledge is an imprint of the Taylor & Francis Group, an informa business

British Library Cataloguing-in-Publication Data
A catalogue record for this book is available from the British Library

Library of Congress Cataloging-in-Publication Data
Names: Spalek, Basia, author. | Spalek, Mark, author.
Title: Integrative counselling and psychotherapy : a textbook / Basia Spalek
    and Mark Spalek.
Description: 1 Edition. | New York : Routledge, 2019. | Includes
    bibliographical references and index.
Identifiers: LCCN 2019001320 (print) | LCCN 2019005572 (ebook) |
    ISBN 9780203732915 (Master ebook) | ISBN 9781138300972 (hardback : alk. paper)
    | ISBN 9781138301016 (pbk. : alk. paper) | ISBN 9780203732915 (ebk)
Subjects: LCSH: Counseling. | Psychotherapy.
Classification: LCC BF636.6 (ebook) | LCC BF636.6 .S73 2019 (print) |
    DDC 158.3—dc23
LC record available at https://lccn.loc.gov/2019001320

ISBN: 978-1-138-30097-2 (hbk)
ISBN: 978-1-138-30101-6 (pbk)
ISBN: 978-0-203-73291-5 (ebk)

Typeset in Times New Roman
by Apex CoVantage, LLC

Printed and bound by CPI Group (UK) Ltd, Croydon, CR0 4YY

Contents

Biographies

Basia Spalek is a Visiting Professor in Conflict Transformation at the University of Derby. She has conducted internationally renowned research on community-based approaches to countering violent extremism. Basia has also taught Integrative Counselling and Psychotherapy to students studying for a Master's degree in Counselling and Psychotherapy at the University of Derby. Basia is a BACP accredited therapist and works part-time for the University of Leicester Student Counselling Service. Basia also has her own private therapy practice at Connect-and-Reflect.org.uk. Basia supervises Counselling and Psychotherapy trainees and practitioners, and she is currently supervising mental health workers in Trondheim, Norway. Basia also enjoys long distance running, having completed many marathons, and she is now a United Kingdom Athletics running coach.

Mark Spalek is a Clinical Hypnotherapist, NLP Practitioner and Self-Help Publisher with a private practice in Leicester, Positive Suggestions, www.positivesuggestions.co.uk. He specialises in working with fears, anxiety, depression and confidence. Mark is registered with the General Hypnotherapy Register and offers a bespoke audio hypnotherapy service at Positiveblossom.com for international clients. Mark has run relaxation and mindfulness workshops for the local community as well as UK-based charities. He has taught confidence building in Further Education and developed training materials for people wishing to get back into employment. In his spare time Mark enjoys running, cycling and reading.

Linzi Allette, Illustrator, is a full-time parent, illustrator, and is currently in the midst of writing and illustrating her own books based upon Islamic teachings for children, young people and adults. Linzi has had a passion for, and involvement with, illustrating for over 18 years. Illustrating for this book has been a great opportunity and experience for Linzi. The complex world of Integrative Counselling and Psychotherapy is very fascinating to explore. Linzi was able to use Basia and Mark's insightful writing to her advantage whilst illustrating, to aid the reader to gain a visual perspective of Basia and Mark's professional approaches as therapists. In her spare time Linzi enjoys a variety of activities: running, boxing, reading, painting and drawing. Linzi welcomes freelance illustration enquiries, and is contactable at: linzi.a@outlook.com

Introduction

Increasing numbers of people in our society are seeking out personal therapy as a way of alleviating some of their emotional, psychological and even physical pain. Therapy is now widely accepted as a means to enhancing mental health and wellbeing. As a result, many thousands of new mental health practitioners are being trained in counselling skills and in therapeutic practice. But what actually is therapy? Is it about one human being with another? Does it involve an emotional, psychological, even physical and meta-physical journey of some kind? Does therapy involve achieving a heightened state of awareness, enlightenment maybe? Does it involve examining the past in order to be able to live better in the present? Does therapy involve practitioners in listening, providing empathy, reflecting back to clients? Is it about connection and relationship? Therapy involves elements of all of these things, and more. Given the profound and complex nature of therapy, what then is integrative therapeutic practice? How does the integration of different therapeutic modalities like cognitive-behavioural, person-centred and relational, enhance effective practice?

We have been motivated to write *Integrative Counselling and Psychotherapy: A Textbook* in order to explore and articulate as clearly as we can our own understanding of integrative therapeutic practice, in order for students who are on counselling courses to be able to learn and understand better what integration involves. We draw upon person-centred, cognitive-behavioural, relational and hypnotherapeutic modalities and integrate these through the presentation of five key integrative concepts: presence, emotional processing, attachment, thinking and the conscious/unconscious. Each of these concepts are explained at length in Chapters 1 to 5 of this book. We then focus the second half of *Integrative Counselling and Psychotherapy: A Textbook* (Chapters 6 to 10) on working integratively with grief and loss, anxiety, depression, relationships, and guilt and shame, which are key issues that clients often bring to therapy.

Each chapter in *Integrative Counselling and Psychotherapy: A Textbook* has many different therapeutic tools that students and other readers can use with their clients and also with themselves. We know that these therapeutic interventions can be effective because we find that they work with the clients that we see. We also present many case studies based on real life clients as a way of illustrating integrative practice, and we provide questions for mental health students and practitioners, which can be used for group work or for individual study.

We have striven to create a book that is engaging to read, and so we have written a number of short stories within each chapter as a way of explaining key ideas and issues. We are keen to convey the creative process that therapy involves, and so what better way to do this than to be creative ourselves when writing this book? We have also included in the chapters considerable space for self-reflection because key to being an excellent mental health practitioner is self-awareness. Both of us have been on significant personal journeys ourselves and so we have brought our own unique histories and experiences when writing this book. We hope that students and other readers have as much pleasure reading the book as we had when writing it. One final thought: we hope that in reading this book you are inspired to be a creative practitioner, for this is really what therapy means to us – being creative with another human being in order to help facilitate kindness, compassion, joy, tolerance and other positive aspects to being human. Enjoy!

Chapter 1

Presence for mental health and wellbeing

An integrative approach

> All of humanity's problems stem from man's inability to sit quietly in a room alone.
>
> Blaise Pascal, *Pensées* (1662)

Introduction

We begin this book by journeying into and exploring presence. The notion of presence comes from a book by Patsy Rodenburg (2007). Her argument is that we each inhabit what might be called three 'circles of energy'. Circle one is primarily withdrawn, like a headache feeling or intense lethargy/shyness, circle three is an uncontrolled release of wild energy, like Friday night drinkers or party dancers, and circle two is a centred 'two way street' of giving out and taking in – an alert cat, or political interviewer, carefully taking in the responses and returning with a balanced challenge – which could also be describing advanced tennis players, Formula One drivers, surgeons etc. Presence is about becoming more balanced and inhabiting each moment; and in relation to Rodenburg's (2007) three circle metaphor, it is about inhabiting energy circle two.

The focus on presence in Chapter 1 demonstrates the centrality of this notion when working therapeutically with our clients, and when considering our own wellbeing as mental health practitioners. It is important to be able to cultivate within ourselves a connection to the present, to the timelessness of each and every moment, and a proactive stance upon the world, and to work with our clients to help them understand and cultivate their own unique experiencing of presence. In today's society there seems to be a constant fragmentation of who we really are, a constant pressure to achieve, a fast pattern of change, a restlessness and lack of focus. It is important to understand these societal stressors and the challenges that they pose for presence, in order to be able to empower ourselves and to effectively work with clients.

In this chapter we introduce you to presence as an integrative concept that can help to capture many different techniques that work within and across different psychotherapeutic modalities. We argue that presence is a useful way of thinking about and drawing together relaxation techniques, breathing techniques, mindfulness, body posture, grounding techniques, and pacing and leading. In this chapter we aim to introduce you to the techniques that we have found useful when working integratively with clients and we suggest exercises to practise these techniques, on ourselves, in groups, and in clinical supervision. We offer suggestions for how these techniques can be applied to clients, drawing on our own clinical experiences. There is also a theory section that links the notion of presence to theoretical concepts endemic to cognitive-behavioural therapies (CBT), person-centred (PC), interpersonal and hypnothera-peutic modalities. These are the modalities that we as practitioners integrate.

Firstly, in this chapter we provide a short summary of contemporary societal dynamics and how these can work against presence. We believe it is important for counselling students and mental health practitioners to know something about the societal pressures that surround our lives because these can overwhelm us. Developing an understanding of the wider social context to our clients' lives is, we believe, critical to working effectively with them. We then discuss presence as an integrative concept and show you techniques that can help you and your clients to experience this, through practising and drawing upon relaxation techniques, breathing techniques, mindfulness, body posture, grounding techniques, and pacing and leading. Finally, we explore presence theoretically.

Society as an attention deficit and hyperactively disordered entity

Inattentiveness, impulsivity and hyperactivity are symptoms that are typically associated with individuals who have been diagnosed as having Attention Deficit and Hyperactive Disorder (ADHD). These symptoms can also be linked to a wider social malaise that has infected our societies. Many of us are constantly under pressure, and this pressure begins early. As therapists working predominantly with adults and young people we are often struck by how much pressure people feel that they are under. This pressure can be in the form of work and academic goals, employment and life goals. A pressure to 'succeed' in life!

Many books have been written about the challenges of our society over constant change, social comparison, isolation, work stress, technological advancements that have increased the pace of our lives, the insecurities of modern life and so forth. Added to this is the increasing capture of our attention by global corporations, disempowering us from simply being with ourselves, day-dreaming, meandering along life's pathways (Crawford, 2016). Perhaps it is unsurprising that mental health issues have reached epidemic proportions in our modern societies. Perhaps we can think about presence as being an important and powerful antidote against depression, anxiety, stress, hyperactivity, and other challenges to our mental health.

We now consider key techniques for developing presence, for ourselves as therapists and mental health practitioners and for our clients. In practising the techniques as discussed below we can experience ourselves as empowered human beings, letting go of past experiences, of any future anxieties and fears, awakening us to embracing the here and now, experiencing the timelessness of each and every moment.

Breathing and presence

A tale of two Jacks

Imagine this scenario: footballer Jack is playing in the biggest game of his life in front of ninety thousand screaming fans. His team are trailing one goal to nil and there are ten seconds left on the clock. Jack's team throw caution to the wind and launch the ball towards the opposing goal where three of their strikers wait in anticipation. As luck would have it the ball reaches one of Jack's players, a tall rangy centre forward who forces his way into the penalty box only to be fouled by a defender from the opposing team [by the opposition]. The stadium erupts into a cry of 'Penalty' and the referee blows his whistle and points to the spot. Jack is the penalty taker.

Suddenly he feels a wave of anxiety wash through him. The cries from the crowd become overwhelming. His breathing is rapid and when he places the ball on the penalty spot his heart is practically breaking out of his rib cage. Jack's legs feel like jelly as he takes a few steps back. His breathing is short and sharp and no air seems to be going in. The referee whistles for Jack to take the penalty, making him start. He must score otherwise there will be no extra time and

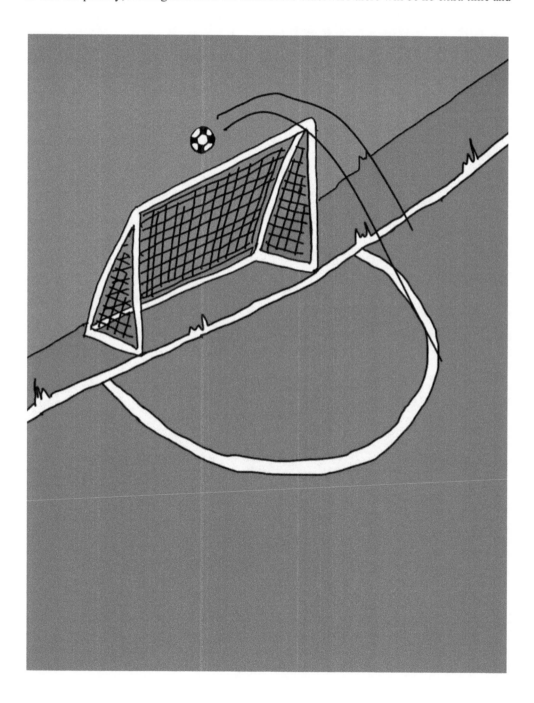

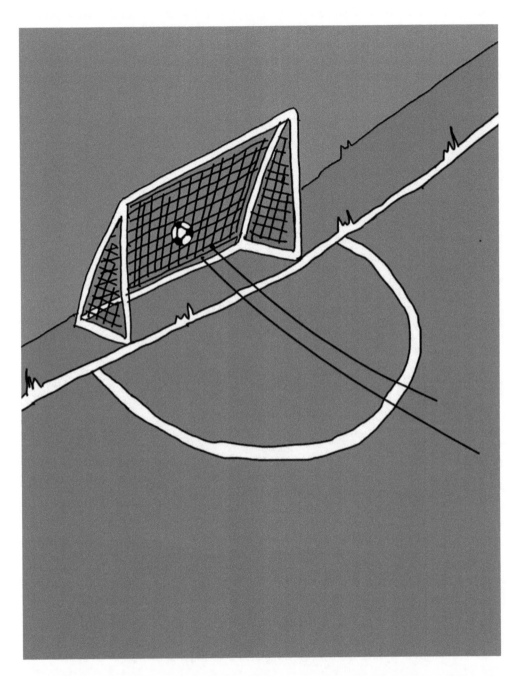

his team will be out of the cup. Jack takes a few tentative steps towards the ball and kicks the ball but it seems that his foot is not part of his body and he has no control over it. The ball soars high above the goal and Jack sinks to his knees in distress. His team have lost.

Now imagine a different Jack. A version of Jack that has practised slow deep breathing as a relaxation technique and can utilise relaxed breathing in stressful situations. A version of Jack that uses breathing techniques that allow him to 'step outside of himself' in situations that are stressful and to empty his thoughts. When the referee blows for the penalty this version of Jack automatically starts to take long slow deep breaths, using his diaphragm to allow the air to flow into his lungs. As he does this, instead of being sucked into the maelstrom of excitement and emotions unleashed around him, he remains focussed, placing the ball on the penalty spot as he mentally rehearses which part of the goal he will aim at. As he takes a few steps back, Jack steadies himself, once more focussing on slow long deep breaths. His breathing is relaxed, his heart beats steadily, he feels in control. He feels relaxed, a direct result of the endorphins that are being produced by the brain because of deep breathing (Loehr & Migdow, 2000). He is in the moment and everything that happens now is fluid, without exertion. He runs towards the ball and strokes it into the top corner of the goal and his team are back in the game!

Through the use of diaphragmatic breathing Jack has remained calm and relaxed, allowing him to focus in on the moment – the situation – as opposed to becoming overwhelmed by it. Here is an example of utilising controlled breathing techniques in order to remain fully present and in the moment. You may wonder whether this breathing technique is outside of our scope or ability but diaphragmatic breathing, or abdominal breathing as it is often referred to, is a natural instinct within us, and very apparent in babies and infants.

As we get older the slow deep natural rhythm of diaphragmatic breathing is usually replaced with rapid shallow chest breathing. For example, if you were to join the army your sergeant major would encourage a military posture based upon standing with your chest out and stomach in, something that most of us get told to do at some point in our lives (Alman & Lambrou, 2012); this type of posture does little to promote deep abdominal breathing. Instead it gets us used to constricting our breath, losing our natural breathing mechanism and this ultimately leads to a loss of presence. After all, how we breathe in and out manifests in how we make sense of the world: our reaction to situations and events, the rich interplay of thoughts, emotions and feelings that encompasses even the simplest conversation, the concept of our very selves and how we appear to others.

How natural breathing gives you presence as a therapist

Jane has a problem with her throat. Since picking up a heavy cold several months ago, she has cleared her throat constantly and it has become a habit, something that she does without conscious thought hundreds of times a day. The habit makes Jane feel self-conscious and embarrassed and it has become so debilitating that she has begun to avoid social situations, forsaking evenings at the theatre for sitting at home on her own. Jane has decided that enough is enough and has booked a consultation with you. As Jane explains her problem in detail you notice that her anxiety increases, she leans forward and her voice rises in pitch, her breathing starts to become rapid and shallow and her throat clearing gets worse. Part of you recognises the importance of building rapport with Jane, of matching her patterns of breathing and posture with your own breathing and posture, so that they align more closely to her reality experience. Yet, another part of you acknowledges that Jane is desperate, that above all else, she wants to get rid of this annoying habit.

Jane wants results and you recognise this. So instead of matching her breathing, you focus on a natural relaxed breath that keeps you firmly grounded and focussed on Jane's every word. Unconsciously Jane may begin to recognise that you are a centred being, that you have a certain presence about you, a calmness, an indefinable energy or aura that suggests you have the skills Jane is looking for. Jane begins to relax and to build her trust. Even though Jane's emotions and feelings may fluctuate throughout the consultation you remain calm and relaxed. There will be opportunities in later sessions where matching Jane's breathing may be beneficial but in this situation it may be more pertinent to unconsciously give out the message: 'I can help you with this'.

How natural breathing can help your client

The sage Patanjali, who developed the oldest text on meditation that we have – the Yoga Sutras – recognised the importance of *pranayama*, the conscious awareness and spiritual emphasis of disciplined breathing. He identified the connection between breathing and mental states: rapid constricted breathing leading to mental illusion as opposed to relaxed natural breathing which promotes clarity and focus (Keen, 1997). Exercises that develop natural breathing can provide a mechanism for a client to experience herself, or particular situations and events, differently. Often we become so wrapped up in a problem that it becomes our world, an internal and external movie where the stage, set, characters, dialogue and scenes evolve around our issues. As a therapist, disrupting the various stages, sets, characters, dialogues and scenes, or introducing new characters, new dialogue and scenes within a client's experience provides a way of breaking up a problem or issue. A good starting point for problem disruption is to empower the client with breathing techniques.

Integrating breathing techniques in sessions is highly recommended. Through getting a client to practise slow deep breathing, a sense of control and focus on something other than, for example, obsessive thoughts or fears, can be fostered. In this way, the client can gradually discover that she can relax and experience herself differently. In a metaphoric sense this can be like shining a light on a painting for the very first time and illuminating all the colours. Taking a step back and assessing a situation or problem or feeling or emotion when calm and relaxed may spotlight a solution, a way out of a predicament, a different scene. Think about a chess grandmaster surveying the whole board as opposed to solely focussing on a single piece. This 'out of self into self' process has at its foundation a relaxed deep breath. We learn to see the wood for the trees by focussing internally. Relaxed breathing is the clients' new vantage point, a place of rest that she can look down from and get a sense of what is really going on in her life.

Recognising the relationship between breathing and internal and external states

Before you begin to recognise and make sense of breathing in others, a good starting point is to get a sense of your own breathing patterns and habits.

Consider the following questions:

When is your breathing rapid and shallow?
When is your breathing deep and relaxed?
Are there situations or events where you find it difficult to breathe?
Does the presence of some people affect the way that you breathe? If so, how do these people affect your breathing?
Which parts of your body move when you breathe?
How often do you notice your breathing during the day?
What is your breathing like when you are angry?

What is your breathing like when you are sad?
What is your breathing like when you are happy?

If you have a good awareness of your breath then you can answer most of the above questions. To develop a better awareness of how you breathe, check your breathing patterns over the next week in relation to the above questions and note down your observations. This exercise will help you discover how your breathing reflects your internal state and the external factors around you.

Notice but don't look

Recognizing how internal and external states affect our own breathing can provide us with a greater understanding of what is going on in a client's worldview, their experience of a problem or issue, whether they accept a suggestion that we have made or not. For example, when describing something traumatic, a client's breathing may become rapid and shallow. When a client is upset or very emotional she may find it difficult to breathe. You notice her breathing not by directly looking at the chest, which is inappropriate, but through peripheral observation of the subtle movements of her clothing, shoulders and abdomen (Battino, 2005). Breathing patterns form part of the client's body language and reading body language well is one of the key skills of an effective therapist.

As a therapist you may make a suggestion to the client that could potentially lead to a problem or conflict being solved or changed in a positive way. A large part of the job is to make suggestions, offer guidance and to provide support for your client as they bring these suggestions and guidance to fruition.

In many ways, this is similar to a salesman making a suggestion to a potential customer that will steer them towards purchasing a car that is more fuel efficient or perhaps safer than their current model. Successful salespeople are exceptionally good at reading the subtle nuances of body language. They will recognise situations where they need to pull back and ease off on the hard sell and situations where they can go full on to effect a sale.

At the surface level, the client may seem to accept your suggestion through her positive vocal response. Yet the way her clothes and shoulders start to move sharply, the way her abdomen starts to rise and fall quickly, suggests rapid breathing. Her breathing seems out of kilter with what she is saying which may indicate anxiety or internal conflict. It may also mean that she is excited about the prospect of trying out your suggestion so take care not to plunge in too quickly and change your course of action. Sometimes a planted seed for an idea or concept may take a while to 'bed in', so rushing with a different idea or reframe should be avoided.

However, if you feel that there is anxiety or internal conflict, then your response, just like the salesman, could be to hold back on the previous suggestion, and try a different tack instead. Always be aware and fully present in each moment with a client. Attention is your best friend. Presence provides this for you.

Finding your natural breath

Imagine breathing in some air as though it's the most natural thing you have ever done. It is, but most of us have forgotten how to do it! Imagine the in breath flowing into you, perfectly fluid and free, and as you do this, think about all the elements of your existence that this inbreath can represent. Think about the situation that you are in, what things you are thinking about in that situation, what responses or moves you want to make, how you appear to someone else, the emotions and feelings that you wish to convey. A natural inbreath gives you focus and control and freedom to be you in all experiences.

The inbreath is half of the journey towards building a solid presence. Now imagine breathing out, imagine a column of air that builds deep from within your abdomen and journeys from the lungs into your windpipe and your voice box before being released through your mouth. As you imagine this, get a sense of the energy that goes into a moment of your experience: your response, movements, actions, words and feelings. Natural unhurried calm breathing allows you to take a step back and assess a situation. It provides you with space to explore your thoughts, emotions and feelings so that you can make incisive decisions and react in a centred, calm manner.

The process of diaphragmatic (abdominal) breathing

Diaphragmatic breathing is common in babies and infants and if you were to observe this process in action then you would notice that as the baby takes in a breath so its abdomen rises gently. During exhalation, when the breath is released, it falls back to its resting position. Let us explore the process practically.

Practising diaphragmatic breathing

1   Find a safe, quiet place and sit or lie down.
2   Place your hands, palms downwards, onto your stomach just below the rib cage.
3   Breathe in slowly through the nostrils for a count of **three** and as you do, focus on inflating your stomach like a balloon. This may not be easy to begin with but, as you focus on your stomach, it will eventually start to rise with each inbreath.
4   As you breathe in, allow your chest and shoulders to remain as still and relaxed as possible. The focus is on maximum utilisation of the diaphragm in order to affect the inbreath (and outbreath), so it should be doing all the work as you relax into each breath.
5   Breathe out slowly for a count of **four**, preferably through the mouth, and allow your stomach to fall and return to its original position. You can feel the rise and fall of your abdomen with each inbreath and outbreath with your hands.
6   Repeat steps 1–5 for a period of two minutes and gradually increase this to ten minutes. Repeat as often as you wish during the day and night.

Diaphragmatic breathing with progressive muscle relaxation

This technique utilises a combination of diaphragmatic breathing and progressive muscle relaxation and is useful in situations when a client may find it difficult to relax. When someone is in a relaxed, focussed state – a present state – they are more likely to accept suggestions that promote positive change. Practising this technique on a daily basis will allow you to relax and ground yourself as a therapist.

1   Find a safe, quiet place and sit or lie down. Sitting is better for this exercise.
2   Focus on abdominal breathing: in for a count of three and out for a count of four. Feel your stomach rise with the in breath and fall with the out breath, releasing that old stale air. Spend a minute just breathing in silence.

3   Now gently contract your muscles with each inbreath and relax your muscles with each outbreath. Start by squeezing your hands into fists as you breathe in for three, relaxing your hands as you breathe out for four. Repeat this three times. Next contract your arms by bringing your hands up to your shoulders as you breathe in for three. As you breathe out, relax your arms by placing your hands onto your thighs. Repeat three times.

4   Go through the rest of your body in this way: lift your shoulders gently to your neck with the inbreath and relax with the outbreath. Contract your chest muscles with the inbreath, relax the chest with the outbreath. Move onto the stomach and do the same. Contract the muscles in your legs by pressing down gently on the floor with the soles of your feet until you feel the muscles in your thighs contract. Relax the legs with the outbreath. Scrunch your toes in with the inbreath, relax with the outbreath. Finally, gently scrunch up your face (eyes, nose and mouth) with the inbreath and release with the outbreath. Remember to repeat three times before moving on to the next part of your body.

5   Finish by focussing on your breathing and noticing any pleasant feelings or sensations.

Mindfulness in presence

The above breathing exercises are the first steps on the path to mindfulness or true presence, where we observe or experience our thoughts, feelings and emotions without attaching to them. Mindfulness allows us to let go of judgmental thoughts; it is a state of being where we are aware of our thoughts and feelings and accept these thoughts and feelings without agreeing with or liking them (Forsyth & Eifert, 2008). This non-judgmental awareness, one of the true essences of Buddhism, is an important component in psychotherapy and psychology in the Western world, from psychoanalytic models developed by Freud through to Gestalt humanistic approaches created by Carl Rogers (Kornfield, 2008).

Mindfulness is key to developing presence. Within the therapeutic relationship, mindfulness enables us as therapists to note and empathise with a client's thoughts and feelings without becoming absorbed by them, giving us enough distance to be able to work effectively with our clients. Mindfulness also helps us as therapists to note the things that a client might be saying that are triggering thoughts and emotions inside ourselves, to be able to put them to one side to explore later in clinical supervision, to then be able to focus our attention back on the client. Practising mindfulness for clients can mean that they begin to sense some distance between themselves and their thoughts and feelings, and to begin to feel that they have some control over these, that they do not necessarily need to respond to their thoughts and emotions but rather to note them and their transitory nature.

The case of Jade

Jade was a 40-year-old mother of three, who began coming for therapy as a result of high anxiety. She could not stop worrying about her children, the relationships that she had with their fathers, and criticised herself constantly for being a 'bad mother'. This anxiety led Jade to drink a bottle of wine each night; she also found it hard to sit and relax and was constantly doing something – the housework, mowing the lawn, doing the washing up and so on.

Mindfulness is something that Jade worked at inside and outside of her therapy sessions. Jade kept a diary of events that triggered in her worrying thoughts and she also made a note of how she felt at the time and how she responded. This enabled Jade to get a better sense of the events that trigger in her anxious sensations and the thoughts that accompanied her anxiety. Jade was also encouraged to sit with uncomfortable thoughts and feelings, to notice when these were happening for her and to imagine her distressing thoughts lifting up into the blue sky above like a balloon. In this way Jade was learning not to fight her thoughts and emotions, but rather to make a note of them and to start to stand back from these and to notice that they were fleeting – even if and when her distress could last a long time. Jade was also taught some relaxation and breathing techniques, which she began to incorporate into her daily life. Over time and with practice, Jade found it useful to notice her thoughts and feelings and to sit with these, and she found that by not fighting her thinking and feelings she was beginning to feel less distressed, less anxious. Whereas previously Jade's coping strategies were drinking wine and keeping busy, Jade found that she was no longer needing to drink as much wine and that she was able to sit and find activities that relaxed her rather than rushing around the whole time. For example, Jade found that eating a piece of toast and having a cup of tea helped to ground her, helped her focus on the here and now rather than getting absorbed by her anxious thoughts. Jade found that her relationships with her children improved and she was able to enjoy spending time with them, playing games rather than ruminating over any housework she previously would have felt that she had to do.

Mindfulness is not attaining a Zen-like state

The key to practising mindfulness is to let go of placing any pressure on yourself. Thoughts and feelings can bombard us, and that is okay. We don't need to criticise ourselves for not reaching a 'Zen-like' state, that is not what the practice of mindfulness is about. Rather, mindfulness consists of acceptance, accepting that as humans we can have many thoughts, some silly, some sinister, some embarrassing. Thoughts are not important, what is important is how we respond to these thoughts, how we behave. Mindfulness encourages us to turn towards our thoughts and our feelings and to embrace them, to calmly notice them and to explore behaviours that we can adopt that we find helpful in grounding ourselves. We are not necessarily seeking inner wisdom or any personal epiphanies, rather, we are just quietly observing ourselves and developing helpful ways of coping. It is okay if some days we find mindfulness easier than other days, if on some occasions we lapse into some of our old, unhelpful, habits.

Mindfulness in thoughts

Imagine that you are a cloud gazer staring up into the skies. You notice the clouds floating on a distant horizon, their different shapes and textures, colours and forms. As you watch the clouds, you notice that no cloud ever stays in the same place, that clouds constantly move and shift. You begin to realise that clouds are just clouds, you cannot touch them (not unless you are 15,000 feet up on Mount Kenya!). All you can do is observe. And as your eyes follow the clouds, eventually the clouds disappear and a bright sun lights up a wonderful blue sky.

The process of mindfulness allows us to experience our thoughts as if they were clouds. We can label our thoughts, for example, 'good thought', 'bad thought', 'positive thought' in the same way that we can label clouds 'Cirrus' and 'Cumulus'. In a state of mindfulness we have a choice: we can attach to our thoughts or we can say hello to them and let them go. We can allow our thoughts – good or bad – to float past with non-attachment. This non-judgmental essence is a very powerful state: it builds our presence, enhances our concentration and makes us better able to listen, counsel, advise, empathise, suggest. More importantly: we are better able to listen, counsel, advise, empathise and suggest, whether we are having a good day or a bad day.

The cloud gazer meditation for relaxation in clients

The cloud metaphor can be utilised with clients who find it difficult to let go of things, for example, anger or frustration towards a work colleague or spouse or situation. It can be a panacea for intrusive damaging thoughts and forms a conduit for eliciting relaxation and calmness. Reducing tension can enhance a client's motivation for healing, while relaxation can be a crucial element of the communication process (King, Novik & Citrenbaum, 1983). A relaxed client is more likely to follow suggestions and complete tasks. When this metaphor is coupled with progressive muscle relaxation, an unconscious message can be planted within the client: I can control my muscles so I can control other things in my life. I can experience my thoughts without reacting to them.

Exercise

Ensuring your client is seated in a comfortable position, go through the exercise 'Diaphragmatic breathing with progressive muscle relaxation'. You can perform this exercise along with your client in order to build rapport.

When the client is comfortably relaxed (notice a relaxed breathing state, relaxed facial muscles, even a faint smile at the corners of the mouth), take them through the cloud-gazing metaphor. A sample script could be as follows:

> 'That's it . . . and now I'd like you to imagine that you're gazing up at the sky . . . watching the clouds float past on a distant horizon . . . notice how the clouds never stay in the same place at any one time . . . notice how they constantly shift and move . . . and as you notice this so you can begin to notice your own thoughts . . . and any thought that pops up in your mind you can begin to label . . . 'good thought' . . . 'bad thought' . . . 'positive thought' . . . and once you have labelled a thought you can let that thought go . . . imagine that thought floating up towards the clouds . . . imagine that thought being absorbed by a cloud . . . and notice that in the same way that you cannot attach to any cloud so you cannot attach to that thought any more . . . you have let it go . . . notice how calm and relaxed you feel . . . just letting all your thoughts go . . . one by one . . . into the clouds . . . and imagine all those clouds floating past . . . imagine all the clouds floating past leaving a blue sky and bright shining sun . . . enjoy the peaceful relaxing warmth of the sun as you focus on your breathing. . . .'

Alter the above meditation as you wish and adapt to include phrases that are congruent with your client. For example, a 'feeling' person may respond better to phrases such as '*feel* the weight of each thought lift from you as you let it go'. An 'artistic' person may wish to explore the colour of the clouds in greater detail than a person who lacks imagination, in which case you can use phrases such as: 'Notice how the colour of the clouds change with every thought that they absorb.'

Practising mindfulness

There are many ways in which we can engage with mindfulness. It is good to practise some of these techniques for ourselves as therapists because not only does this give us a better sense of what we are asking our clients to do, but also instilling mindfulness within ourselves helps us experience presence, which, we have argued, is a key integrative therapeutic concept.

Walking mindfully

Imagine a cat slowly, purposefully, treading through long damp grass. This particular cat, a grey bushy-tailed cat, doesn't enjoy getting his paws wet. He therefore looks to place each paw on the driest parts of the lawn. How does he do this? By walking mindfully. Slowly he picks up his front left paw and places it gently onto a patch of grass and at the moment of connection with the grass, this cat decides whether to fully put his paw down or whether to withdraw his paw and find a slightly drier spot. Whilst doing this, his whiskers are touching the high blades of grass surrounding him, giving him more sense of where the wet patches are. Upon committing himself with his left paw to a patch of grass that is acceptable to him, this cat moves his body slightly forward and to the left, with the rhythm of his front step. The cat then picks up his right paw and begins the process all over again.

In the above scenario the cat is walking slowly and is focussing his full attention on what is immediately around him. He doesn't hurry any steps and takes his time to figure out the best route to take. We can try ourselves to walk mindfully by copying this cat's way of negotiating his space. Practise the following:

> Find a safe space where you would like to walk mindfully.
> Focus your attention on the ground below. Notice the surface and any obstructions you may need to navigate.
> Then look up ahead of you and focus your attention on anything you see.
> Then take note of anything you hear or smell in your safe space.
> Pick up your left foot and place it slowly down on the ground in front of you. Notice what you feel through the soles of your shoes or through your socks or even bare-footed if the ground that you are walking on is soft and without obstacles. Notice any thoughts that you have; don't fight them, just notice them.
> Pick up your right foot and place it slowly on the ground in front of you. Again, notice what you feel through the soles of your shoes or through your socks or even underneath bare feet. Notice any thoughts that you have; don't fight them, just notice them.
> Do this exercise for five minutes. Notice how you feel at the end. Do you think that there might be opportunities to try this activity in your daily life, at home or even at work? What might be the obstacles preventing you from practising mindful walking? Note these down and think about how you might be able to set these obstacles aside.

Setting the table for dinner or lunch mindfully

Here is another exercise in the practice of mindfulness:

> When setting the table for a meal, slowly pick up one fork at a time and slowly place it down on the table. As you touch the fork, notice how this feels in your hands, note the

appearance of the fork, its colour, the materials it has been made from, think about the process involved in making this fork and the number of people potentially involved – from those quarrying the materials out of the ground, to those individuals involved in the production and packaging processes. Consider how heavy or light the fork feels in your hand. Repeat this exercise with any knives, spoons or plates that you may be using. Take your time and notice your breathing. Note any thoughts that automatically arise in your mind. Do not criticise yourself for these thoughts, rather, notice them and picture them rising above you into the expansive sky. Then when you come to eat your meal notice whether, how, and in what ways you feel different about the food that you are eating. If you like, you can practise mindfulness as you eat, as will be explained below.

Eating mindfully

Take a look at the food that you are about to eat. Notice how it looks, think about the processes and people involved in getting this food to you – the farmers, farm pickers, factory workers, market traders, shopkeepers, delivery staff. Slowly pick up the item of food, with your hand or a utensil, and place it into your mouth. Notice how this piece of food feels on your tongue, how heavy or light it is, note the flavour that comes through – sweet, salty, spicy. Chew slowly, there is no hurry to swallow. Then when you feel that you have chewed this item of food enough, swallow it. Notice how you feel after you have swallowed the piece of food. Note any thoughts that come into your mind; do not hold onto these thoughts but try to see yourself stepping outside of your thoughts as your thoughts come and go. Again do not criticise yourself for any thoughts that you may have; the important thing is to notice without judgment, without attaching to any specific thought that may arise.

Mindfulness can help to slow our minds and our bodies down. It can help us to become more aware of the myriad of thoughts that we have each day, and moreover, can enable us to distance ourselves from our thoughts – thoughts as fluid, as not defining who we are. By practising mindfulness as therapists we can find it easier to focus on the present, and not be consumed by our own thinking patterns and internal struggles. Mindfulness can help clients who are experiencing wide-ranging challenges: anxiety, depression, eating disorders, anger, addiction and so on. Often clients can be stuck in their thinking patterns, which can generate uncomfortable emotions in them, thereby perpetuating their psychological and emotional distress. By practising mindfulness, clients can come to experience how it is that thoughts come and go, and how it is possible to slow things down for themselves. Clients can suggest activities that they would like to carry out mindfully – the above are just examples. Thus, some clients might like to try stroking their animal companion mindfully, others might want to empty a dishwasher mindfully. The type of activity doesn't matter, what is important is that it is meaningful to the client, and some clients will suggest their own activities, whilst others will take prompts from the therapist. By being present as a therapist, this allows us to remain open to a client – whether they want to practise their own suggested activity mindfully or whether they would like to practise an activity that the therapist suggests, or both.

Listening and presence for the therapist

Listening with full attention to someone who is pouring their heart out, or is communicating an in-depth account of their difficulties, forms the foundation of effective therapy. Yet unless you are a musician or a music producer, this is a skill that is rarely taught. The following exercise helps you focus and improve your listening skills with clients:

A listening exercise

1   Watch a TV programme where there are two presenters, for example, newsreaders or chat show hosts, actors or sports commentators. It can be any programme as long as there is more than one person on the screen.
2   Focussing on **only one** of the presenters/hosts/actors/commentators, try to listen to every word that they say to the exclusion of the other person. Notice the pitch of their voice, their tone. Does the voice change at any point – does it become louder or softer? Do they pronounce certain words in a characteristic way? Does their tone change?
3   Once that person stops talking, focus all your attention on your breathing: the inbreath, the outbreath. As you focus on your breathing, detach your attention from the other person or people who are talking.
4   When your chosen person starts to talk again, once more focus all your attention on their voice. Notice as much about their voice as possible (pitch/tone/emotion). When the person stops talking, once more shift your focus towards your breath.
5   Repeat steps 2–5 for five minutes.

As you practise the above exercise regularly, you will begin to notice a gradual improvement in your listening skills. You can also try this exercise with radio shows too for variety or if you don't watch TV.

Posture and presence

Janet is a new client who has a problem dealing with her husband's infidelity. During her consultation with Tim she crosses her legs, leans forward and holds her hands out when talking about her husband. Tim, on the other hand, sits in a laidback pose with his arms folded across his chest and his legs splayed out. His movements and posture do not fit into Janet's world. Janet starts to feel self-conscious although she doesn't know where the source of this feeling stems from. Tim would be better off leaning forward slightly and crossing his legs in a subtle manner to more closely match Janet's actions.

Consciously matching or pacing certain elements of a client's posture, her movements, certain vocal nuances and breathing can allow a therapist to become more present in the client's world which makes it easier to lead clients out of emotional and physical states. Matching behaviours is a natural occurrence in humans. If someone speaks to you in an animated fashion then you will usually reply animatedly. We often match our footsteps with the person walking with us so that we both have similar rhythms and strides. If you lean against a garden fence while chatting to your neighbour then the chances are he will do the same. Subtle matching of behaviours is recommended so that it does not become obvious that you are changing your posture or voice in a way that may be perceived as insulting. For example, if a client shouts when they speak, then raising the volume of your voice slightly is all that is needed. You do not need to cross your legs as soon as your client does; wait a few seconds and then cross your legs. Timing is what makes matching truly effective: as the musician Tommy Shaw once said, 'Timing is everything.' Avoid copying regional accents or dialects. The key to effective matching in pacing is to execute it in such a way that the client is not consciously aware of what you are doing but registers the changes to posture, vocal nuances and breathing unconsciously.

A matching exercise

The following exercise can be practised with two or three people, where person A is the client, person B the therapist and C the observer who will provide feedback with regards to the quality of matching.

Scenario: Information gathering during consultation

1   Client A and Therapist B sit opposite each other in chairs. Observer C sits some distance away and between A and B.
2   Client A will start proceedings off by saying something simple such as 'I'm Jane and I suffer from anxiety.' She will imagine herself as anxious and act out her posture, breathing and vocals to reflect this.
2   Therapist B will ask questions, matching A's posture, breathing and vocal nuances.
3   The discussion will continue and as A changes her physical, breathing and vocal states so B matches these changes.
4   At the end, C can provide useful feedback to B regarding the quality of matching. If there are only two of you then Client A can provide feedback.

Grounding techniques are another key aspect to achieving presence, as will be discussed below.

Grounding techniques as a fundamental tool for presence

Grounding techniques are a key therapeutic tool and can be used for wide-ranging clients with a myriad of different issues and complexities. In order to get a better sense of what a grounding technique is, think about a time in your life when you felt extremely nervous – before a driving test, or exam, speaking publicly, or before going to the dentist, for example. It is likely that you would have had a fast beating heart, your breathing would have been quicker and more shallow, you might have sweated more than you normally do, and you might even have noticed yourself shaking or trembling. In this situation you are likely to have struggled to find focus and calm, your thoughts might have been racing, and you might yourself have felt like running away or vomiting or you might have felt that what was happening around you was nor real, that somehow you were disconnected from your experience and surroundings.

Clients may come to you and talk about how they feel disconnected from their surroundings, how anxious or cut off from the real world they feel. Clients may also tell you about how difficult it is for them to go to places and be with people, how they can become emotionally distressed by events or the thought of certain events. Clients can also experience flashbacks of traumatic events, substance cravings, uncontrollable self-criticism, a craving to self-harm. Clients may also become emotionally distressed during a therapeutic session.

Grounding techniques can help clients, and ourselves, to cope with distressing feelings and situations. In being able to cope with our own distress, we can become more present to the here and now. There are many different grounding techniques and some will be suggested below.

It might be that clients suggest their own grounding techniques – essentially these are techniques to help people to deal with emotional and psychological distress.

Physical grounding

Physical grounding might be thought of as doing things physically that help deal with emotional and psychological pain. It is important that the physical things are not inherently harmful, such as:

Holding and gently squeezing the index finger of our left hand with the index finger and thumb of our right hand.
Touching any piece of furniture that we are sitting on or close to.
Running cold water from a tap over our fingertips.
Holding ice cubes in our hands.
Holding and squeezing a pebble or stone that we have specifically chosen to help ground us.
Feeling the ground beneath our feet as we stand or sit.
Touching any objects that are lying around us – books, keys, pens.
Squeezing a soft ball or sponge.
Stretching our limbs.

Imaginary grounding

This involves using our minds to help take our attention away from our emotional and psychological distress (Najavits, 2017). Again, clients are likely to suggest and find their own images and mind-games that they see as effective for them, but the below are some suggested examples that can also be used:

Counting from one to ten, over and over again.
Noticing an object and describing it in detail – its colour, shape, texture, what people use it for.
Imagining being in a safe place, a place of peace and calm, somewhere where we feel secure. This can be a real place or a made-up place.
Describing a route from one location to another – noticing if there are any trees, flowers, birds, animals, houses and so on along the way.
Describing the environment around you in a lot of detail – what you see in front of you, to your left and right, what you can hear, what you can smell.
Repeat a positive mantra to yourself over and over again – for example, 'I can do this', 'This is not my fault'; 'I believe in myself'.
Imagine being your own best friend and imagine what you would say to yourself – for example, 'You are a good person', 'You are kind', 'You are generous'.

The key to grounding is that it may not immediately work. It takes time and it takes practice, particularly if a client is experiencing very high levels of distress. It is therefore important to practise grounding regularly, not to wait until emotional distress is felt but rather, incorporating it into daily life so that we can draw on this when distress arises.

Grounding in therapy

We can help clients to explore and develop grounding techniques. These can be used for clients experiencing anxiety, stress, depression, unhelpful or extreme mood swings and mood disorders such as bipolar disorder. Grounding techniques can also be used when working with trauma, abuse, dissociation (feelings of unrealness that clients may have), substance cravings, self-harm, and eating disorders. Grounding techniques are an essential tool in a therapist's toolkit.

It is important to explore with the client what is happening for them – their feelings, physical sensations, thoughts and behaviours. Exploring how they experience their emotional and psychological distress takes time and patience because every individual client will experience this uniquely. This is why it is important as a therapist to cultivate and practise a sense of presence so that we are open to what our clients are telling us, rather than being distracted by our own thoughts or feelings. Some clients may experience their distress in very complex ways and it can take time for us as therapists to understand this distress. The following is a case study based on a client that one of us was seeing. This case study serves to illustrate the importance of listening and understanding because it shows that whilst there tend to be generic symptoms associated with diagnoses, each individual human being will be experiencing these symptoms in their own unique ways.

The case of Alex

Common symptoms of depression include: low mood (feeling sad or empty), little pleasure in everyday activities, significant weight change (gain or loss), difficulty sleeping, lethargy, rumination, and suicidal ideation. Alex is a 25- year-old young man who comes to counselling because he has had thoughts of self-harm and suicide. Alex says that although he has thought about jumping in front of a train, he would never do this because he would let his family down; furthermore, although he has thought about cutting his arms he has not done this and believes that he will not do this. Although Alex has a supportive and stable family, mental health issues are not discussed. Upon further exploration with Alex, it becomes clear that he has experienced episodes of depression from an early age, around 10. Furthermore, he has never shared his experiences of depression with anyone and so is unsure whether what he has been experiencing perhaps two or three times a year is 'normal' or not. During an episode of depression, Alex finds it hard to sleep; he also finds it difficult to get out of bed and do anything and he has thoughts of self-harm and suicide.

This case study demonstrates the importance of a trusting relationship between a therapist and a client because it is only through trust that a client will reveal things that they have never told anybody. In this case Alex spoke about what it feels like to him when he is depressed. He spoke about how he experiences depression like 'white noise' – he can hear what people are saying to him but he cannot understand them and finds it very hard to communicate. Alex also described how he can feel cut off, or dissociated from himself – he feels like he is going through the motions of getting up and going to work but that somehow he is not in his body and is outside of this looking at what he is doing. Alex described his depression as like being under a rain cloud that is funnelling down torrential rain on him but that he cannot be bothered, or has given up trying, to run away from this cloud. Alex also spoke about how he cannot look into a mirror when he is depressed because what he sees there is, he feels, not him.

The case of Alex clearly shows the complexity of depression and the importance for the therapist to try to understand this complexity. It was important for Alex to know that he was not 'going mad' and that what he was experiencing were symptoms associated with depression. By being able to identify these symptoms, Alex is better able to understand what is happening to him and thus is less fearful of future depressive episodes. Moreover, in exploring and talking about his depression Alex can then think about what some coping strategies might be to better deal with his particular set of symptoms. Indeed, Alex may already be engaged in coping strategies but is just not aware of this.

Alex also found it useful to draw the raincloud that represents his depression and to shrink it in size and colour it in different colours as a way of feeling more in control of his depression – Alex felt that he was no longer a victim of low moods, but rather, a person with bouts of depression with a deeper understanding of these and of himself. This case also shows that it is critical for a therapist to explore risk in relation to self-harm and suicide. If a client has had thoughts of harm, it is crucial to find out whether the client has ever tried harming themselves or others, whether they have ever put in place any specific plans for suicide, and if they have then to put together a safety plan with the client.

The case of Alex further suggests that pacing is key when working with clients – therapists must not hurry the work that they do. Being present with Alex, the therapist here was able to give Alex the time to narrate his own unique experiences of depression and to come up with an image to symbolise this. This meant the therapist holding back at times, remaining silent whilst fully present in that situation with Alex. Clinical diagnoses have sets of symptoms associated with them but ultimately every individual client will experience their particular mental health challenge or challenges uniquely, and it is important as a therapist to bear this in mind.

Let's get theoretical

Now that we have explained how presence is linked to key therapeutic tools like mindfulness, leading and pacing and grounding techniques, we turn our attention to theory. In particular, we explore presence in relation to CBT, PC, relational and hypnotherapeutic modalities and how integration is the process of connecting theoretical ideas across these modalities vis-à-vis presence.

Very simply, CBT brings together thoughts and behaviours – that how we think has a direct influence on how we feel and behave. CBT is the combination of behaviourism (Watson, 1924 in Buckley, 1989) with cognition (Beck, 1989), with the emphasis being upon the notion that behaviour and maladaptive cognitions are learned and therefore can be unlearned (Kuyken, Padesky & Dudley, 2011). CBT is about exploring with clients their thought processes and about raising clients' awareness and understanding of these.

CBT has increasingly incorporated mindfulness and relaxation techniques, demonstrating the importance of cultivating presence within this therapeutic modality. There is mindfulness-based cognitive therapy (MBCT) (Segal, Williams and Teasdale, 2012 in MBCT.com 2017), Acceptance and Commitment Therapy (ACT) (Hayes & Smith, 2005), and Compassionate Mind Training (CMT) (Gilbert, 2009). Firstly, taking MBCT, there are three broad elements to MBCT – cultivating mindfulness; an acceptance of experience and the development of a healthy interest in this; and developing an understanding of one's vulnerability through mindfulness and acceptance, particularly in relation to depression. MBCT seeks to de-centre one's relationship to one's thoughts, to see thoughts not as facts but as relating to one's thinking processes (Crane, 2017). The techniques associated with ACT relate to three core areas: mindfulness, acceptance and values-based living. ACT offers to help people to put them in touch with the lives that they want to live, according to their values. ACT is also about acceptance of one's suffering, living one's own experience authentically (Hayes, 2005). Clearly, both MBCT and ACT draw on the notion of presence – developing an awareness of one's self, one's environment and being open to one's own experiences rather than rigidly following unehlpful thoughts that a person may have learnt. Thus, through MBCT and ACT presence is developed as a way of exploring thinking patterns, distancing oneself from unhelpful thinking processes and becoming more focussed on the present. CMT uses relaxation and breathing techniques and safe space imagery as a way of cultivating presence within the client. According to CMT, our minds and bodies have evolved to have three emotional regulatory systems: a drive/excite/vitality system which involves wanting, pursuing and achieving; a content/safe/connected system that is experienced as soothing, and a threat focussed system that is about protection and safety seeking (Gilbert, 2009). Compassion focussed therapy raises awareness within individuals about the nature of their brains and bodies and how individuals' threat systems can be over-stimulated. Techniques to encourage social safeness are promoted in order to encourage our self-soothing systems. Within CMT clients are encouraged to be still with their thoughts and emotions and to imagine feeling compassion and self-compassion. Thus, for CMT presence is about experiencing self-compassion and through this clients can begin to stimulate their content/safe/connected regulatory system. Being able to self-soothe ourselves enables us to be more alive to the present because our bodies and minds are no longer locked within a threat focussed system, and it is an over-stimulated threat focussed system that can sustain anxiety, depression and other challenges, which prvent us from experiencing the here and now – with an openness and acceptance.

The notion of congruence is central to PC therapeutic approaches. Congruence is about being genuine, about encouraging us to experience ourselves as we truly are, and for our clients to experience themselves as they truly are (Rogers, 1951). Congruence also links to self and self-concept. Within person-centred approaches the self-concept is seen as being developed over time in relation to how others view and relate to us. The self, on the other hand, is closer to who we really are, our innate abilities and qualities, which may be suppressed by our wider environment. Presence – being open and balanced in each moment – is thereby developed and understood by person-centred approaches through congruence and the self/self-concept. Congruence is achieved by helping ourselves and our clients to question the self-concept and to explore what our 'true self' may be. By experiencing our true selves we are more likely to have presence – emotional balance and inhabiting the present.

Relational modalities within counseling and psychotherapy place human relationships at the centre of analysis. Key to these approaches is that humans are relational beings and so a large aspect to therapeutic work is a focus on understanding and developing our clients' experiences of relationships – with themselves, with family members, intimate partners, colleagues, friends and others. Attachment theory underpins relational modalities in that the attachment bond is seen as crucial to the bonds that human beings form with each other. John Bowlby first introduced us to the importance of the relationship between the infant and their primary care-giver (in Holmes, 2014). Bowlby found that where this relationship was strained, this influenced a child's internal working model of themselves, other people and the world around them, and such internal working models then persist into adulthood. Mary Ainsworth carried out various experiments to document different attachment styles in children and she and her colleagues found predominantly five styles: secure, preoccupied, anxious ambivalent, avoidant and disorganised. A secure attachment style is experienced by children who have had responsive caregivers, validating them and their experiences. When these children grow up they are likely to be adults who can form and maintain trusting relationships, adults who have a healthy relationship also with themselves, believing that ultimately 'everything will be okay'. A preoccupied attachment style is seen to be the result of parents who are overly intrusive in their child's life. An anxious ambivalent attachment style is also a type of preoccupied attachment style, but here the child is angry as well as anxious. Adults with preoccupied attachment styles experience relationships as anxiety-provoking and can be overly concerned by what others think, feel and how they behave. Adults with an anxious ambivalent attachment style may also become angry when they believe that they have not had the response from a person that they should have. A child with an avoidant attachment style is considered to have had parents who dismiss or avoid their emotional distress. As a result, when the child grows up, they come to rely on themselves for their emotional needs and they tend to avoid becoming attached to other people, very fearful of being rejected (Holmes, 2014). Attachment-informed therapy includes a focus upon helping the client experience and develop a secure base, as well as processing anger and loss (Holmes, 2001). Attachment theory also involves discussing significant attachments and/or relationships clients have in childhood and adulthood (Holmes, 2001). Attachment styles can change throughout life, and are therefore quite fluid, and so therapy can really help to provide clients with their own secure base. Within attachment focussed therapy, therefore, presence might be viewed as the therapist and client cultivating within themselves a secure base from which to experience, build and maintain healthy relationships. Here, the cultivation of presence is important in that this can help clients to become more balanced within relationships with other people, being more open to each encounter within a relationship, rather than the person being influenced by unhelpful, unhealthy and often deep-rooted thinking and behavioural patterns that lead to challenging and disempowering relationships with others. So we can often project onto others our own unhealthy expectations and beliefs about relationships, and in that way cause ourselves and others emotional distress. Through presence we can be open to each new encounter with an individual, without prejudice or judgement.

Hypnotherapeutic modalities utilise strategies and techniques that explore relaxation, mindfulness, enhanced self-awareness and experiential processing: all of these elements draw upon presence. The term *hypnosis,* as suggested by psychiatrist Milton Erickson in Rossi & Ryan (1998), can be defined as a means of communication of ideas by the therapist to the client, utilising the clients' ability to enter a relaxed state of awareness and mindfulness: the relaxed mind is a receptive mind, capable of absorbing new information and learning that promotes positive change and self-development.

Direct hypnosis strategies rely upon structured techniques such as utilising a countdown in order to deepen the relaxed state and the use of direct suggestions (Kroger & Yapko, 2008), where the therapist makes suggestions that can focus on the client's own unique traits of motivation, personality, values and belief systems. Presence through relaxation and mindfulness is a key component of this process, helping facilitate the acceptance of positive suggestions without conscious resistance. A leading pioneer in approaches with hypnosis and psychotherapy, Erickson developed his own unique methodology and techniques. Not only utilising direct suggestions, *Ericksonian hypnosis* involves the use of indirect suggestions, metaphors and storytelling to facilitate therapeutic gains, often outside the client's own conscious awareness.

A relaxed mindful state can involve heightened awareness and conscious detachment where the conscious mind can be occupied with each present moment while suggestions are made by the therapist. Erickson recognised that we often shift from conscious to unconscious awareness, for example, thinking about the shopping while 'unconsciously' driving the car from work. Knowing how to tap into these unconscious states was a part of Erickson's presence as a therapist, the ability to utilise a client's inner resources a key element in addressing thoughts, values, emotions, memories and beliefs in his/her life.

Studies indicate that there is no overall advantage of using direct or indirect suggestions in relation to eliciting behavioural responses (Matthews et al., 1985). Some people respond more effectively to direct suggestions while others prefer the more permissive indirect approach (McConkey, 1984). The aspects of presence that therapists such as Erickson engender within their methods allows them to individualise approaches and techniques dependent on the requirements and characteristics of the client.

Cognitive Behavioural Hypnotherapy (CBH) involves the integration of cognitive behavioural therapy (CBT) and hypnosis to enhance treatment of emotional states and promote changes in feelings, thoughts, perceptions and behaviours. When dealing with stress related issues such as Acute Stress Disorder a combination of CBT and hypnosis can be more effective than either CBT alone or supportive counselling (Bryant et al., 2005). Utilising relaxation and mindfulness in cultivating a state of presence, a client can be exposed to a particular conditioned fear stimulus that would otherwise prove difficult or unacceptable, for example, when someone has a phobia of vomiting (Wijesinghe, 1974). Relaxation and mindfulness through hypnosis can help cognitively restructure a client's experience of the various triggers for a particular fear. As the client visualises or experiences these triggers in their mind, he/she can explore the emotions surrounding them with the therapist. A high state of emotional arousal can be induced and maintained and this can then be progressively reduced as the patterns of association to the fear stimulus are transformed in the hypnotic state. In this way, the individual learns to feel safe in situations that would previously have elicited anxiety (Bryant, 2008).

The above modalities rely upon forming strong therapeutic alliances through building and maintaining a state of presence that works in conjunction with the client's own positive attitudes and beliefs about the treatment. Suggestions for enhancing confidence and self-esteem can be utilised for ego-strengthening so that a client can start to believe that they can overcome a fear or addiction, or deal better with thoughts, feelings, emotions and physical sensations such as pain. Hypnosis provides a way of widening a client's experience of the past, present and future in order to address dysfunctional belief systems, cognitions and perceptions (Alladin, 2008) and central to this is presence: a relationship between the client and therapist that incorporates relaxation, mindfulness, empathy, acceptance and trust.

Presence is also key when considering the therapeutic relationship, which lies at the heart of PC approaches. Carl Rogers (1951; 1961) highlighted the importance of the relationship between the therapist and the client in therapy. For Rogers (1951), the therapeutic relationship is so key because this enables the client to take down their defences, and so the client feels able to be themselves. According to Rogers (1951), an ideal relationship for therapy is one where there is empathy and complete understanding by the therapist of the client's attitudes and feelings as they perceive and experience them to be. Research has demonstrated the importance of the therapeutic relationship to healing and growth (Prochaska & Norcross, 2009). Even within therapeutic approaches in which the therapist plays a more directive role, such as CBT approaches, the importance of the therapeutic relationship has also been stressed. According to Kuyken et al. (2011), for example, the effectiveness of CBT is improved when therapists develop and sustain a positive therapeutic alliance. A positive therapeutic alliance is correlated with positive outcomes in therapy (Kuyken et al. 2011). For Mearns & Thorne (2012), in person-centred counselling the therapeutic relationship is one of equality between the therapist and the client in that there should be no hierarchy and so the therapist should not assume the role of 'expert'. Rather, the therapeutic relationship is about developing intimacy and involvement between the therapist and the client (Mearns & Thorne, 2012).

Conclusion

In our work, presence is key to developing a strong therapeutic relationship with our clients. By being emotionally and psychologically centred as therapists, through the practice of relaxation, mindfulness, pacing and so on, we are able to be open to what our clients are saying to us, as well as what is underpinning or what is behind their conversation. Through presence we remain aware of each moment with our clients and when we do become distracted we are able to see this to be able to come back to focussing on our clients. This helps us to build a strong therapeutic alliance with clients because they experience us as therapists who are genuinely listening, empathic and understanding of their experiences. Presence gives us confidence to be creative with our clients – rather than dogmatically following a particular set of steps we integrate different modalities and different techniques to make the therapy as effective and enabling as possible. Presence is also key to integrative practice in that by practising presence clients are able to cultivate a way of non-judgementally and compassionately being with their issues. The strategies that help cultivate presence are excellent strategies for clients to use as part of a toolkit for their mental health and wellbeing. As such, introducing the techniques outlined in this chapter fairly early on with clients can be extremely effective and beneficial.

References

Alladin, A. (2008) *Cognitive Hypnotherapy. An Integrated Approach to the Treatment of Emotional Disorders*. Chichester: Wiley.

Alman, B. M. & Lambrou, P. (2012) *Self-Hypnosis: The Complete Manual for Health and Self-Change*, 2nd edition. New York: Routledge.

Battino, R. (2005) *Metaphoria: Metaphor and Guided Metaphor for Psychotherapy and Healing*, new edition. Carmarthen: Crown House Publishing.

Beck, A. (1989) *Cognitive Therapy and the Emotional Disorders*. London: Penguin.

Bryant, Richard A. (2008) 'Hypnosis and anxiety: Early interventions'. In Nash, Michael R. and Barnier, Amanda J. (Eds). *The Oxford Handbook of Hypnosis: Theory, Research, and Practice*, pp. 535–547. New York: Oxford University Press.

Bryant, R., Moulds, M., Gutherie, R. & Nixon, R. (2005) 'The additive benefit of hypnosis and cognitive-behavioural therapy in treating acute stress disorder', *Journal of Consulting and Clinical Psychology*, vol. 73, pp. 334–340.

Buckley, K. (1989) *Mechanical Man: John Broadus Watson and the Beginnings of Behaviourism*. New York: The Guilford Press.

Crane, R. (2017) *Mindfulness-Based Cognitive Therapy*. 2nd edition. London: Routledge.

Crawford, M. (2016) *The World Beyond Your Head*. London: Penguin Books Ltd.

Forsyth, J. P. & Eifert, G. H. (2008) *The Mindfulness & Acceptance Workbook For Anxiety*. Oakland, CA: New Harbinger Publications.

Gilbert, P. (2009) *The Compassionate Mind: A New Approach to Life*. Oakland, CA: New Harbinger Publications.

Hayes, S. with Smith, S. (2005) *Get Out of Your Mind & Into Your Life: The New Acceptance & Commitment Therapy*. Oakland, CA: New Harbinger Publications.

Holmes, J. (2001) *The Search for the Secure Base*. London: Routledge.

Holmes, J. (2014) *John Bowlby and Attachment Theory*. London: Routledge.

King, M., Novik, L. & Citrenbaum, C. (1983) *Irresistible Communication*. Philadelphia: Saunders.

Keen, S. (1997) *Hymns to an Unknown God: Awakening the Spirit in Everyday Life*. London: Piatkus Books.

Kornfield, J. (2008) *The Wise Heart*. London: Rider.

Kroger, S. & Yapko, M. (2008) *Clinical and Experimental Hypnosis in Medicine, Dentistry, and Psychology*, 2nd edition. Philadelphia, PA: Lippincott Williams & Wilkins.

Kuyken, W., Padesky, C. & Dudley, R. (2011) *Collaborative Case Conceptualization*. London: The Guilford Press.

Loehr, J. E. & Migdow, J. (2000) *Breathe In, Breathe Out*. London: Time-Life.

Matthews, W. J., Bennett, H., Gallagher, M. & Bean, W. (1985) 'Indirect versus direct hypnotic suggestions — an initial investigation: A brief communication', *International Journal of Clinical and Experimental Hypnosis*, vol. 33, no. 3, pp. 219–223.

MBCT.com (2017) 'Your guide to mindfulness based cognitive therapy'. Available at www.mbct.com (accessed 21 June 2017).

Mearns, D. & Thorne, B. (2012) *Person-Centred Counselling in Action*, 3rd edition. London: Sage.

Najavits, L.M. (2017) *Seeking Safety: A Treatment Manual for PTSD and Substance Abuse*. New York: The Guilford Press.

Pascale, B. (1662) *Pensées*, www.goodreads.com/quotes/19682-all-of-humanity-s-problems-stem-from-man-s-inability-to-sit (accessed 1 June 2018).

Prochaska, J. & Norcross, J. (2003) *Systems of Psychotherapy: A Transtheoretical Analysis*, 7th edition. London: Thomson Learning.

Rodenburg, P. (2007) *Presence: How to Use Positive Energy for Success in Every Situation*. London: Penguin Books Ltd.

Rogers, C. (1951) *Client-Centered Therapy*. London: Constable.

Rogers, C. (1961) *On Becoming a Person*. London: Constable & Robinson.

Rossi, E. & Ryan, M. O. (1998) *Life Reframing in Hypnosis. The Seminars, Workshops and Lectures of Milton H. Erickson Volume II*. London: Free Association Books.

Wijesinghe, W. (1974) 'A vomiting phobia overcome by one session of flooding with hypnosis', *J. Behav. Ther. & Exp. Psychiat.*, vol. 5, pp. 169–170.

Chapter 2

Processing emotional and psychological distress integratively

> I love the colour red. It is dynamic and symbolises what I feel. Passion, anger, love, rage, sensuousness. A colour so filled with internal contradiction that I can't help but relate to it.
> Danielle Boshoff, 'Diagnosis Bipolar II' (personal journal)

Introduction

Love them or hate them, we cannot ignore emotions. From time immemorial humans have experienced their physical and social worlds emotionally, because within our mind/body systems are complex organic processes that help create feelings. Without emotion, as a human species we would not survive because without a sense of fear, for example, we would not know what things to avoid or fight against. Without pleasure from certain activities, such as sexual intercourse, we would not be as motivated to perform them. Emotions have therefore played, and continue to play, a key role in humans and within societies.

Within a therapeutic setting, emotions are a key aspect of the therapeutic relationship, alongside any clinical work that we do with clients in relation to helping them understand, process and cope with their emotions. At the same time, understanding how and in what ways our own emotions can be triggered by our clients is a key aspect of our own professional and personal growth, and is a key aspect of clinical supervision. Working with clients' emotions is central to many different therapeutic modalities. For example, some CBT based approaches distinguish between healthy and unhealthy emotions; whilst relational modalities might view emotions as being triggered by key childhood experiences.

This chapter aims to look at what emotions are and how these can play out within clinical, therapeutic, settings. We discuss how clients may come for therapy because they are overwhelmed by different emotions; whilst others may come to therapy because they do not feel anything and would like to experience more emotion. We look at how emotional processing might be approached integratively, through person-centred, relational, CBT and hypnotherapeutic modalities. We also present some fictional case studies of how we might work with clients in relation to emotional processing. Finally, we look at how as therapists it is important to maintain a strong awareness of our own emotional landscapes and how we also as therapists can better manage and process difficult emotions.

Firstly, we begin with focussing upon the emotional upheaval of a character in a world best-selling book that was originally published in 1846, a story about unrestrained and out of control emotions, of love, passion, jealousy and hatred, set in the tumultuous historical period of A.D.54–68 when Nero's corrupt era in Rome was coming to an end, to be replaced by early

Christianity. The character comes from *Quo Vadis*, a best-selling classical novel written by Henryk Sienkiewicz (Sienkiewicz, 1806), who received a Nobel Prize for Literature for this work. The character we are focussing on is Marcus Vinicius, a young Roman, a handsome noble man, who falls passionately in love with a young woman called Ligia from a different country and culture, who was handed over to the Romans as a hostage by the Lygians as a way of keeping peace with Rome.

Marcus Vinicius and his uncontrollable emotions

In *Quo Vadis*, Marcus visits his uncle Petronius, a rich and influential nobleman living in Rome who has the confidence of the emperor Nero. Marcus is desperate to talk to Petronius about a young and beautiful woman that he recently encountered whilst staying at another noble man's house to recuperate from a battle wound. Marcus describes how the first time he set eyes upon Ligia he fell head over heels in love, and now is all-consumed by his passion and lust for her, being unable to think about anything else. Marcus is desperate to see Ligia again and even to try to marry her, even though this would be frowned upon by his family and his peers, because Ligia comes from a tribe that is considered to be barbarian by the Roman nobility.

Looking at Marcus through a psychotherapeutic lens, it is clear that Marcus has lost control of his emotions, and is in considerable distress. He is overwhelmed by passion, love and lust. He is craving the attentions of Ligia, and is unable to separate himself from the strong emotions that Ligia has aroused in him. It is clear that Marcus has become very attached very quickly to Ligia, and has lost sense of himself as a separate being who can accept he is experiencing emotional distress (even if at times this is being experienced as euphoria) whilst not being completely subsumed by this. Moreover, Marcus does not seem to have the capacity to ground himself and to connect with any other emotions that he might have been experiencing prior to seeing Ligia – sadness, boredom, contentment, joy, and so on. Thus, Marcus is currently out of balance emotionally and as a result is behaving with little consideration of any wider consequences. He is visiting his uncle and telling his uncle about his newly found passion, knowing full well that his uncle has the ear of Nero, the Emperor of Rome. In this way Marcus is setting in motion actions that may have fatal consequences for Ligia and for himself, because Marcus' uncle is likely to use his influence with Nero to strategise to ensure that Ligia leaves the house where she currently resides and where she is happy, to move her closer to Marcus and his household. All of this without any consultation with Ligia!

The character of Marcus illustrates how dangerous uncontrollable emotions can be. Emotions, when experienced acutely, can be distressing and can make people behave in unethical and even dangerous ways. Out-of-control emotions can lead to harming and self-harming behaviours and so working with clients to recognise, understand and process intense emotions and figuring out coping strategies with them is a key aspect of therapeutic practice. Working therapeutically with Marcus would involve exploring how he experiences the intense emotions, where he feels them in his body. This would help Marcus to see that his emotions do not just appear but rather they comprise of a series of physiological sensations. By drawing attention to Marcus' physical sensations, this would enable him to perhaps feel that he is more in control of his feelings, that he can experience these without necessarily acting upon them. Marcus could also be encouraged to keep a record of when he feels most passionate and to explore how he might respond to such feelings in ways that do not harm him or others. Mindfulness, relaxation, these are techniques that could be usefully introduced to Marcus in order for him to practise sitting with his emotional distress and to notice when the intense feelings

become less intense for him. Marcus could also be encouraged to think about times in his life when he has felt contented or calm. Marcus could be encouraged to imagine people, animals, objects or places that have inspired in him contentment or calmness as a way of balancing out his intense lustfulness. This would all, of course, take time. Marcus' attachment style could also be explored. Might it be that Marcus has a preoccupied attachment style, and so has difficulties seeing himself as an individual with his own experiences and perspectives? At the moment he seems to attach himself to other people and to become absorbed by them. Through developing a strong therapeutic relationship with Marcus, it might be possible for Marcus to begin experiencing a secure attachment style, with his therapist. Marcus could then be encouraged to adopt this attachment style in relation to other people. Marcus could be encouraged to discuss what having a secure attachment to Ligia might look and feel like. In this way, Marcus might begin to see that he has become too attached to, and too preoccupied with, Ligia. Marcus could also be facilitated to view Ligia as her own person, detached from him, and this could also help with discouraging Marcus from telling his uncle about Ligia, so as to reduce the potential for a damaging set of consequences for Ligia and for Marcus. Thus, in providing Marcus with therapeutic interventions and practice, this might completely change the outcomes of Quo Vadis!

Whilst Marcus and Ligia are fictional characters, they do demonstrate the potentially distressing and harmful effects and consequences that emotions can have on people. There are hundreds of different words in the English language that express a myriad of different emotions. Perhaps some of these emotions are more in evidence within therapeutic settings than other emotions are – sadness, guilt, shame, fear, anger, jealousy and craving/desire are perhaps commonly found within therapy. As therapists we help clients to identify what emotions they might be feeling and what kinds of physical sensations those emotions evoke. We also help clients to process these emotions so that they are less intensely experienced in the future; we also help explore with clients when particular emotions are triggered and what they may be linked to, thereby increasing clients' understandings of their feelings. We work with clients to help them to be able to sit with distressing emotions, to increase their tolerance and acceptance of these. We also work with our own emotions as therapists.

Therapy can be a powerful tool in dealing ethically with emotion, not only impacting upon individuals themselves but also upon the wider social context. We now discuss what emotional distress is. We also explore what emotional processing is and the challenges to this. Challenges include clients who repress or deny their emotions, clients who may be afraid of their emotions, the role of substance abuse in dampening down emotion. We present some key therapeutic tools for helping clients to process their emotions, before looking at the emotions that we as therapists can experience within the therapeutic relationship. As therapists it is key for us to understand our own emotional triggers, and to practise emotional processing ourselves as a way of clearing our own distress and reconnecting with a sense of inner balance, or presence as explained in Chapter 1.

Emotional and psychological distress: Dealing with our shadow side

Within the context of Shamanism the uncontrollable jealousy and lust experienced by Marcus Vinicius in *Quo Vadis* could be considered part of our 'shadow side': that part of ourselves where destructive emotions, limiting beliefs, prejudices, hatred and fears reside. In art forms and certain religions the 'dark' shadow has symbolically been linked to the concept of Evil, for example, in the film *Star Wars*, where Luke Skywalker is encouraged by Darth Vader to turn to the 'dark side' (Madden, 2009).

This link between our unconscious 'shadow' and the concept of 'darkness' has direct implications upon self-awareness, self-empowerment and healing. The powerful symbolism of darkness and Evil teaches us to ignore, even to suppress difficult emotions and feelings within – affective states that are to be feared and avoided. Not only are we taught to ignore powerful emotions, *instinctively* we utilise suppression and dissociation as strategies for emotional avoidance, as manifested in trauma victims (Briere & Scott, 2006).

Often we are unaware or ignorant of these powerful emotions and feelings, hidden in the unconscious, until they manifest themselves through triggers, flashbacks, thoughts or factors outside of conscious awareness. We can often be too afraid to face emotional and psychological distress; instead of healing our distress we let it fester and grow powerful. Once a runaway train reaches a certain speed and momentum it can be almost impossible to stop. Then our anger is unleashed or our shame is acted out or our guilt is fuelled. Our actions and reactions can often feel as though they are not even part of us. Sometimes we can 'lose it' with our anger or suddenly feel completely worthless if someone says something that triggers emotional distress within us. It can feel as if that person is controlling a 'bad person' within us using a switch or remote control.

Balancing darkness is light and the concept of working with powerful emotions and psychological distress in a way that allows greater self-awareness and acceptance of what is going on within us, providing opportunities for healing to take place. Presence with distressing emotions is a way of gathering information; detective work that can provide vital clues regarding emotions such as anger, shame, guilt, repression and depression. What is their purpose? Why do we experience that particular emotion? What does it tell us about ourselves? Where is it located in our body? Does it have a form or symbol or colour associated with it? Can I feel differently towards that emotion or state? Can I live with the emotion or state without it harming me? Can I take a step back from an emotion or state instead of becoming attached to or consumed by it?

Addressing the above and similar questions can begin to free us from the shackles of emotional distress. Becoming open to our emotions and feelings, as opposed to locking them up and throwing away the key, brings opportunities and possibilities for growth. Within therapeutic contexts, it opens the door to helping a client, for example, to challenge and dispute irrational beliefs and to notice the effect of these disputations. It can shine a light on why a certain thought or flashback triggers a certain emotion or feeling. Reframing the context or meaning of a particular thought or event or memory that triggers distressing emotions can change its impact profoundly and can help change a client's belief in relation to emotions such as anger or shame or guilt.

Emotional processing

Emotional processing can be defined as a process where distressing or disturbing emotions are assimilated or reduced so that they no longer affect or interfere with normal daily functioning. In his 'Model of Emotion', Baker (2007) provides a simple representation of the various stages that comprise our emotions, suggesting an **input – experience – expression** sequence that is involved in expressing and regulating emotions.

Input event and appraisal of its meaning

This is the emotion-provoking event itself and our interpretation of the event. For example, a manager may say something at work that we may interpret as 'belittling us' or making us feel 'inferior and unworthy'. Interpretation of the event can be complex and based upon many different components such as values and belief systems, past experiences and memories and input from other people; interpretation can include unconscious as well as cognitive elements.

Emotional experience

This component relates to the emotions that we experience as a result of our interpretation of the input event, for example, feeling anger or frustration as a result of what our manager said. The emotional experience can encompass emotions and physical sensations that together can result in producing 'psychological meaning'. For example, 'After the manager said those things I was absolutely fuming; I could feel my blood boiling . . . I've never felt so small in my life. He completely belittled me in front of others. . . .'

Emotional expression

This stage relates to how our emotional experience, for example, 'feeling angry', is expressed. Do we express our emotions instantly or do we have a more controlled approach such as taking a step back and assessing the situation, our thoughts and feelings surrounding it? Do we address the person who has caused us upset directly or do we vent our anger in an indirect way such as hitting a wall? Do we bury our emotions instead of expressing them?

Control of emotions

Emotional processing within the therapeutic framework not only relies upon an awareness of the different stages involved in the emotional sequence but also how these stages are *controlled* or *regulated*. People with phobias or anxiety disorders may control the input event by avoiding situations that provoke their fear, for example, enclosed spaces, tall buildings, driving on motorways, doing a presentation in front of others. Regulating the emotional experience through emotional detachment or numbing can result in the inability to experience positive emotions, and is a common symptom of Post-Traumatic Stress Disorder (PTSD). Controlling emotional expression by, for example, taking a step back and assessing a particular situation and our reaction to it, even though we carry the anger within us, can be more beneficial than unleashing our anger immediately. Punching your manager is not recommended!

Processing emotional and psychological distress: Hypnotherapeutic modalities

Hypnotherapeutic modalities utilise a range of strategies and techniques for processing emotional and psychological distress. Through teaching a client to relax their mind and body using breathing techniques and guided mental visualisations or experiences, the concept of imagination can be brought out. The power of imagination cannot be underestimated within therapy: it provides a vehicle for the client to *re-imagine* rather than *re-live* certain thoughts, feelings, situations and events which caused distress in a way that influences the thoughts and feelings surrounding these events in a positive way.

Guided imagery techniques can facilitate self-understanding of emotions: where is the emotion located in the body? Does it have a shape? What does it look like? What does it feel like? Can you describe the emotion in words? Imagine taking the emotion and placing it behind you – how does that feel? Imagine taking the emotion and changing how it looks, for example, making it very small and fuzzy at the edges – how does the emotion feel now? Imagine placing the anxiety in a box, putting a lid on the box and throwing the box far away from you – how does the anxiety feel now?

A whole scene that causes distress in a claustrophobe, for example, sitting in a train that suddenly stops on a track, can be 'played out' on an imaginary movie screen where the client imagines himself watching a version of himself dealing with the situation in a different way. He can imagine being calm and relaxed and focussing on happy positive thoughts that make the situation more pleasant. He can imagine focussing on the pleasant feelings and sensations that he is experiencing in the state of hypnosis, as opposed to fear and panic. He can imagine entering this hypnotic state whenever he sits in a train. Through seeding the mind with positive experiences, the client is creating a store of 'imagined' positive memories that can create the association of calmness and relaxation, happiness and contentment within a train. This can help with diminishing the catastrophic 'what if' thoughts that presage a future trip on a train.

Through hypnosis, systematic desensitisation and cognitive restructuring of difficult in vivo situations using imagination can gradually release the fear or anxiety, changing the experience and disarming emotional distress. A client who is terrified of birds can start by imagining a version of themselves on a screen in a situation where birds are present. This should be the least anxiety provoking experience in the hierarchy of anxiety provoking situations. Over a period of several sessions, the client gradually lets go of the fear and anxiety and becomes more confident that they can deal well with the situation, as well as lose the fear of birds. They can then be instructed to imagine the situation in a way where they are actively experiencing it as opposed to watching a version of themselves on a movie screen. The therapist can take the client through subsequent events that are higher in the hierarchy; firstly in a dissociative manner and then through fully associated imaginations of situations. The fear surrounding the 'input event' can disappear, replaced with more positive associations such as calmness, relaxation, positivity and confidence. Ego-strengthening suggestions can be included in order to boost confidence and self-esteem so that any reservations that the client may have about overcoming their fear can be released.

In some cases it can be useful to use age regression techniques in order to take the client back to an initial event that triggered a fear or anxiety that developed into a phobia during later life. This technique should be performed in such a way that the client is dissociated from the event, for example, by imagining that they are 'above' the event and 'watching in' as though the event is a 'stage' below them. A middle-aged client with bird phobia in relation to pigeons regressed to a memory of an uncle who had a pigeon with one wing and encouraged his niece to tease the bird by throwing popcorn at it. By imagining this memory through the adult lens, the client was able to calm and comfort the young child forced to do this horrible act and this started the process of breaking apart the phobic response to pigeons. During subsequent sessions, feelings of guilt and shame associated with the act were acknowledged and reframed in order to process powerful and destructive emotions in a way that instilled self-calming and self-nurturing. The client was able to accept the uncle was a powerful family figure using fear as a tool to make her tease the pigeon and that she was too young to have a different response to him. She acknowledged that she 'felt terrible teasing the poor bird' but that she also 'deliberately missed the bird with the popcorn as a way of getting back at her uncle'. Guilt and shame were released through the understanding that none of what happened was her fault and under hypnosis she was able to imagine herself treating the bird with love and kindness. She also imagined pigeons as being small and cuddly. Gradually she became less and less afraid of pigeons and eventually was able to go to places where pigeons were present.

The above visualisation and experiential techniques can bring emotions and feelings to the point of conscious awareness. In cases where a negative habit is performed 'automatically', for example, placing an online bet, the emotions and feelings underpinning the period *before* the bet is placed can be explored and determined using hypnosis. Emotions and feelings *during* gambling can be investigated and the subsequent thoughts, feelings and emotions *after* the gambling has stopped can be uncovered. Becoming conscious of thoughts, feelings and emotions surrounding powerful compulsions can help break the cycle of unconscious behaviour, introducing the element of choice. In the case of a gambler the choice is whether to place a bet or whether to stop himself doing so. Often the understanding that a person has a choice over a habit can be empowering; where once the compulsive habit or behaviour seemed all-powerful and consuming, the notion of conscious choice in performing the habit or behaviour can weaken its influence and value.

Re-imagining events or memories versus recalling events or memories

In certain situations, for example when dealing with trauma victims, care should be taken not to cause the client suffering or distress. Rather than focussing upon reliving horrific events, interventions can be directed towards helping the client process their wounds instead. *Re-imagining* events and memories in order to change their meaning or context in some positive beneficial way is a better strategy than recalling events or memories, since direct recall could reinforce any distorted cognitions that a client may already have about that particular event or memory.

Processing emotional and psychological distress through CBT, PC and interpersonal modalities

Drawing upon a CBT based framework, emotional and psychological processing is undertaken through structured activities that raise awareness within clients of patterns of trigger events, thoughts and behaviours that are linked to the different distressing emotions that they may be experiencing. Clients are often asked to keep a 'thought log' that helps them track events, thoughts, emotional states and behaviours. Clients are asked to keep the log updated in between counselling sessions so that during a therapy session the therapist works with the client to explore and identify any patterns between triggers, thoughts, emotions and behavioural responses. Clients are then encouraged to think about ways in which they might change any unhelpful or rigid thoughts into more helpful thoughts, which may lead to a reduction in emotional distress. For CBT, there is a direct connection between thinking – thinking content and patterns – emotions and behaviours (Joseph, 2009). Clients can also be encouraged to map their moods on a daily, weekly or monthly basis so that they get a better sense themselves of their 'highs' and 'lows'.

Such structured activities enable clients to understand themselves better, and it might be argued that by challenging some of their thinking, clients are processing distressing emotions by seeing that their emotions are linked to their thoughts. Changing thoughts can bring about a change in emotions – this can be liberating for clients!

PC modalities offer a more non-directive approach to emotional and psychological processing. What is important here is for the therapist to work with the client at the client's own pace. Key counselling skills such as listening, empathy, reflecting back and summarising (Mearns & Thorne, 2012) enable clients to explore themselves, their lives, their emotions. It is important for the therapist to check in with the client regularly, to ensure that they understand what the client is telling them. Questions like 'Am I getting this right?' 'Is this what you mean?' 'Is this what is happening for you right now?' help the therapist check out that they are psychologically and emotionally connecting with the client, achieving relational depth (Mearns & Cooper, 2005).

When a client is experiencing emotional distress, they may not be able to articulate what is happening for them. In this instance it is important for the therapist to help the client explore and understand their emotions during the therapy session. For instance, in the case of a client who stops talking midway and looks at their hands and rubs their hands together, the therapist might say something like 'I notice that when you said . . . you then stopped speaking and looked down at your hands and were rubbing them. Can you talk about what is going on for you right now?' Clients may experience emotional and psychological distress through bodily reactions and so it is important for therapists to see physically what is taking place for the client: 'I notice that your neck gets very red as you talk about. . . .' Clients themselves may have little, if any, awareness of their bodily sensations and so bringing awareness of this within a therapeutic setting can be a helpful way of clients understanding their distress, what this might be linked to and how this might be played out physically for them. 'How would I know if you were angry/sad/anxious?' can be a useful question to ask a client. This not only raises the client's awareness of how to recognise their various emotional states, but also can provide vital information about what signs to look for as a therapist, to help the therapist know what emotional state the client may currently be experiencing.

Within PC modalities, the therapist may also invite the client to imagine what particular emotions look like for them – any colour, shape or object for example. Metaphors can be a further useful tool in helping clients to explore and process their emotional and psychological distress. It is important for therapists to listen out for images that clients may be using as a way of representing their experiences and how they are feeling. A therapist can also encourage a client to re-imagine a setting or object or any other image that might helpfully reposition their distress. With complex conditions, it can take clients many years to figure out who they are and what it is that they are experiencing and so as a therapist it is important not only to help clients identify strategies that they may find useful to explore, understand and process their emotions, but also to learn about any strategies that clients may have developed themselves for understanding and documenting their moods. Some clients may be used to expressing their emotions in creative ways – through poetry, music, writing a journal, and these can be brought into the therapeutic environment. Clients can be encouraged to express themselves emotionally through the use of tools that encourage creativity, and they can also be encouraged to bring to the therapy session any material that they have used or produced themselves as a way of releasing different emotional states. A therapist can then help the client to explore this creative output of emotion. Some therapists use mood cards for clients who experience difficulties in communicating their emotions. Mood cards can certainly be a useful tool, and some therapists create their own unique set of mood cards.

Relational therapeutic modalities tend to focus upon key trigger events in childhood, events that produced significant emotional distress. The idea here is to find the initial trigger for a particular emotional state in order for the client to identify this and then link this to current emotional difficulties that they may be experiencing. For example, a client who feels anger towards her manager may actually be experiencing the anger that she initially felt towards her father, when her father abandoned her. It may be that the client's current manager is triggering this and other emotional states within the client. Exploring childhood experiences, particularly in relation to strong emotional states, can therefore be helpful.

When clients come to realise that what they are feeling right now has a deeper, historical, basis, then they gain a broader perspective upon their current emotional distress. The therapist can also help the client explore how they felt as a child, before then asking the client to step into their adult self and to explore what their adult self might say or do for their child self in order to soothe away any emotional distress. This type of work is often referred to as 'working with the inner child'. Basically, the proposition here is that as adults we all have an inner child, a child-like state that continues to feel the emotional and psychological distress that we felt when we were growing up. It is only by accessing our adult self and using this to soothe and help and empower our child self that we can understand and process distressing emotions so that our feelings are no longer as overwhelming, as overpowering. This therapeutic work is very sensitive and needs to be done with caution, and at a pace that suits the client. Some clients may not want to connect with their 'inner child' because if they were neglected and/or abused as children then this can access a very painful place for them, and they may be fearful of accessing their inner child. The therapeutic rationale here is for therapists to help clients to understand their 'inner child'; to help, support and love their 'inner child' as a way of soothing and healing any emotional or physical or sexual abuse; and to integrate the 'inner child' back within the adult so that the client is no longer overwhelmed by emotional distress.

'Inner child' work

Here are some approaches to working with a client's inner child that you may find helpful:

- Take Maslow's hierarchy of needs and explore with the client which needs were met at which age and who met those needs. Ask the client to then think about how they might meet some of their unmet childhood emotional and psychological needs now, in adult mode. Encourage the client to act within adult mode to meet some of their needs now,
- Explore with the client some key feelings that they currently experience that cause them distress. Explore with the client whether they can remember feeling like this as a child. Then ask the client what their adult self might do in order to help alleviate the distress that their child self feels.
- Encourage the client to write a letter to their child self. What might the client like to say to their inner child? How might they like to soothe their inner child?
- Explore with the client what things they might like to do with their inner child who might be afraid, or alone, or in despair so as to help ease these painful feelings. Consider helping the client to support their inner child – for example, through imagination opening a door with a client and helping the inner child to leave a painful place behind, a place that the client equates with loneliness and despair.

This type of therapeutic work can be emotionally draining for a therapist because the therapist may feel the presence of a client's inner child, a child that is deeply hurting. This work should only be carried out once a strong therapeutic relationship has been developed with the client.

At the same time, it is important to prepare the client for 'inner child' work. Preparation might involve teaching the client distraction techniques and tools for mindfulness and relaxation, as set out in Chapter 1. Preparation might also involve helping the client to imagine a safe space for themselves, as a way of grounding them if they become overwhelmed by emotions. It may also become important to have a signal that the client provides (like a raised hand) if they feel they want to stop the counselling session at any time. Therapists should never force clients to undertake anything that clients do not want themselves to do. It is also important to consider the history of the client and their current environment and any challenges that they may be facing. If a client has a history of complex trauma (for example, child sexual abuse) then it may be that inner child work is not undertaken because this could be potentially experienced as overwhelming by the client, potentially re-traumatising them. It may be that a client's current life situation is full of distressing events – divorce, house move, job loss, bereavement etc. – and so inner child work may not be appropriate at this time. It is important for a therapist to take into consideration a client's past as well as the current challenges that they may be facing and this should form part of the assessment as to what sort of therapeutic work to undertake with the client.

The tale of the graceful hare

Harry the hare is a beautiful, long-legged, long-eared, soft brown furry creature, with big amber coloured eyes. Harry lives in at times a tough and at times a fun environment. In winter Harry is constantly hungry because there simply isn't enough food to go around and the ground beneath him is often frozen, making it very difficult for him to eat the grasses and roots that he needs. In spring and summer time, on the other hand, Harry takes great joy in boxing with his hare companions, and racing through the fields, enjoying the freedom of simply being and breathing in the fresh clean air that surrounds him in the countryside.

Whenever Harry hears a sound that makes him afraid, a sound that might mean a predator is nearby, Harry simply freezes. He stops dead in his tracks, sits up on his hind legs, and listens, listens and listens even more. If Harry reckons that the predator is far away enough from him then Harry will run away as fast as he can, and will keep on running until he is able to find a safe place to hide. If, on the other hand, the predator is just too close to Harry then Harry will have to decide whether to fight off the predator or whether to remain frozen in position, playing dead. All of these decisions and processes take place naturally for Harry, because they have a long evolutionary and biological history. Luckily for Harry, his memory and sense of self are not as highly developed as in human beings, and so if Harry survives his encounter with a predator he will not be going back over events, blaming himself for what he should or should not have done.

Interestingly, humans have also evolved to have a fight, flight or freeze response to dangerous and traumatic situations. Our bodies and minds are also involved in complex decision-making processes to try and make us safe. We too run, fight or freeze when there is danger around us; the main difference is that because our minds our more evolved than a hare's mind, we are left with complex associations, memories and responses if we survive a traumatic and dangerous event.

As therapists it is important for us to know that humans have a fight, flight or freeze response because we will see this in our clients. In many situations we may argue, fight or flee our way to safety. However, there are many situations whereby this is not possible, and so our minds and bodies take on the freeze response, which can be linked to the notion of dissociation. Dissociation, which is the process of us disconnecting or separating from our experiences, is an important survival mechanism in the face of threat. Thus, when faced with a life-threatening event or series of events, many of us will dissociate from this experience, whereby we may feel that we have left our own bodies, or that the traumatic event that is taking place feels like a film rather than reality. This allows us to survive experiences that are simply too traumatic to engage with psychologically and emotionally. Within a therapeutic setting, dissociation is an important aspect to consider when looking at emotional processing. Dissociation plays an important role in enabling individuals to cope with emotionally distressing experiences, because the process of dissociation protects people from having to take on the full extent of the emotional distress. However, what can then happen later on, once the trauma has ended, is that a person continues to struggle with symptoms associated with dissociation – perceptions of there being an unreal world, perceptions that somehow a person is not connected to their bodies, a person struggling to have any feelings at all. It may be that in these situations normalisation and containment, rather than emotional and psychological processing, are the therapeutic approach, especially if a therapist is not trained to work with specialised dissociative disorders. So it may be that therapeutic work here involves normalising a person's dissociative symptoms so that they feel that they are not 'going mad'. At the same time, therapeutic work may involve coping strategies to help clients manage their experiences of dissociation and any associated feelings of guilt or shame. Therapeutic work may also involve raising awareness of an individual's body and how emotions might be experienced in their body. The following case study demonstrates how we might work with dissociation.

Janet

Janet is a forty-year-old woman with two grown up children. Janet divorced an abusive husband ten years ago and since that time has been living alone. Janet received counselling within a year of leaving her husband; the therapy here focussed on her processing the emotional and physical abuse that she had experienced from her husband. Eighteen months ago Janet suffered a trauma. She was walking back from the pub at night on her own, when she was attacked. Janet cannot remember much about what happened, but she does remember a man trying to rape her and she also remembers receiving blows to her head. Somehow Janet managed to stay alive and a passing taxi driver called an ambulance. Nobody has ever been caught and prosecuted for this crime. Janet has come to counselling saying that she would like to explore what happened to her on the night of the attack and her reactions to this. Janet says that she finds it difficult sleeping, she finds it hard to concentrate, she has had to leave her job as a sales person. Janet also talks about feeling numb all of the time and not really having any emotions anymore, and how the world around her doesn't seem real, how people seem like robots to her.

In the above case, the therapist began by spending a few weeks building a strong therapeutic alliance with Janet, and exploring her current life circumstances. Quite quickly the therapist also gave Janet some psycho-education about trauma and its effects on the body and how this might link to the symptoms that Janet was experiencing. In this way the therapist was helping Janet to normalise her reactions. The therapist also provided Janet with a safe space in which she could explore her perceptions about what she thought had happened and how she had responded to the attack. Janet revealed that she felt guilty for not having fought off the attacker. Janet talked about how she should have pushed him away, kicked him with her stiletto heels, how she should have scratched and screamed at him. Janet perceived herself as weak because she had simply frozen. She perceived herself as failing to fight or to manage to run away from the attacker. The therapist helped Janet to explore these perceptions and also to consider the body's natural freeze response. Over time, Janet began to see that actually her body had frozen as a way of protecting her, as a way to ensure her survival and so Janet became less critical of herself. In this case the therapist had to decide what work, if any, to do regarding Janet's dissociative symptoms – her emotional numbing. As explained previously, dissociation is a coping mechanism, and so if in therapy we dismantle this for a client we are potentially dismantling the client's own coping strategy, potentially leading to worse outcomes for the client like self-harm or suicide. In the case of Janet, the therapist had to assess Janet's history of abuse and her current circumstances. It may be that normalisation and containment is better for Janet rather than processing her traumas. The therapist spoke with Janet about dissociative symptoms, what these are, and explored with Janet her experience of dissociation. In this way Janet became more understanding of her emotional numbing and surreal experience of the world. Janet was encouraged to keep a diary where she could express her perceptions and experiences and in this way Janet built up a good picture of how the intensity of her dissociation rises and falls on a daily and weekly basis. The therapist also explored with Janet coping strategies that she might find helpful during those times when her dissociative symptoms were at their strongest – grounding techniques like counting to 100, or describing a piece of furniture in detail, or imagining a list of her favourite sweets. Janet used to like running when she was younger and so she suggested that she would try to start doing this again. Janet found that running gave her a routine and also produced feel-good hormones in her body (serotonin), which further helped with her dissociative symptoms. In future the therapist might work with helping Janet to process fully the trauma that she had experienced; however, this work will proceed only if and when Janet feels ready, and only if and when the therapist also assesses that Janet has enough coping strategies and enough stability in her life to be able to deal with any distress that processing the trauma may produce in her. It may be the case that in processing Janet's trauma her dissociative symptoms will reduce even further. This case study illustrates the complexity of working with dissociation and trauma. Just because a client is experiencing emotional numbing, this does not mean that therapy should try to restore a client's emotional experience. Dissociation is a coping strategy and so therapists should proceed with caution when working with this. It may be better to normalise and contain dissociation rather than try to challenge or overcome it.

The following is another case study, this time looking at an integrative approach to empowering a client to process their emotions.

Simon

Simon was a single man in his early fifties who had a daughter from a relationship that ended several years ago. Throughout his adult life, Simon had drifted from job to job, never feeling fulfilled or rewarded in his work. He felt as though life was passing him by and struggled with confidence and self-esteem; the overwhelming belief that he was 'not good enough' pervaded his thoughts each day. Simon looked after his daughter's pet budgerigar, something that started when his pregnant daughter went into hospital to have her baby, and used this as a reason for stopping him from applying for jobs in other parts of the country. Whenever he thought about returning the bird back to his daughter he felt guilt, so powerful that he 'couldn't possibly' hand the bird back. Simon acknowledged that he had had a difficult relationship with his father, now deceased, who had emotionally abused him when he was a child and teenager. Simon came to therapy in order to work on his confidence and self-esteem and to overcome the barriers within him so that he could apply for jobs that he knew he was capable of doing. He wanted to let go of the negative emotions he felt towards himself, to let go of the emotions from the past and to 'start a new chapter in his life'.

During the information gathering stage, the therapist asked questions surrounding Simon's experience of his confidence and self-esteem: How does it feel to have low confidence and self-esteem? If he could explain the low confidence and self-esteem in terms of words what would they be? What situations/events triggered his low self-esteem? Does the lack of self-esteem have a form, a shape, a feeling, a colour? Where is it located in the body? Has there been a time when confidence and self-esteem were better? How would Simon know if he was confident and felt good about himself? Would his friends or family notice a difference?

Questions such as these allowed the therapist to build up an awareness of what it was like to be Simon and how Simon felt when he experienced low confidence and self-esteem. As he asked each question the therapist carefully observed Simon's posture, his facial expressions, breathing, voice timbre. The therapist asked Simon about anything that he was proud of achieving, any successes that he had forgotten about. Simon remembered a time when he used to cycle in the countryside on his own for miles and miles, and the wonderful feeling of achievement that he experienced at the end of the ride. The therapist noted this memory and the positive way in which Simon responded in terms of his posture and voice timbre, utilising it within subsequent sessions in order to help Simon elicit and associate positive thoughts with positive feelings and emotions, something that Simon had found difficult to do.

During the first two sessions Simon was taught breathing and progressive muscle relaxation techniques that would help ground him whenever his thoughts started to spiral out of control. In a relaxed state, he was taught how to be aware of his thoughts and how to externalise any uncomfortable thoughts through visualisation exercises. It was important to determine when Simon felt strong enough to deal with the emotions from the past, particularly in relation to his father, in order to avoid upset or distress. By the fourth session of therapy Simon felt as though he was making good progress and feeling more centred and relaxed so the therapist used age regression with dissociation to search through difficult memories in order to process and let them go emotionally. On an imaginary movie screen, Simon was able to experience a younger version of himself sitting at a kitchen table with his father who was jabbing a finger at his chest and yelling at him, saying things like Simon 'was a useless piece of shit' and that he 'wouldn't amount to anything'. Through reframing and soothing the younger version of himself with his adult self, Simon was able to process the complex emotions of guilt and shame and anger associated with the relationship with his father; emotions that had long been buried within and had manifested in problems with confidence and self-esteem were released in a dissociated way so as not to cause suffering. Simon understood that 'being the good boy' that he was, he had unconsciously fulfilled the suggestions of 'useless' and 'worthless' instilled by his father and that throughout his adult life had sabotaged various situations in order to remain 'useless' and 'worthless'. After all, good boys always listen to their father.

Simon wasn't a writer but he could draw so the therapist suggested that he keep a notebook where he sketched any negative emotions or thoughts that he felt at the time, but in such a way that they were very small and black and white drawings, almost insignificant on the page. Next to the small drawing he was instructed to sketch a large image of the way he would like to feel or think instead, for example, the drawing of a large golden heart to represent his kindness and compassion to others. He was to make these drawings as big and bold and bright as he could, time permitting. Cognitively challenging emotions and thoughts through art was something that Simon had never considered, but after a few weeks he came in with a notebook filled with beautiful drawings. Some of the best drawings he would cut out and stick around his home; the therapist encouraged this and suggested that he should frame some of them, which he subsequently did.

After several sessions of processing memories, emotions and feelings from the past, Simon felt that he had cleared his mind with regards to his father and his father's influence, and that it was time to 'move on'. The focus of therapy changed towards imagining being 'the most confident person in the world' and through hypnosis Simon was able to experience himself as a confident, outgoing person who was capable of dealing with situations in a positive way; lots of associations of future success and the wonderful experience of cycling that Simon had talked about during the consultation were created, with help from the therapist. A self-hypnosis audio recording of positive experiences during sessions was provided so that Simon could further reinforce therapeutic work at home. Through the use of relaxation and hypnosis Simon was taught to access his own 'wise inner advisor' and this helped him to build a solid relationship with himself that could sooth during difficult situations. Simon began to accept that he was a unique individual with qualities that no one else possessed, and his self-esteem began to grow. Simon discovered that it was time to hand the budgie back to his daughter, which he did.

Age progression techniques under hypnosis were used in the final sessions of therapy in which Simon created a blueprint of the way that he wanted to be: someone with strong confidence and high self-esteem, someone who felt good within themselves and worthwhile. Imagining a future job that he really wanted brought up images of boats and travel. Simon left therapy with the promise of contacting the therapist a few months later in order to let them know how he was getting along. The last contact with the therapist established that Simon had found a job which involved travelling the world in a ship.

The above case study illustrates the impact of unconscious emotional processing; how negative and damaging suggestions by figures of authority can become integrated in such a way that a cycle of avoidance or sabotage is established, often early in life, in order to stay true to the suggestions. Utilising the client's world and his experiences and capabilities, in this case through art and visual imagination, can begin the process of redemption and recovery. It is about finding something within the client that they can begin to work with; this can be anything, even something seemingly insignificant such as a hobby or a favourite colour or food, and working with it. Water a seed regularly and it grows into a tall strong tree. In the above example a combination of hypnotherapy, cognitive behavioural therapy and arts therapy was utilised in order to overcome barriers to growth and development, allowing the client to experience a world that they truly felt part of and belonged in.

The angry therapist

Tim was a therapist with a good reputation and lots of clients, specialising in stress and anxiety and using a range of different modalities and techniques that he developed over many years of practice. Gradually, things started to happen in Tim's life that made him angry. Not realising that he was carrying anger within him, and that this anger was getting progressively worse,

Tim started to notice that a lot of his clients were, in fact, quite angry. This affected his thera-peutic relationship with clients and got in the way of interventions: he couldn't treat this person for anxiety unless they 'lost the anger', he couldn't treat that person because 'they were always losing it in his session'. This fixation on anger in his clients meant that Tim eventually lost a lot of them and he was left even more angry as his practice became smaller and smaller. The lesson to learn from this is that as therapists we need to be mindful of our own emotions and feelings to avoid the possibility of projecting these upon our clients.

At the same time, as therapists we may be picking up and feeling emotions that our clients are feeling. For example, as a therapist you might feel anger in your body when working with a client. Interestingly, the client may say to you that they are fairly calm and do not tend to get angry very much. As a therapist it is vital to be noticing what emotions are stirred within us when we work with clients because it may be that we are feeling emotions that our clients are repressing for themselves. Thus, by being alert to our own emotions we are also alert to the possible feelings that our clients may be containing through denial, repression, dissociation and so forth. It is therefore important for us as therapists to develop ways of processing our own emotional states and experiences. Physical activities, creative expression, communicat-ing with supportive colleagues, friends and family members, engaging in therapy ourselves, these are all mechanisms through which we can stay alert to, and express and process, our own inner emotional landscapes. Both of us are keen runners and we subscribe to the viewpoint of Thaddeus Kostrubala, a medical doctor and psychiatrist, who stated the following in 1976: 'I have come to the conclusion that running, done in a particular way, is a form of natural psychotherapy. It stimulates the unconscious and is a powerful catalyst to the human psyche' (Kostrubala, 1976: 119). We both go on many runs as a way of helping ourselves to process our emotions and as a form of self-care. Indeed, there are many books now written about the emotional and psychological positive effects of running.

As therapists it is vital to find what works for us, how we can process the harrowing stories and experiences that clients share with us. We have to be creative and draw upon coping strat-egies that work for us. This may involve simply being in and with nature because as the next section illustrates, the emotions we feel are not only created by other humans, but by animals and nature itself.

Not all emotions are caused by humans

Not all the emotions that we experience during our lives are a direct result of humans or rela-tionships with humans. Witnessing the red disk of sun as it sinks below the edge of the ocean can stir feelings within us. Anyone who has experienced a sunrise or a sunset, a dark canvas of night lit up with stars, anyone who has sat on top of a hill with a peaceful breeze would find it hard not to experience some kind of emotion; perhaps a connection with the universe and beyond, something profound and indescribable, unconscious yet tangible, perhaps a feeling of peace and contentment or at the other end of the scale excitement and bewilderment. Some-times these emotions are powerful and distinct, other times distant and unfathomable. As a therapist building awareness and understanding that emotions can be experienced through con-nection, unconscious processes, instincts, non-human interactions, light, dark, sound, smell, texture, everything else in the world and beyond means that we can focus in on our clients and the way they feel and what they are trying to say and how their representation of the world builds and influences their emotions, with greater insight and added purpose.

Exercise: Building awareness of emotions due to connection with the world

1   Sit in a dark room and listen to the rain pattering against the windows. What emotions does this experience stir within you? How do you feel? Do your emotions and feelings change when you turn on the light?

2   Experience a sunset and sunrise. How does each of these make you feel? What emotions are there? Do your feelings and emotions change in relation to the weather?

3   Think about the vastness of the universe and note your emotions and feelings. Do you feel connected or disconnected or somewhere in between within the universe?

4   Watch a bird closely, notice how it behaves, the things it does. What emotions does the bird elicit within you? How do you feel when you see a bird fly?

5   Sit in a garden and listen to the wind rustling the leaves. What emotions stir within you? Smell the flowers in the garden. How does each different smell make you feel? Does the smell of some flowers bring back powerful emotions?

6   Taste something nice. What feelings does this bring? Taste something not so nice. How do this make you feel?

Conclusion

In this chapter we have looked at emotions and their relevance for therapy. We have considered the distressing and unethical aspects to emotions, or the 'shadow side' to our human nature. We have highlighted the importance of processing emotions so that they do not come to control us and our responses to other people and the world around us. We have looked at CBT based, relational, person-centred and hypnotherapeutic modalities for the insights that these bring into emotional processing. We have presented some case studies of integrative psychotherapeutic work in relation to clients and their emotions. We have considered the importance of dissociation when thinking about emotions and that therapeutic work can focus upon normalising dissociative symptoms for clients. We also consider the importance of us as therapists being mindful of our own emotions so that we do not allow these to interfere with the therapeutic relationship and also with therapeutic processes. Finally, we have considered how non-human factors can also influence our emotions. Ultimately, this chapter has demonstrated that key to integrative psychotherapeutic practice is an understanding of the significance of emotions, for our clients and for ourselves.

References

Baker, R. (2007) *Emotional Processing: Healing Through Feeling*. Oxford: Lion Hudson Books.

Briere, J. & Scott, C. (2006) *Principles of Trauma Therapy: A Guide to Symptoms, Evaluations, and Treatment*. Thousand Oaks, CA: Sage.

Joseph, A. (2009) *Cognitive Behaviour Therapy*. Chichester: Capstone Publishing Ltd.

Kostrubala, T. (1976) *The Joy of Running*. San Francisco: Ora Press.

Madden, K. (2009) *The Book of Shamanic Healing*, 6th edition. Woodbury, MN: Llewellyn, p. 147.

Mearns, D. & Cooper, M. (2005) *Working at Relational Depth in Counselling & Psychotherapy*. London: Sage.

Mearns, D. & Thorne, B. (2012) *Person-Centred Counselling in Action*, 3rd edition. London: Sage.

Sienkiewicz, H. (1806) *Quo Vadis: A Narrative of the Time of Nero*. Warsaw: Gebethnera & Wolffa.

Chapter 3

Attachment as an integrative concept

Nurturing a client within therapy offers them experience with the healthy attachments which can be felt within a nurturing family environment, thus enabling them to experience for themselves what is secure and what is not.

Robina Zafar, Integrative Psychotherapist

Introduction

Attachment is a core integrative concept. Without a profound appreciation for attachment, and without an engagement with attachment-related issues and disorders, our therapeutic work cannot be as dynamic, creative and effective as it needs to be. Attachment lies at the very essence of human wellbeing and existence, and so it is crucial that we take the time to consider attachment through the integration of CBT, person-centred, relational and hypnotherapeutic modalities.

In this chapter we build on the attachment-related work that we set out in Chapters 1 and 2. We consider healthy and unhealthy attachment and bring exercises that can be used with our clients. These exercises can also be used for ourselves, as therapists and other mental health practitioners, to consider our own healthy and unhealthy attachments. We look at non-attachment and consider its links to meditation, mindfulness and also Buddhist principles, given the popularity of these Eastern-based approaches to mental health and wellbeing. Indeed, it may be that through the practice of non-attachment we can develop and cultivate healthy attachments and attachment styles, with ourselves, other people, animals and objects. We also explore how clients can strive to maintain and enrich the healthy attachments that they may have, as anchors for their lives. This is particularly important given the socio-political challenges of the current era for human existence. We look at attachment and relationships, and some issues to consider for counselling concerning relationships. Finally, we consider attachment through the lens of CBT, person-centred, relational and hypnotherapeutic schools of practice and set out some case studies of how we have worked integratively with attachment.

A cycle ride around Rutland Water

Rutland Water is a 26-mile nature reserve in the East Midlands of England, in the county of Rutland. At the centre is a human-made reservoir with crystal blue water, around which fauna and flora and wildlife exist. Cycling around this beautiful environment it is impossible not to notice attachment-related behaviours amongst the birds and animals that reside here. Wildfowl are in abundance and when cycling during the early hours of the day or during sunset a regular experience is watching the birds taking off from one side of the reservoir, to fly fast and free above the water, to then land on another part of the reservoir's shore. It is exciting to hear the gaggle of wildfowl and to listen to their powerful wings brushing across the sky. Importantly, the birds follow each other in droves – as the first few take off into the air, they are followed by more and more birds. Essentially, this is attachment behaviour within wildfowl. The birds keep themselves safe by ensuring that they are attached to a wider flock, behaving in unison as a large entity rather than individually doing their own maverick thing. As one pedals around the reservoir, one also notices the sheep there. During lambing season it is obvious to the eye

that lambs generally are attached to their mothers or other significant females for shelter, safety and food. To view and experience attachment-related behaviours in non-human species it is therefore well worthwhile taking a cycle ride around Rutland Water!

Attachment seems to have an evolutionary, biological rationale. Attachment-related behaviours can be seen in wide-ranging animal and bird species. Within humans, attachment also plays a significant evolutionary and survival role. However, in human beings attachment is complex and we can have both healthy and unhealthy attachments, with ourselves, other people, objects, animals and other real or imagined phenomena. It seems crucial, therefore, for us to explore unhealthy and healthy attachments, before focussing on the idea and practice of non-attachment.

What is unhealthy attachment and what attachment disorders might there be?

Clients who come for therapy will often have challenging attachment-related behaviours, perceptions and emotions, and they are likely to be experiencing unhealthy attachments in their lives. At the same time, some clients that we see may be viewed as experiencing various attachment disorders. Adults with attachment disorders might be viewed as experiencing the following symptoms:

- An inability to trust other people.
- Anger, hostility and aggression towards self and others.
- An inability to connect with other people.
- Social isolation.
- Various maladaptive coping strategies such as substance abuse and other kinds of addictions.
- Co-dependent relationships whereby each individual within the co-dependency is over-dependent on the other person or people for their self-identity and for meeting their needs.
- A lack of boundaries between self and other people, an over-familiarity.

It may also be that individuals who have been diagnosed as having autistic-related symptoms and traits, including individuals with attention deficit hyperactive disorder (ADHD), experience disordered attachment-based symptoms. It is important to acknowledge that our clients will have different attachment-related styles and issues and for us to accommodate their needs effectively. Often trainee therapists are told that clients with an avoidant attachment style tend not to come for therapy. Whilst this may be the case, it is not the case with all clients. Some clients may have a predominantly avoidance attachment style and as therapists we need to be aware of this and work appropriately. For example, with an avoidant client it may be that we need to be more flexible in terms of last-minute cancellations. We may also need to be more patient as therapists in terms of building a therapeutic relationship with an avoidant attachment style client. Within sessions, patience is key because it may take the first 40 minutes of a 60 minute session before any significant issues are discussed by the client. We also may need to be more open to the client not committing to, or avoiding, any tasks or exercises that we ask them to undertake in between sessions. With clients who have an anxious attachment style then it is important to keep strong boundaries. It is also important to place the locus of control (Rotter, 1954) with the client rather than with ourselves. An anxiously attached client might be prone to looking to us as therapists for 'an answer'. It is therefore important for us to give the client control in terms of their own decision-making and actions. With any clients exhibiting co-dependent relationships with significant others in their lives (for example, with their mothers or their partners), we as therapists need to tread very carefully because as the client grows in therapy and begins to become more aware of their co-dependency, they may become very fearful of implementing changes in their lives and may become angry towards us as the therapist. It is important for us as therapists not to get stuck within complex family dynamics, but rather to remain boundaried and professional, and even err on the side of caution here. There is now also a large amount of research and policy development around good practice when working with children and young adults with attachment disorders. Children who are adopted or in foster care raise particular attachment-related issues. For further information, see guidelines by the National Institute for Clinical Excellence (NICE, 2015).

The girl in the sweet shop

Picture a girl aged 13 who lived in a sweet shop. This girl was sickly, bedridden and she was told by doctors and by her family that she could not and should not eat any of the sweets in the shop because she was extremely allergic to sugar. The girl was allowed to sit in her bed, which was brought downstairs, and she was able to watch the customers come and go as they bought pear drops, cola cubes, sherbet lemons and other delights. The girl's family often ignored her because they were so uncomfortable about her illness and were terrified of becoming too emotionally close to her in case she died. As a result, this girl spent the next five years of her life mostly in bed and alone. Her comfort was observing the customers in the shop, particularly the regulars. The girl would remember their names and she would listen to what they were saying. The girl would also notice every detail of their clothing, their bodies and their facial expressions and when these customers left the shop the girl would imagine to herself the perfect lives that these customers led – lives full of laughter, love and value. The girl often felt a strange emptiness inside herself and it was only through obsessing about other people and their lives that she could feel real, through their imagined and idealised lives this girl could live and exist. One day this girl grew up and decided that she would leave the sweet shop and leave her family and that she would go out into the wider world. Nonetheless, despite managing to find a job and a flat to rent, this girl-woman led a lonely existence. She did get married and she had children; however, this never felt real for her. Therefore, this girl-woman carried on focussing on other people, on their lives, their bodies, their minds and she imagined perfection. For this girl-woman, other people mattered more than she did to herself, other people were of greater value than her own children; through the imagined lives of other people this girl-woman lived out the rest of the days of her life.

The above story serves to illustrate the challenges of working with clients with attachment disorders. Clearly, the girl in the sweet shop was denied experiencing any sort of secure attachment style. Her family exhibited a preoccupied, or anxious, attachment style towards her because they were frightened that she might die. At the same time, her family avoided her and so exhibited an avoidant style of attachment to her. Unable to access and to experience any supportive, caring and stable relationships, this girl developed attachments to the customers who came to the shop. However, because the girl never really interacted directly with these customers, she was forced to interact with them in her mind, through her imagination. This girl imagined the customers being perfect people who lived perfect lives and so the girl became very attached to near strangers. This dysfunctional attachment process meant that the

customers became more important to the girl than herself and her own family. In this way, the girl grew into an adult with an attachment disorder because she was unable to securely attach with her husband and her children, but rather spent most of her time and energy attaching to near-strangers, whereby she imagined them as perfect individuals and it was this perfection that she was intoxicated by, almost like an addiction. A client like this might even harm themselves during times when they feel their inner loneliness and worthlessness, or they might dissociate and regress back to a child-like state where they are unable to reflect upon the psychological and emotional processes that are taking place for them. Therapeutic work with such clients can be challenging, complex and long-term. Whilst clients' attachment styles can develop and change, for clients with attachment disorders this is particularly difficult.

What is healthy attachment?

Given the complexity of the attachment disorders and unhealthy attachments that our clients may be experiencing, it is important to consider how we might understand healthy attachments and healthy attachment styles. As therapists it is crucial that we exhibit healthy attachments and attachment styles, within and outside of the therapeutic setting. Not only is this beneficial for our clients, but is also an essential aspect of our own self-care and ethicality. So what is healthy attachment in relation to our relationship with ourselves and with other people? Perhaps this involves elements of the following characteristics:

- Being boundaried with other people – not needing to share everything in our lives with everyone that we know or meet.
- Having a strong sense of our own agency, or locus of control.
- Being open and flexible to various changes and challenges in our lives.
- Knowing what our own emotional, physical and psychological needs are and catering to these as much as is possible.
- Accepting that all relationships we have with other people will be strained at times and that this is okay.
- Having a strong sense that we are okay, that we can fix any difficult challenges that happen in our lives.
- Having a strong sense of self-worth.
- Valuing ourselves and others.
- Having self-compassion and being compassionate to others.
- Not being overly concerned about what other people think or say about us.
- Being able to connect with others and build relationships with them.
- Having a strong sense of our own identity and the various roles that we play in life.

Non-attachment and Buddhism

Within the principles of Buddhism lies the concept that all suffering comes from attachment: attachment to ideas, principles, objects, theories, beliefs, things, emotions, feelings and thoughts that build up our unique experience of life. Buddhists believe that positive experiences such as pleasure or enjoyment can also cause suffering. For example, eating a piece of chocolate can bring us pleasure while bingeing on lots of chocolate can lead to suffering through addiction to sugar as well as obesity and related health problems.

Some attachments that we form are physical, such as addictions to certain drugs; if you drink a lot of strong coffee each day and subsequently stop, you may experience caffeine withdrawal symptoms such as headaches, lethargy and even depression. Other attachments can be less tangible and oriented towards our own perceptions of reality, the 'external universe' out there and how we relate and process or model this within our own 'inner' mind.

Attachments based upon individual perception, values, belief systems and distorted realities can be much more complex and difficult to address or redress within the therapeutic environment. Based on sensory information of the external world and universe, our minds process the visual, auditory, kinaesthetic, olfactory and gustatory data gathered in order to create an experience of this outside world within our brain. Since unconscious processing of the external world begins from the first moment of birth, attachment styles can be encoded during the early years of life before the development of speech (Briere & Scott, 2006) and can result in firmly ingrained beliefs. For example, a child may be psychologically abused by a parent from an early age and consequently develop an unhealthy attachment style that presupposes that he/she is unattractive and has always been unattractive and that there is no way that he/she will ever be attractive. To the individual concerned, the external universe, whose perception she holds internally within her mind, is an environment where no one is to be trusted and where aggression to others is right and appropriate in trigger situations.

A therapist may find it very difficult, if not impossible, to change this person's internal perception of the outside world simply by telling the client that she is attractive and that most people are okay and can be trusted and that there's no need to get angry in certain situations. Getting the client to understand how and why his/her attachments persist and, in many cases, the causalities behind the development of their attachments coupled with reframing can be more useful in breaking patterns of behaviour.

Nurturing the concept of non-attachment can be useful in empowering the client, providing them with choice: the choice to attach to something and the choice to let it go. Buddhists pursue the idea of non-attachment as a way of ending suffering, a way of eliminating the craving or thirst (*tanha*) that causes clinging or attachment (*upadana*). Since craving leads to clinging, Buddhists believe that suffering ends when craving disappears (Komagata, 2010). In order to get rid of craving, the process of mindfulness meditation is used by Buddhists.

The boy in the sweet shop

There was once a young boy whose uncle owned the biggest sweet shop in the city. Every weekend the boy would make the trip to visit his uncle by bus, looking forward to scoffing his face with chocolates, bonbons, lollipops and toffees. His uncle would always have a little surprise in store for the young boy: a bag of sweets left under the counter or tied to one of the tall plants that stood either side of the entrance. On this particular occasion, however, when the boy arrived at the shop there was no sign of his uncle. The boy called out his name, 'Uncle Tom! Uncle Tom!' But no reply. What was the boy supposed to do? Then his eyes alighted on a glass jar on top of the counter. The jar was filled with gobstoppers, large and round and tasty looking. The boy made his way to the jar. He knew that he shouldn't put his hand in the jar without his uncle's permission but the call of the gobstoppers was too loud. Turning his head slowly one way and then the other the boy decided to pilfer a gobstopper. Sliding his hand in through the narrow neck of the jar he grabbed one of the sweets. But when he went to pull his hand out of the jar he found that it was stuck. Try as he might he couldn't slide his hand, grasping the gobstopper, out of the jar. His face turning scarlet, the boy tried shifting the angle of his hand but to no avail. His hand was trapped in the jar, grasping the gobstopper. He didn't know what to do. The young boy stood with his hand stuck in the jar until his uncle appeared from the back of the shop. A faint smile melted the shopkeeper's features when he noticed the boy's predicament. Eventually the boy let go of the gobstopper and slid his hand out of the jar. 'What a beautiful morning to learn an important lesson!' the shopkeeper declared.

The above story highlights the principles behind the concept of craving: the boy desires the sweet so strongly that he craves it beyond anything else. Because of the craving the boy is then trapped, his hand stuck in the jar. Craving leads to suffering. Through meditation and nurturing mindfulness, Buddhists strive to recognise and respond more healthily to desires, mediating the cravings that can arise and preventing the suffering.

Mindfulness meditation and attachment

In Chapter 1 we introduced the idea of mindfulness and presence within the framework of integrative therapy and now consider how mindfulness meditation can be utilised by therapists and clients in order to become better aware of how our senses lead to craving and attachment. Nurturing non-attachment through meditation can start to open us up to the external universe, aligning our own internal perceptions with healthier belief systems; for example, letting go of the desire and craving for material things by letting go of the belief that these things will make us happy. Instead of buying the best car we can or cannot afford, we learn to simply enjoy the pleasure of driving a car without the belief that we need the actual car in order to make us happy; in this concept it is the driving experience that makes us happy rather than the model of car.

The following meditation can be performed by therapists in order to familiarise themselves with their own attachments. It can also be given as homework to clients with attachment disorders, as a process of building the client's own self-awareness and understanding. By performing this meditation at home, the client can monitor their experience in a continuous daily way that does not rely on being present with the therapist in an office. The client can then report any findings that they discover within themselves to the therapist at the next session.

A meditation for non-attachment

1   Find a safe quiet place and sit down in a comfortable position.
2   Focus on your breathing, the inbreath and the outbreath, relaxing your muscles as you do. Imagine any stress or anxiety floating away from you like balloons.
3   Begin to get a sense of an attachment that you have. For example, an attachment to a physical object such as a car or an emotional attachment to a partner or friend, perhaps someone at work. It can be a recent attachment or something that you have carried within you for a long time.
4   With every breath that you take, imagine that you are a detective hunting for clues as you go deeper into the attachment. What is its purpose? How did it start? What are your emotions and feelings surrounding this attachment? What does the attachment tell you about yourself? What do you hope to get out of grasping the desire, object, feeling, emotion?
5   Begin to sense the bigger picture surrounding the attachment by breaking it down into its constituent parts. For example, if you crave a car, think about the car as the sum of many different components put together in a factory. Imagine the machines and men building the car. Imagine the car being painted and the seats being put in. Get a sense of the many different stages in the process and the many different people involved: designers, manufacturers, advertisers. As you get a deeper experience of the attachment, so the attachment can begin to change in some way.
6   As you focus on your breathing, begin now to sense yourself without the attachment. Imagine your world without the desire or craving that you have been dwelling on in this meditation. Imagine how it would feel to let go of the attachment. For example, imagine yourself driving and just enjoying the experience of driving itself and not the car. Make your experience without the attachment as real as you can, as though you are there, seeing what you see, hearing what you hear and feeling what you feel.
7   Begin to acknowledge any positive sensations and feelings that you have now that you can experience yourself without the attachment. Acknowledge to yourself that you can feel happy without the attachment. Acknowledge to yourself that you wish to let go of the attachment and imagine it floating away from you along with any emotions and feelings associated with the attachment. Begin to acknowledge happiness without desire or craving or clinging. Get a sense of this positivity and turn it up in your mind and body as though you have a remote control within you that enhances your strength and resilience, your happiness and wisdom.
8   Focus on your breathing once more and return your attention back to your surroundings.

Regular meditation and reflection in this way can loosen the grip of unhealthy attachments allowing the seed of non-attachment to grow and prosper. As therapists we often absorb a great deal of information from our clients, some of which is complex, often disturbing and upsetting, and which can trigger our own unhealthy attachments. A simple 5-minute meditation such as the above exercise can be performed between client bookings as a way of cleansing and reenergizing our mind, body, thoughts, feelings and emotions. It can provide the therapist with a way of letting go of attachments as well as building greater self-awareness of any trigger points for attachments to form or resurface.

Attachment and psycho-emotional and physical boundaries

Many counselling skills books include a focus upon boundaries between therapists and their clients. Establishing and maintaining clear and consistent boundaries is seen as essential, as a way of protecting both the client and the therapist, and for developing and maintaining a strong therapeutic relationship (Amis, 2017). It is important to link attachment with the issue of boundaries because as therapists we need to be mindful of our own attachment styles to ourselves and to others in order to have a better understanding of what challenges these bring for remaining boundaried with clients. As explained in Chapter 1, preoccupied/anxious attachment style to self and/or to others involves an individual being overly focussed upon themselves (preoccupied attachment style with the self) and/or an overly anxious preoccupation with how other people perceive us (preoccupied attachment style in relation to others). If, as therapists, we are not aware of this in ourselves then this could translate into unethical and unboundaried practice. Thus, if we are too anxious about ourselves then this means that we are unable to sufficiently focus upon our clients. During a counselling session we may be thinking anxious and repetitive thoughts like, 'I am feeling anxious', 'I feel myself losing control'. We may also have thoughts like, 'I wonder what the client thinks of me?' 'Am I coming across as helpful?' If this happens too frequently during a therapy session we are giving with a client, then this leads to ineffective and even dangerous clinical practice. Having nerves initially as we train to be therapists is normal and fine, which is why a lot of time is spent on counselling courses practising and developing counselling skills with our student colleagues in a safe environment. At the same time, it is important to check in with the client fairly regularly, perhaps after every other session, whether they are finding the counselling useful or not. However, if we find that we continue to have interruptive and frequent anxiety-provoking thoughts about ourselves, then this may indicate a preoccupied attachment style. It is important to deal with this rather than simply ignore or push it to one side. Equally, if we have an avoidant attachment style with ourselves or with other people, then this can also impact on any therapy that we are providing. As discussed in Chapter 1, an avoidant attachment style involves ignoring or avoiding our own emotions and/or the emotions of other people. If, as therapists, we allow this attachment style to predominate within a therapy setting, then this potentially means we are avoiding certain topics of exploration with our clients because these topics make us feel uncomfortable, and so we avoid them, even though the client might actually want to be, or benefit from, exploring them.

The discussion above suggests that as therapists we cannot simply play the role of a secure base. Rather, we need to be reflecting upon our own attachment styles outside of the work that we do in order to work with these so that they are less likely to impact upon our practice. It is possible to change our attachment styles, as well as to become much more aware of them so that they are less likely to impact on our thoughts, feelings and behaviours. We can learn about our own attachment styles through undertaking personal therapy, which many counselling students do. Additionally, it is possible to access questionnaires that focus on our 'attachment styles'. For example, there is the Adult Attachment Interview (George et al., 1985). It is also well worth reading and engaging with *Reinventing Your Life*, a book by Jeffrey Young and Janet Klosko. This book helps people to identify their 'life traps', which are patterns of thoughts, feelings and behaviours that begin in childhood and continue on into adult life (Young & Klosko, 1994). Two critical life-traps that counselling students and practitioners often have are the abandonment and the subjugation life-trap. The abandonment life trap involves feeling that the people you love will abandon you and that you will always remain emotionally isolated; you will always be completely alone and will never be able to make up the gap of the person you have lost. The subjugation life-trap involves feeling that you have little or no control over your fate; you are eager to please other people and have difficulty in not responding to all the demands and the needs that other people make on you (Young & Klosko, 1994). It is important essentially to identify our own life-traps, to understand their childhood bases, to understand how we cope in relation to these life-traps and to then challenge these. Interestingly, life-traps can be linked to attachment styles because it might be, for example, that the abandonment and subjugation life-traps are linked to any preoccupied and/or avoidant attachment styles we may have. These can substantially impact upon our work with clients, and yet many counsellors are unaware of their attachment and how this can impact on their approach to working with clients. This brings us to the issue of boundaries.

Psycho-emotional and physical boundaries are there to protect us and our clients. These boundaries protect the space for therapeutic practice, work that is often emotionally, psychologically and physically demanding. Boundaries enable therapeutic work to take place through relational depth, intimacy and connectivity, because boundaries contain the work that we and our clients undertake. Without boundaries, strong emotions and psychological processes would not be contained, potentially leading to unethical relationships being developed between client and therapist, and unethical behaviours. This is partly why clinical placements are required to provide a private and safe location for therapy to take place, with there being clarity regarding contracting with clients, how notes are safely stored, and clear procedures for breaking confidentiality with clients. Often counselling students will express surprise and even negative judgement regarding hypothetical cases where boundaries between client and therapist could be blurred. Nonetheless, it is important to highlight that boundary issues often creep up on us unawares because in reality we cannot anticipate things that may happen that can place a strain on boundaries, particularly if then also throwing into this mix the complexity of attachment issues.

Consider the case of a client who is unable to attend a session because she is reliant on her son to take her to the counselling service. The client is potentially in a co-dependent relationship with her son because her son likes to insist that he help her out, to then have the power to back out of commitments that he has made regarding his mother. The mother telephones the counselling service to say that she cannot come for her session with you. The counselling service responds by saying that they will pass on the mother's message to you and that you or the counselling service will contact her. When the manager of the counselling service calls you, the therapist, to ask you whether you would like to telephone the client directly yourself to speak to her or whether you would like the service to schedule in another appointment with the client, what will you do? In many ways, how you respond to this question and this situation will be partly determined by your own attachment style and your attachment to the client. If you have a predominantly preoccupied attachment style then you may decide to call the client yourself. The risk here is that you end up providing an unscheduled counselling session over the telephone, which leaves you feeling exhausted and rather annoyed that you have given a counselling session from home during your personal time! In this situation it would be better to telephone the client but to make it clear that you are calling to reschedule the session with her. If you have an anxious ambivalent attachment style then perhaps you would like to initially contact the client, but at the same time you feel aggrieved, even angry, that she did not attend the last session with you. Perhaps you decide to tell the counselling service manager to contact the client on your behalf and then perhaps in your next session with the client you will continue to be annoyed with them. In this situation, it is important to seek advice from your clinical supervisor, to express your thoughts and feelings so that these do not come into the therapeutic setting with your client. If you have an avoidant attachment style, perhaps you tell the manager of the counselling service that you are happy for them to contact the client. Perhaps at your next session with the client you tend to avoid mentioning that the client did not attend last week; or perhaps you avoid talking through your thoughts and feelings around the client's non-attendance with your clinical supervisor. This discussion serves as an important illustration about the kind of boundary issues that clinical work can raise and how our responses can be partly influenced by our attachment styles.

There will inevitably be times in our practice where boundaries are challenged. This is why, not only is it so important to have regular clinical supervision, but also to be aware of our own attachment styles and to lead an authentic life. By this we mean it is important to grow as a person if undertaking counselling and psychotherapeutic training. It is important to accept that how we view ourselves and others, and the relationships that we have with other people, will inevitably change whilst we train to be counsellors. Some trainees resist change, believing that somehow it is possible to reflect a secure base within a therapeutic setting without necessarily having a secure base in other parts of their lives. This is not possible because clients will trigger our own deep-seated attachment issues through the things they say or do, and so it is important to develop a secure base for ourselves in all aspects of our lives. We now encourage you to spend a few moments reflecting upon the following set of questions as part of your journey into understanding and processing attachment:

- List the people that you feel you are attached to in your life.
- List the animals that you feel you are attached to in your life.
- List the objects that you feel you are attached to in your life – this could be your car, your mobile phone, your computer for example.
- Now, for every person/animal/object, consider whether this is a healthy or unhealthy attachment using the list of healthy and unhealthy characteristics mentioned already in this chapter.
- Consider how you might change an unhealthy attachment into a healthy one.
- Consider whether there might be some unhealthy attachments that you want to be rid of, and consider what the challenges might be to ridding yourself of these.
- Consider how you might boost your list of healthy attachments.

The long walk to non co-dependency

There was once a young man who lived in a kingdom where the weather would change on an hourly basis, so that one moment it might be freezing cold with snow, whereas the next moment it might be breezy and mild. The rapid changeability of the weather kept this young man very much obsessed by it, and very unsettled because he did not know from one moment to the next what to expect – wind, heavy rain, thunder, fog, heat, cold, snow, what next ? Every day the young man would take the short walk to the only hilltop in his kingdom where he would sit and look out and try and spot what weather system was about to arrive. The young man would also bring offerings to this hilltop – fruit, chocolate, flowers – in the hope that these might placate the Weather Wizard. This young man's life was dominated by his thoughts, feelings and behaviours in relation to the Weather Wizard. What wonderful gift could he bring to make the Weather Wizard happier? What song might he sing to the Weather Wizard in order to get some sunshine? What other form of flattery might he draw upon to get the Weather Wizard's attention? Now and then the young man's efforts were rewarded, and for a few moments the sky above would become crystal-like blue, and the sun would shine neither too strongly or too weakly, and for those few seconds the young man felt comfortable and well. It was these few moments of wellbeing that kept this young man coming back to the hilltop, for he yearned, even needed, the blue sky and the sunshine to appear, no matter how briefly or how sporadically. This young man's greatest fear was leaving the hilltop, his kingdom and the Weather Wizard, for what would he have then? Beyond the Weather Wizard, the young man could not imagine a life for himself; all he could picture was a blank piece of paper, nothingness.

One night the young man had a vivid dream. In this dream appeared a swallow, who sang him a beautiful song and somehow the young man could translate the bird's melody into words. The words told him about another kingdom that existed at the end of a long trail, a trail that began on the East side of this young man's kingdom. The swallow sang about how this trail led through woodland, through fields, around rivers and lakes, but that eventually, the trail stopped and that where it stopped the weather was much more stable, it didn't constantly change. In fact, the weather system in this second kingdom was reliable, dependable – yes it changed as all weather systems do but there was a stability about it, a reassurance that any change in temperature or moisture levels would come about gradually, and moreover, when the sunshine appeared it would stay for weeks, even months. The young man awoke terrified, yet with a desperate need to find this magical trail that would take him away from his kingdom to another place in the universe. He got out of his hammock and packed a rucksack with items of food and clothing, and he decided not to visit the hilltop that day because he might get stuck there, not wanting to upset the Weather Wizard now that he was leaving.

The young man stepped out of his dwelling and began walking due East. At that moment, the weather changed from being cloudy and humid, to gale force winds blowing and heavy rain lashing down. The atrocious weather conditions made the young man think about the Weather Wizard, and made him criticise himself for not having taken any gift to the hilltop that morning. Thunder and lightning encompassed the young man, and he began to doubt himself and his ability to reach the kingdom that the bird had told him about in his lucid dream. 'I'm not good enough' is a thought that kept repeating itself as the young man kept on putting one foot in front of the other. 'I should have gained the Weather Wizard's permission to do this' is another thought that the young man berated himself with. This lasted for days. The young man was almost driven to insanity by his fear-driven thoughts, but he kept on going further and further East, having found the mythical trail that the swallow had promised him existed.

Then one day the young man awoke to discover that it had stopped raining, and that instead of hurricanes there was a gentle breeze blowing. The young man smiled to himself, then stood up, stretched out his arms and skipped around the lake that was beside him, where he had spent the night tucked up in his tent. The young man laughed and cried and shouted out 'I am free', and for the first time in his life he felt like an individual person – out of the grasp of the Weather Wizard. The young man got a piece of paper out of his tent and wrote a brief note, 'Goodbye Weather Wizard', on it. He tied the note to a jagged rock and threw the rock into the lake, watching it as it plunged down into the deep water. At this point, a town appeared on the opposite side of the lake. The young man quickly gathered up his things and ran over to the town, where he noticed that the sky was blue and the sun was shining and that there was an air of calm. Th young man decided that this was where he would spend the rest of his life, because in this place he felt secure in himself, and any previous thoughts that he had had about the Weather Wizard completely disappeared. In this new kingdom the young man also discovered that the people there were calm and helpful, without expecting any offerings from him. More-over, the people here did not bully or manipulate others and so the young man discovered that he could truly be himself and could live out the rest of his days embracing his own uniqueness. This new kingdom is where the young man finally relaxed and took delight in being himself. He had made the long journey from the *Kingdom of Co-Dependency* to this new *Kingdom of Independency* and he was loving it!

Attachment through an integrative lens of person-centred, CBT, relational and hypnotherapeutic modalities

Attachment as a concept can be thought of integratively because it transcends different psy-chotherapeutic modalities. Working with person-centred theory, attachment can be viewed as helping clients to explore and accept their 'real selves' as opposed to them clinging to, hating or not understanding their 'self-concepts'. As explained in Chapter 1, clients will often come to therapy stuck with 'self-concepts' that they either are unaware of consciously, or are aware of but do not feel are really who they are. The self-concept is, after all, how others perceive us, and how others value us. Thinking around attachment, it seems reasonable to suggest that a person experiencing a secure attachment with themselves and with others is a person who is in touch with, understands, accepts and values their 'real self', the self that is part of who they really are, their innate qualities and attributes (Rogers, 1951). An individual who values them-selves for who they are – with the 'good, the bad and the ugly' – is able to be their own 'best friend', their own secure base and as a result is able to build boundaried and secure relation-ships with other people. Attachment can also be linked to person-centred approaches, in the sense that the person with a secure attachment style is likely to have an internal locus of con-trol, being motivated to act upon the world through their internal views and their own decisions rather than being overly influenced by other people's actions or viewpoints. Where individuals have had conditions attached to their sense of self-worth, then these individuals are unlikely to have developed a secure base because they are likely to rely on other people's judgements and as such are likely to have anxious or avoidant attachment styles. This can be linked to rela-tional psychotherapeutic modalities, in that if a person has experienced others in unboundaried and unhelpful, even bullying and/or abusive, ways then they are unlikely to have experienced any secure base for themselves and as such will have anxious or avoidant attachment styles. At the same time, a chaotic or unstable and/or traumatic childhood means that an individual is less likely to be able to develop and draw upon rational thinking processes. As a result, they are less able to display meta-thinking, which is 'thinking about thinking'. This can compound any anxious or avoidant attachment styles that they have because they are unlikely to be aware of their own feelings, thoughts and behaviours in relation to themselves, other people and the world around them, and as a result will continue to repeat various life-traps. This links nicely to CBT-based approaches because these tend to be structured and directive, often involving helping clients to set their own goals and to work through various tasks.

Tasks that involve the process of writing or drawing or creating an image of our thoughts and experiences can be an important aspect to helping us to develop mentalisation, where mentalisation involves understanding our own mental states and that of other people. Thus, by working with a client through a CBT based approach, this can help them to develop their own rational thoughts and can help them to learn how to articulate these, rather than simply being overwhelmed by, or reacting to, their various emotional and psychological states. Experiencing a secure base is about having the ability to articulate one's own thoughts, feelings and behaviours, and as such CBT approaches can help clients to learn to be able to mentalise. This can be an important step to clients experiencing a secure base within themselves. It is also important to note that mentalisation can help clients to have a secure attachment style because this involves having an understanding that other people experience different states of mind. A client with an anxious or avoidant attachment style is perhaps likely to attribute other people's behaviours as being due to them – 'It's my fault'. Mentalisation enables an individual to begin to appreciate that other people's behaviours might be due to their mental states rather than anything that that individual has or has not done. Fonagy (1987, in Wallin, 2007) calls this reflective function – we are able to respond to others not just on the basis of their actions but also on the basis of their underlying mental states. Thus, a client who sees her daughter as being aggressive and rejecting of her can, through the process of mentalisation and reflective functioning, see her daughter's behaviour as being underpinned by depression. Mentalisation can thus enable an individual to experience a secure base for themselves and can help to create and maintain secure attachment styles with others. Through hypnosis, a solution focussed approach to attachment disorders can be facilitated, where the client's own unique subjective experience of his/her relationship difficulties can be utilised to instigate change. The use of age regression in hypnosis can allow an individual to drift back in time and gain an understanding of the cause of his/her unhealthy attachment style, whether avoidant, ambivalent/anxious or disorganised. This in turn can open up the therapy towards reframing an unhealthy relationship or relationships from the past, as well as promoting understanding and insight surrounding experiences of attachment that may have become 'buried' in the unconscious. Hypnosis offers the ability to release unhealthy attachments from the past and the corresponding emotions and feelings surrounding these; as Erickson and Rossi (1979) suggest, under hypnosis a person's learned limiting beliefs can be dissociated from their limitless mental potential, associations and resources, allowing these to be utilised for solving problems. Goals for healthy relationships can be developed through age progression, again under hypnosis, where the client can start to experience what it would feel like to have a healthy relationship with strong boundaries. Within a deeply relaxed state, suggestions for secure attachment can be presented to the unconscious mind, bypassing critical processing and judgement from the conscious part (Yapko, 2011). Negative thought processes and feelings can be challenged and the client's own internal resources can be utilised in a positive way. For example, the capacity to love securely and to experience secure love can be experienced through mental rehearsal utilising visual, auditory and kinaesthetic modalities. This experiential awareness can be heightened within hypnosis as the mind learns how to focus. The deeply relaxed state of mind and body that comprises the essence of hypnosis offers the individual an experience of themselves external to any attachment. This process is similar to meditation and mindfulness, shifting the focus internally and challenging beliefs, thoughts, feelings, actions and emotions in a way that is beneficial to the client and their representation of attachments.

A CBT based exercise in mentalisation

We can encourage clients to keep a diary of events in relation to how other people behave around them, and to log their automatic thoughts, feelings and behaviours. For example:

Event – A work colleague walked past me without saying 'hello'.
Automatic Thought – 'I must have done something wrong'.
Feelings – Shame, guilt, nervous.
Behaviour – Being extra nice to the colleague, or avoiding the colleague.

We can then explore the above with the client and also ask them to imagine the reasons for their colleague's behaviour beyond any immediate thoughts they have. We can encourage the client to write down a list of reasons underpinning their colleague's behaviour:

- The colleague is short-sighted and did not see me.
- The colleague was busy.
- The colleague was day-dreaming.
- The colleague had just had an argument with their son and was absorbed in thinking about this.
- The colleague was tired, having had very little sleep the night before.

We can then explore with the client how they might feel and behave differently if considering one of the above reasons for their colleague's behaviour. This exercise can really help a client to perform reflective functioning, which as explained previously, can be an important building block in clients' experiencing a secure base.

Working integratively with attachment disorders through hypnotherapeutic, cognitive and solution focussed modalities

Simon came to therapy, a 39-year-old man with low self-esteem, low self-confidence and attachment issues. Simon wanted to let go of the negative thoughts surrounding life and his future within it, thoughts such as 'I'm not good enough' and 'I'm a fake and one day I'll get found out'. Simon wanted to build his self-esteem and confidence as well as relax his mind. Simon's mother died when he was very young and his father subsequently re-married a further three times so the child experienced a series of stepmothers. His father was often away on business but whenever he was around he would put his son down, reinforcing within Simon the message, the hypnosis, that 'he wasn't good enough'. As a result, the little boy felt insecure and every time a relationship ended between his father and the boy's latest stepmother he would blame himself, thinking that it was down to him that the marriage had failed. The boy began to form unhealthy, anxious, attachments with each new stepmother, trying to be the good little boy and always fearful that the new stepmother would leave. He began to rely upon his grandmother for emotional support but then his grandmother died so he was left feeling 'groundless, like the rug was pulled from under my feet'. An overwhelming feeling of abandonment 'washed over me' as he re-experienced this memory in his mind. Twenty years later Simon now found himself in an unhealthy relationship with a partner who drank heavily. The relationship had fragmented to the point where Simon had issued an ultimatum: stop the drinking or leave. Simon had come into therapy believing that although the choice he presented his partner with was firm and unequivocal, he did not believe that he had the strength and confidence to end the relationship if his partner did not stop drinking.

During the first session, after practising grounding techniques with the client that included progressive muscle relaxation, breathing exercises (in for three, out for four) and visualizing a safe relaxing place, the process of *age progression* was used under hypnosis to determine how the client would feel *without* low self-esteem, low confidence and attachment issues. Age progression can be likened to time-travel into the future using the mind as opposed to something mechanical such as the Tardis used by Doctor Who. It allows an individual to project his/her self to some point in the future where they are free of the issues and difficulties that they currently experience, and where they can imagine a more pleasant environment (Wolinsky, 1991). Very often the client is so 'stuck' within the problem that it feels that the problem is their whole world. Using age progression to take the client away from the problem, even for a short while, can begin the process of seeding the mind with the powerful concept that things can, and indeed, do change; that the cycle of suffering can be broken, that a viewpoint or understanding or learning of a current difficulty can be different in time. Since age progression involves going into the future and thinking about a current issue/problem that is now in the past, this new viewpoint allows the client to utilise the concept of *hindsight* to resolve a conflict (Erickson, 1998); this shifts the responsibility for change onto the client and opens up new possibilities and understandings that can lead to self-empowerment.

To further underpin the principle of looking at a problem from a different perspective the metaphor of experiencing a TV in many different ways was introduced during the first session:

> Sit in front of the TV and you can experience the programme and the sound coming straight at you. However if you *shift your position* to one that is experiencing the TV from directly above it, as though you are hanging off the ceiling, the TV will look like a thin horizontal line of plastic that makes sound but has no picture. *Changing the perspective* once more so that you stand and observe the TV from the side, you will experience a vertical line of plastic that makes sound but has no picture. Due to sound bouncing off the various surfaces in the room producing reflections, the sound from the side of the TV will *be different* to the sound experienced above it. From the back of the TV you will see some connectors and connections and hear sound but again no picture, while the sound may be muffled depending on where the speakers are. So *your experience can be altogether different depending upon your perspective*.

The above metaphor illustrates that you can *experience something in more ways than one*. The italicised phrases indicate indirect suggestions that were said by the therapist in order for the unconscious mind to *make the connection* (more on this in Chapter 5); a slightly deeper voice was used for these phrases so that the client's mind would unconsciously recognise these subtle changes in tone and *make the connection*.

At the end of the first session the client reported that through age progression he had experienced himself as living in the moment, feeling happy and not caring about the past or the future. The building blocks for the way he wanted to be were starting to arrange themselves.

During the second session, another pseudo-orientation in time was utilised using hypnosis: *age regression*, in order to try and determine the origin of the negative thoughts experienced by the client. Since the client had not experienced physical or sexual abuse and wanted to know where these thoughts stemmed from, the therapist deemed this a suitable intervention. Under hypnosis, the client was taken back in time and a memory appeared of him sitting on a sofa with his father telling him that his stepmother – the first of the three stepmothers – was leaving. In the memory the young boy was feeling terrible: feeling that the breakup was something to do with him. In sessions three and four, the therapist worked with the client, once more utilising age regression, in order to lift the negative emotions and feelings surrounding the memories. In this way the client was able to start to lift the burden of negativity that he had held within him for many years, along with the insecurity and feelings of 'not being good enough'. The therapist encouraged the client to give himself permission to think differently about himself, to realise that he was not to blame himself for any of the marriage breakdowns that he had experienced in his father's house. The adult version of the boy was able to 'time-travel' to the past and let that little boy know in no uncertain terms that his father's relationship breakdowns were nothing to do with who the little boy was and how he behaved. The client was able to reframe the traumatic events he had experienced in a more appropriate way: 'Actually I was probably the glue in most of his marriages because he was a toxic person and they would have broken down sooner if I wasn't around.'

The client, under hypnosis, was guided to moments in his life when he felt more positive and confident: he remembered himself as a teenager working at a seaside fair, earning money for a trekking holiday. He felt happy at this point; the therapist noted this for future reference: here was a memory to revisit in order to build positivity and confidence utilizing the client's own experience and internal resources.

Gradually the client developed his sense of mindfulness and self-awareness and over the next few sessions reported feeling better able to deal with knock-backs and rejections as well as gaining a sense of confidence and an improved self-image. He was able to recognise and let go of negative thoughts through breathing and visualisation exercises. He felt as though his relationship with his partner was improving and they were able to share more experiences together as opposed to living separate lives, albeit under the same roof.

However, things can change very quickly in therapy. At the beginning of session eight, the client came into the office in an upset and agitated state. He had discovered that during the episodes of drinking, his partner, now sober, had had an affair with his friend. This inevitably brought up the old issues of trust and insecurity, and the presenting problems were now close to paranoia with the client constantly tormented about whether his partner would cheat on him again. At this point the therapist suggested that, since the playing field had changed, a new set of rules had to be *written* that would better suit these changes. Thus a cognitive behavioural element was introduced into the therapy where troubling thoughts were written down and challenged with alternative viewpoints and understandings.

The client was instructed to relax while the therapist asked him *magic wand questions* where the client was oriented to a future where his situation with his partner was resolved. Questions such as these do not target the specifics of getting to a particular future but are useful in getting a clearer picture of goals as well as building the presupposition that success will manifest itself (O'Hanlon & Beadle, 1997). For example, 'Imagine you had a magic wand and waved it in front of yourself and your partner and things worked themselves out. What would be different about you? What would be different about your partner? How would things be different in the relationship?'

The client was handed a notebook and asked to consider each question carefully, writing his answers down. After reflecting on the answers, the client had imagined a future self where he had got rid of the anger and resentment over his partner, where a bond of trust could be built and healthier boundaries developed. The client had reported that his partner would often stay up into the early hours of the morning, contacting people on various apps which she would justify by explaining to him that they were just friends. The client wanted to set clear boundaries and have the confidence to keep these in place. The answers to the magic wand questions became the goals and targets for therapy.

Through mindfulness and presence (see Chapter 1), the client was able to imagine himself creating a strong sense of self within the relationship with his partner. The therapist encouraged the development of healthy boundaries, which the client visualised as an invisible shield around him protecting his inner self: a bright light within his heart. Utilising his imagination, the client visualised situations at home where clear boundaries needed to be set; he imagined situations where his feelings of insecurity and paranoia were manifested and began to find his own solutions, for example, setting the clear boundary that contacting friends through social media apps late into the night was unacceptable and would not be tolerated. Sessions nine, ten and eleven were focussed on building the sense of identity and self-awareness as being distinct from his partner, and the client reported that he felt less enmeshed within his partner's world. His partner had agreed to stop using social media (recognizing that it was causing hurt) and, just like with the alcohol, was sticking to her promise. The relationship was improving, they were communicating better with each other, and the client was ready to work through processing residual anger over the affair.

The next two sessions were focussed on parts therapy, which is based on the concept that our personality is a sum of many different parts, some of which we are conscious of and some of which remain in the unconscious (Hunter, 2005). When these parts pull us in opposite directions then internal conflicts can result, for example, a person who binges on snacks may wish to eat healthily but another part of that person's mind provides pleasure whenever they eat crisps or chocolate. Utilising hypnosis, the client was able to communicate with the part responsible for his anger and to gain a sense of its meaning: that it was there to protect him in some way. With this knowledge in mind, the client was able to start to accept that anger was a natural part of the process of forgiveness and that that part would eventually trigger compassion towards his partner instead. Gradually he was able to release the anger and this in turn released his own suffering, allowing him to start to trust. The last two sessions were focussed on enhancing the strong sense of self that the client had started to nurture as well as his growing self-esteem and confidence that things could and would work out.

Case study questions on integration

Can you identify a core belief the client had in the case study above and how might this link to his negative automatic thoughts?

What attachment styles could the client above be displaying and how would you work with this as an integrative therapist?

Conclusion

A focus on attachment styles and attachment-related issues can be an important aspect of integrative therapeutic practice. Clients often come to therapy not understanding why it is that they may be repeating certain patterns with themselves and in relation to others, and so working with and through attachment can be incredibly empowering for clients. This chapter has shown that attachment is an integrative concept – many different schools of therapeutic practice focus on attachment, even though they may not necessarily label this as such. This chapter has shown that it is possible to work integratively with attachment – through person-centred, CBT based, relational and hypnotherapeutic modalities. This chapter has also encouraged us as practitioners to consider our own attachment experiences and styles. It is important to take stock of our own attachments to other people, animals and objects and to explore the role that these play in our lives. The idea of non-attachment has been explained through drawing upon Buddhist principles. Ultimately, this chapter has demonstrated that attachment styles are malleable and open to change, which means that therapy focussing on attachment can lead to huge beneficial impacts for clients.

References

Amis, K. (2017) *Boundaries, Power and Ethical Responsibility in Counselling and Psychotherapy*. London: Sage.

Briere, J. & Scott, C. (2006) *Principles of Trauma Therapy: A Guide to Symptoms, Evaluations, and Treatment*. Thousand Oaks, CA: Sage.

Erickson, M.H. (1998) *Life Reframing in Hypnosis. The Seminars, Workshops, and Lectures of Milton H. Erickson.* London: Free Association Books.

Erickson, M., & Rossi, E. (1979) *Hypnotherapy: An Exploratory Casebook.* New York: Irvington.

Fonagy, P. (2001) *Attachment Theory and Psychoanalysis*. New York: Other Press.

George, C., Kaplan, N. & Main, M. (1985) *The Adult Attachment Interview*. http://www.psychology. sunysb.edu/attachment/measures/content/aai_interview.pdf (accessed 20 August 2017). California: University of Berkeley.

Holmes, J. (2001) *The Search for the Secure Base*. Hove: Routledge.

Hunter, R. (2005) *Hypnosis for Inner Conflict Resolution: Introducing Parts Therapy*. Carmarthen: Crown House Publishing.

Komagata, N. (2010) *Attachment and Non-Attachment: Attachment Theory and Buddhism*, http://nobo. komagata.net/pub/Komagata09-Xtachment.html (accessed 29 January 2019).

O'Hanlon, B & Beadle, S (1997) *A Guide to Possibility Land. Fifty-One Methods for Doing Brief, Respectful Therapy*. New York: Norton.

NICE (2015) 'Children's attachment: Attachment in children and young people who are adopted from care, in care or at high risk of going into care', https://www.nice.org.uk/guidance/ng26/documents/ childrens-attachment-full-guideline2 (accessed 29 January 2019).

Rogers, C. (1951) *Client-Centered Therapy*. London: Constable.

Rotter, J.B. (1954) *Social Learning and Clinical Psychology*. New York: Prentice-Hall.

Wallin, D. (2007) *Attachment in Psychotherapy*. London: The Guilford Press.

Wolinsky, S. (1991) *Trances People Live*. North Bergen, NJ: Bramble Books.

Yapko, M. (2011) *Mindfulness and Hypnosis. The Power of Suggestion to Transform Experience*. New York: Norton.

Young, J. & Klosko, J. (1994) *Reinventing Your Life*. London: Penguin Books.

Chapter 4

Thinking, through an integrative therapeutic lens

> The Owl said to the Pussycat, 'We are lost; we will never find our way to the land where the Bong tree grows.' 'Nonsense', responded Pussycat.
>
> With apologies to Edward Lear, 'The Owl and the Pussycat' (1871)

Introduction

Thoughts matter. Working therapeutically with clients involves a focus upon both the content and patterns of their thinking. Clients may come for therapy as a result of distressing thoughts that make them feel guilt, shame or other unhelpful emotions; they may come because they feel that they have little control over their thoughts, which may be underpinned by anxiety or depression; they may come for therapy out of having little awareness of the thinking that underpins issues they present with: addictions, phobic behaviours, eating disorders and so on.

As therapists it is important for us to consider thinking and how to work with this therapeutically with clients. Trainee counsellors often struggle with focussing upon thinking with clients – content and structure – because many trainees are more concerned with building a therapeutic relationship and with being empathic, and so targeting thoughts initially can be viewed as something that detracts attention away from providing clients with a safe space in which to explore their concerns and their lives. This, of course, is important, but as therapists we need to have a highly attuned ear for the content and structure of our clients' thoughts.

There are many different ways of looking at thinking. Viewed through an integrative lens, clients as thinking beings is inherent within person-centred, relational, CBT and hypnotherapeutic modalities. The question is how we approach thinking through the integration of these modalities. The following chapter considers content and patterns of thinking through person-centred, relational, CBT and hypnotherapeutic modalities and then looks at how we might work integratively with clients in relation to their thinking. We will also consider thinking with respect to relationships, connecting with the phrase that began this chapter involving the poem by Edward Lear, 'The Owl and the Pussycat'. First of all, the chapter considers the relevance and importance of working with thinking and how as therapists we can focus on this without it taking anything away from building and maintaining a strong working alliance with our clients.

Rebecca and Amy

This was Rebecca's first ever time seeing a counsellor. She was lucky in that she could afford to go to see a therapist privately. 'No need to have to wait six months or even longer for an

NHS-funded therapist!' Rebecca thought to herself as she arrived at the house of a local counsellor, whose details she had found online.

As she stepped out of her car, Rebecca felt a bit apprehensive, so she thought about the photo that she had seen on the counselling website.

'Amy looked warm and kind', Rebecca reassured herself as she banged on the front door of the counsellor's house. Within seconds the door opened.

'Hello. Please come in', said Amy.

Rebecca immediately noticed the shoes that Amy was wearing – a pair of flat shoes, no heels, yikes.

Rebecca followed Amy into a small room at the side of the house.

'The room's a bit cold', 'She hasn't offered me a cup of tea or coffee', 'The room is smaller than I had expected'. These were some of Rebecca's thoughts as she quickly scanned the room before sitting down in one of the armchairs. 'Look at that, a piece of cat fur on the carpet – not just me then.'

'Welcome' said Amy. 'My name is Amy and I am an accredited therapist and have been practising now for a number of years. I work integratively with clients, and this can mean that sometimes I will give you homework to do as this can really help with the sessions here. Before we look at the counselling contract, maybe we can begin by you telling me a little about yourself and what brings you here?'

'Well I am 38 years old, I am a medical doctor working in A&E. I've got a good life – friends, family, I enjoy going skiing every winter and surfing during my summer holidays. I enjoy my job, it's tough but I like the adrenaline kicks it provides. What I am struggling with at the moment is not having a life partner. I have been in and out of relationships my whole life and feel now that it is time that I found someone to settle down with because my biological clock is beginning to tick tock away.'

'Can I ask, how many relationships you have been in and how long has your longest relationship lasted?'

'Well, hard to say really. I had about three different boyfriends whilst a trainee medic at university. Then, when I was a junior doctor for four years, I saw a few men on and off, nothing serious, you know. I forgot to mention that I've had an abortion, when I was in my twenties. Basically, I was in a casual relationship with a builder – I like men to be muscular – and got pregnant and there was no way I was going to throw away my career over a baby, so I aborted it. Anyway, a few years passed by and I then got myself a Senior Registrar position at a highly respected hospital, so I felt good in myself, financially secure.' At this point Rebecca sat forward, lifted both hands into the air and pressed her index and middle fingers down, whilst she said, 'That is when I would say I had my first *proper relationship*.'

'It lasted about three years. The break up was not nice at all. He had started shagging a physiotherapist at the hospital where I was working, had met her at a social event that we had both attended, and so when I found out about his affair I threw him out of my apartment. Maybe I should have waited for his response, to see if I could mend things? That way I might not be looking down the barrel of 40 and being childless. Peter earned less than me. Would you believe that he was a plumber? He was doing some contractual work at the hospital and that is how I met him. Again, nice body, that's what drew me to him, nice big brown eyes. I liked buying him stuff and taking him out to nice restaurants, places he couldn't afford on his wages. I felt in control. So how dare he sleep around like that? There was no way I was going to put up with that.'

'Put up with that?'

'Put up with him coming home late and not telling me where he had been. Sometimes I could smell her perfume on him but if I said anything he would just tell me I was being paranoid and that he'd been working at a female customer's house.'

'How do you feel now about Peter's behaviour?'

'Outraged. Angry . . . Annoyed with myself.'

'Annoyed with yourself?'

'For having ended the relationship with Peter without thinking through the implications of my biological age. I mean, he had good genes and I think that we could have created a beautiful baby together.' At this point Rebecca sat back in the armchair, breathed out heavily and said, 'I take it I can't smoke in here?'

Amy smiled.

Let us take a few minutes to explore the above exchange between Rebecca and Amy, particularly in relation to both Rebecca's and Amy's thoughts. The paragraphs above make it relatively easy for us, the readers, to identify Rebecca's thinking patterns, but of course from Amy's perspective as the therapist not all of Rebecca's thoughts have been articulated. Rather, Amy not only has to listen carefully to what Rebecca is saying but she also needs to be mindful of Rebecca's body language, which may give away some of Rebecca's unspoken thoughts. Firstly, let us take Rebecca's spoken thoughts. These are some of Rebecca's key thoughts that Amy might pick up on during this session:

> 'my biological clock is beginning to tick tock away.'
> 'got pregnant and there was no way I was going throw away my career over a baby, so I aborted it'.
> 'got myself a Senior Registrar position at a highly respected hospital, so I felt good in myself',
> 'That is when I would say I had my first *proper relationship*.'
> 'Maybe I should have waited for his response, to see if I could mend things?'
> 'looking down the barrel of 40 and being childless'.
> 'I liked buying him stuff and taking him out to nice restaurants, places he couldn't afford on his wages. I felt in control.'
> 'he had good genes and I think that we could have created a beautiful baby together'.

The content of the thoughts above can give us a clear picture of Rebecca's approach to relationships, her priorities in life and also some of the self-doubt that engulfs her. Importantly, it is not just the content of Rebecca's thoughts that matter, or even how she articulates these – for example when she raises her hands in the air. Rather, we might be able to detect particular patterns of thinking that may not be very helpful for Rebecca. For example, it seems that Rebecca has an all-or-nothing thinking pattern. That is, something is either all good or all bad; something is black or white rather than grey. An example of this all-or-nothing thinking would be when she says, 'got pregnant and there was no way I was going to throw away my career over a baby, so I aborted it'. This is not to judge Rebecca on whether or not she had an abortion, but rather to notice that for Rebecca a baby signified to her the 'end of her career'. This also links to catastrophic thinking, whereby individuals automatically think about the worst case scenario rather than other alternatives. An example from Rebecca's thinking would be 'looking down the barrel of 40 and being childless'. Amy as the therapist might therefore not only be taking into consideration the content of Rebecca's thoughts but also styles of thinking that might be repeating for Rebecca, potentially disempowering her.

Amy might also have picked up on some of Rebecca's unspoken thoughts. Thus, as Rebecca entered Amy's counselling room, maybe she noticed that Rebecca stared at her carpet and had noticed the bit of cat hair there, maybe Amy would also have noticed Rebecca tightening up her cardigan, at which point Amy might have asked whether Rebecca was warm enough and whether she would like the electric heater to be switched on. This illustrates that as therapists we can detect our clients' unspoken thoughts by their body language and by their actions. It might also have been the case that Rebecca had coughed, and at that point Amy might offer her a glass of water, some tea or coffee.

Another key aspect to the interaction between Rebecca and Amy are Amy's thoughts. Amy is a trained and accredited therapist but this does not necessarily mean that she will be a passive vessel, holding all of Rebecca's thoughts without generating any thoughts of her own. The following might be some unarticulated thoughts that Rebecca has generated in Amy:

> 'This client is very educated and articulate, am I a good enough therapist?'
> 'I wish I had vacuumed the carpet this morning.'
> 'I am 35 years old myself and ended with my boyfriend six months ago, should I be panicking about my own body clock?'
> 'What if I never have children? I need to take this to supervision.'

The thoughts that clients generate in us we have little control over, and we cannot predict as therapists what thoughts we will have during a session with a client. The key to effective practice is to be mindful of our own thoughts, and to take the key ones to supervision or to our own personal therapy so that these do not interfere with the therapeutic process for the client. So Amy might decide to see her supervisor about Rebecca in relation to working with her and how Rebecca's dilemma may be affecting Amy; Amy might also decide to see her own therapist about issues and anxieties concerning motherhood. This enables Amy to remain boundaried and professional in her work with Rebecca.

The above section demonstrates how important it is for therapists to not only be building a therapeutic relationship with their clients, and being empathic, but also for therapists to notice spoken and unspoken thoughts that clients have. It is then a question of timing – the therapist deciding when it is appropriate to reflect back a client's thought, when to challenge a particular thought, and when to highlight thinking patterns that a client may be consistently applying to their understanding of themselves, other people and the world around them. In the case of Rebecca and Amy above, it might take a few sessions before Amy begins to challenge some of Rebecca's catastrophic thinking, for example. In order to challenge the content and style of thinking that clients demonstrate, it is important for us as therapists to feel that a strong enough working alliance has been built between ourselves and our clients. To challenge clients' thinking too soon might potentially rupture any therapeutic relationship that has been built, leading to clients becoming disengaged from the therapeutic process.

Thinking in relation to the integration of person-centred, CBT, relational and hypnotherapeutic modalities

Within person-centred approaches, trying to understand a client's worldview is central. Carl Rogers (1961) developed a person-centred approach because he fundamentally disagreed with therapeutic modalities that placed the therapist in the leading role, as an interpreter of clients' experiences. For Rogers (1961), it is extremely important for clients to spend time articulating their perceptions and experiences as they see them rather than waiting for a therapist to give them the meaning, the answer concerning their life and life's challenges. Therefore, person-centredness is about giving time and space to clients, for them to articulate their thoughts, their experiences, their sensations. Importantly, for Rogers (1961: 108), underpinning people's experiences and life challenges are three key thoughts: *Who am I really ? How can I get in touch with this real self, underlying all my surface behaviour ? How can I become myself?'*

As discussed in Chapter 1, striving for presence can help declutter our minds so that we are able to focus on what our clients are telling us without bringing in our own prejudices. As Rogers (1961: 185) argues:

> the therapist is able to let himself go in understanding the client; that no inner barriers keep him from sensing what it feels like to be the client at each moment of the relationship; and that he can convey something of his empathic understanding to the client. It means that the therapist has become comfortable in entering this relationship fully, without knowing cognitively where it will lead, satisfied with providing a climate which will permit the client the utmost freedom to become himself.

The above quotation would suggest that as therapists we need to be mindful that we are not directing our clients in any particular way, that we are open to not knowing – not thinking – about the 'end result' of therapy. Being person-centred is more than simply passively listening, however. Excellent listening and communication skills are both essential within person-centred approaches (alongside other therapeutic modalities), and so trainee counsellors are often placed into triads when at college and are encouraged to develop their listening and talking capabilities through role-play.

Being person-centred is extremely challenging because it demands much concentration and effort on the part of the therapist. Person-centredness is not a lazy option but the danger is that trainee counsellors often equate being person-centred to being passive. As a result, trainees often struggle to reflect back or challenge or summarise for the client – these being key counselling skills. It takes time to develop an acute sensitivity and an ethical responsivity – listening carefully to what is being said and thinking about what may be left unsaid by the client, and reacting to this from an empathic position which boundaries out one's own thinking.

Being person-centred does not mean that a counsellor cannot make notes during a session. Sometimes it is important to capture key thoughts that the client has and to write these down with a view to returning to these for greater exploration, either in future counselling sessions or later on in that particular session. It is also important to not make any assumptions about what a client may or may not be thinking because our assumptions may actually just reflect our own thinking biases. Rather, it is better to check out with a client whether we understand what they are telling us, whether we have noted down the content of a thought correctly. Within person-centred approaches it can be important to explore a client's thinking in relation to who they think they are (self), how other people view them (self-concept), what roles they think they play in life (e.g. mother, daughter, teacher), and who they think they would like to be (ideal self). An important aspect of person-centredness in therapy may also be exploring a client's thoughts around their life journey – key events that have happened to them – does the client think that these events are positive or negative and in what way? It can also be useful to explore a client's thinking around whether they have any perception of self-growth or self-awareness. Key interventions which have a person-centred aspect here include: a timeline which is used by a client to plot key moments in their life; a picture or illustration where the client is encouraged to write down key roles they play, which roles they would like to reject in their lives and future roles they would like to play; and a pictorial representation of the self, self-concept and ideal self whereby the client is facilitated to write down thoughts concerning these three concepts. These three interventions perhaps clearly demonstrate person-centredness.

When approaching the notion of 'thinking' through relational modalities, perhaps the work by Berne (1964), and later by Harris (1973), best summarises how relational therapeutic approaches bring in thinking. Berne (1964) introduced transactional analysis, which essentially suggests that in our interactions with other people there are three essential ego states: Adult, Child and Parent. Relationships whereby inappropriate ego states are employed by the actors (for example, where a parent acts out a child role whilst a child acts out a parent role) are dysfunctional and can involve arguments and game playing between people. Harris (1973) took Berne's ideas and then suggested that we are often stuck in a child ego state (I'm not okay) and relate in a dependent way to others as though they are parents (You're okay). Therefore, it is important to explore a client's thinking around their relationships with others, which can comprise of the following set of dynamics:

I'm okay	You're okay
I'm not okay	You're not okay
I'm okay	You're not okay
I'm not okay	You're okay

As therapists, we are helping clients to explore the consequences and any advantages and disadvantages of any of the above thinking patterns. For example, it might be that a client who is stuck in the thinking mode of 'I'm okay, you're not okay' with their partner might be highly critical of their partner. This client may also be overly intrusive in their partner's life, unboundaried, and may also be idealising other people and placing them on pedestals, with the thinking mode potentially being here 'I'm not okay, you're okay'. Healthy relationships and healthy dynamics between people come from the thinking mode of 'I'm okay, you're okay'. This thinking mode enables individuals to respect each other, to communicate their needs, to remain boundaried and to also hear what the other person is saying, rather than acting dismissively or aggressively or passively. It can be useful to work with clients by creating a table of these thinking modes and asking them to plot where they think they are in their relationships – with their father, mother, sister, husband and so forth. It can then be useful to explore what 'I'm okay, you're okay too' might look and feel like for the client, and what potential challenges there might be to bringing this thinking mode into any specific relationship that they have. Thus, it can be extremely challenging for a client to start relating to another person in the 'I'm okay, you're okay' mode if that other person is stuck in their own thinking mode of 'I'm not okay, you're not okay'. It can take time for relational dynamics to change and grow, and as therapists we can support our clients and help them explore changes in their relationships over time, as they begin thinking differently about themselves and others in those relationships. It might be that co-dependent relationships are very much based on the thinking mode of 'I'm not okay, you're not okay' and so it can take time for a client to begin to experience themselves as 'I'm okay' before they can then relate to the other person through 'You're okay' thinking mode.

CBT based approaches are probably the modalities that most directly work with thinking. As mentioned previously in this chapter, CBT based practitioners often distinguish between the content and the pattern of thoughts. Regarding the content aspect to thinking from a CBT based perspective, distorted thoughts are the target of therapy whereby clients are encouraged to firstly identify their distorted thinking and then to challenge this so that more empowering thinking is experienced. Distorted thinking encapsulates negative automatic thoughts (NATS), underlying assumptions (rules for living) and core beliefs. This means that a CBT based approach can focus on identifying, challenging and helping to create more helpful NATS, underlying assumptions and core beliefs. It is often the process of therapy with a client that determines which out of the three are focussed upon, and indeed often all three are explored. CBT based therapists will draw on a number of tools to identify and challenge distorted NATS, underlying assumptions and core beliefs. For example, a thought diary can often reveal unhelpful NATS and underlying assumptions that people have. In order to get to clients' core beliefs, one useful technique is to ask the client 'If this were true then what would this mean?' This question, when applied to NATS and underlying assumptions, can help uncover deep-rooted core beliefs that clients have about themselves – for example, 'I am not good enough'. It is then important to draw upon tools in order to facilitate a client to challenge unhelpful core beliefs, to replace these with healthier core beliefs and a range of cognitive and behavioural tools can be used to do this. For example, if one core belief that a client has is 'I am incompetent', then the client might be encouraged to challenge this core belief through making a list of things that they have done that shows a certain level of competency. It is also helpful here to challenge 'all or nothing' thinking, in that we are neither completely competent nor incompetent as individuals. This points to the usefulness in also focussing upon the pattern of thoughts that clients can exhibit. According to CBT based approaches, the following are some unhelpful thinking patterns:

All-or-nothing thinking – thinking in totalities rather than in shades.
Catastrophising – expecting the worst case scenario.
Filtering – focussing on the one negative aspect, ignoring positive aspects.
Comparing – comparing ourselves negatively to other people.
Must and should – rules that we have to follow no matter what.

The way that we think therefore is rather biased. We may think that our thoughts constitute reality when actually our thoughts are simply perspectives with no one necessary truth. This can be deeply troubling initially for a client who believes that what they think comprises of 'the truth'. It can therefore take time to highlight and challenge distorted thinking. Furthermore, it is important to stress that as therapists we are not trying to disassemble thinking content and patterns because this can be extremely anxiety provoking for clients. Rather, our role as therapists is to facilitate clients to explore their thinking, to challenge, to create more helpful thinking at a pace that they are comfortable with.

Hypnotherapeutic modalities rely upon the procedure of hypnosis, defined by Gerrig and Zimbardo (2009) as a deeply relaxed state characterised by susceptibility to suggestions for changes in perceptions, sensations, motivation, thoughts or behaviours. The process of hypnosis can enhance mindfulness, promoting focus and awareness of thinking patterns, beliefs surrounding thoughts, and actions and feelings resulting from thoughts. This narrowing of attention and increased responsiveness to ideas and impressions (Hadley & Staudacher, 2001) can begin to reframe a client's thoughts in relation to their worldview and beliefs. Direct and indirect suggestions can be made that are designed to desensitise the client to destructive and intrusive thoughts; since the client is in an altered state of awareness, as a direct result of relaxation, the critical judgments from the conscious part of the mind can be bypassed, allowing the unconscious to absorb and make use of these suggestions. Imagery can be utilised under hypnosis in order to provide powerful symbolisms for letting go of negative or destructive thoughts. For example, the client can imagine cutting a cord from themselves and their thoughts; they can imagine altering the dynamics of a thought in relation to its volume, location, pitch and tone so that the impact of the thought is lessened. Hypnosis can also promote an experiential awareness of a positive future without the negative thoughts, utilising suggestions and positive goal imagery. A client can gain a deeper understanding of their thoughts and with the use of post-hypnotic suggestions, defined by Yapko (2001) as a way of associating new learnings within the desired circumstances of a person's life, can alter thinking patterns in relation to triggers that in the past would have caused the cycle of negative thinking.

Thinking, relationships and trainee therapists

Edward Lear wrote a famous poem in 1871 about an owl and a pussycat who go sailing and find the land where the Bong tree grows. Once there they buy a ring from a pig and they get married, dancing by the light of the moon. It is a very warm and endearing poem about friendship and love between two creatures. Of course, most of us would like this kind of 'happy-ever-after' ending, or fantasy, for our most intimate relationships. The only words that the owl and pussycat say to each other in this poem are positive and flattering:

> O lovely Pussy! Oh Pussy my love, what a beautiful Pussy you are. . . .'
> Pussy said to the Owl 'You elegant fowl! How charmingly sweet you sing!'
>
> (Lear, 1871)

In reality, as humans we bring to our relationships sometimes complex and unhelpful thinking content and structures. Without even knowing consciously about this, for example, individuals will bring certain 'rules for living' that they have and will apply these to their relationships. These 'rules for living' can place great pressure and expectations on their relationships, and can be a source of conflict within relationships. For example, one rule a person has may be 'I have to be right all the time'. Couples and relationship counselling can involve exploring and making visible previously invisible rules. Individuals can then decide which rules are helpful and which are unhelpful, and how to build their relationship around an awareness of this.

When undertaking counselling training, students often become aware of their own thinking styles and content. This can be a challenging time for students because they can begin to see that some of their thinking processes are not helpful, are limiting and even distorted. Trainees can begin to change the ways in which they think and this in turn can influence their feelings and behaviours. Naturally, this will impact on the relationships that trainees have. A good proportion of trainees will begin to experience discomfort through the changes to their relationships that they are experiencing. At the same time, students can also become more aware of the thinking styles and content of significant others in their lives. This can create tensions within their relationships.

Our advice to students often is to give their relationships time to adjust to change being brought about by heightened awareness of self and others, particularly in relation to their thinking patterns. It can also be important at times to challenge distorted thinking if we believe that this restricts the relationships that we are in, if we think that we are being controlled or manipulated or placed in a fearful or anxious state. We don't have to challenge through a position of anger or distress; however, we can challenge by being robust and fully present, and articulating a helpful thought as a response to an unhelpful thought that a partner, family member or friend has articulated. Thus, think back to the 'Owl and the Pussycat' poem. If owl were an anxious character full of catastrophising thinking patterns then the pussycat might like to respond to this robustly and with respect. So if the owl were to say to the pussycat, 'We are going to starve to death because we can't find any food on the land where the Bong tree grows', the pussycat might respond to this by saying, 'Yes, it is a concern that we haven't yet seen any food on this island. However, I can see a helpful pig over there and so let us ask him where he gets his food supplies from.' In this instance the pussycat is not becoming angry or vengeful towards the owl, rather, the pussycat is acknowledging the owl's concern without being overwhelmed by this and is applying a more rational thinking process to try to solve the situation that they are both in. Sometimes we find that our loved ones take on board our changed thinking and begin to challenge and change their own thoughts. Sometimes we find that some of our family members, friends and significant others do not change their thinking processes. In this situation it is important to decide to what extent we continue to have a relationship with that person, how boundaried we can be with them, and to make sure that our own thinking is not negatively influenced by their distorted thinking. This can be a life-long challenge !

Back to the future to the present to the past to the future to the now

In the early hours of morning, a runner sets off as a fingernail of sun pokes through the curtain of cloud. As the music plays through the headphones and each step becomes another, so the runner begins to time-travel in his mind, to an imaginary moment where he is giving a speech at his own book launch. In this movie in his mind, the runner, standing on a stage in a wine bar, is thanking a particular friend for the support he has provided over the years with regards to writing. As he imagines this scene so a new song starts to play on his iPod: a song that reminds him of *another* friend. This friend, within the runner's internal worldview, is not as supportive and has never encouraged the runner to write, nor congratulated him for gaining a publishing contract, nor indeed, for having a successful career as a therapist. The scene within the movie of the book launch changes abruptly, with the runner now imagining himself on the same stage pointing towards and telling that particular 'unsupportive' friend: 'you know you could have been a bit more supportive . . . God knows your friends have provided you with enough help over the years. . . .'

The association between the song and the friend has set off a pattern of destructive thoughts within the runner's mind and now his emotions and feelings are being sucked into the internal movie in the space between his ears: the fiction, instead of the reality: the run. Each step now begins to elicit anger and resentment and the runner loses himself from the essence of the run itself. He loses himself from himself.

But the runner is aware and mindful, recognizing the fiction that is being created through his lens of distorted thinking. Instead of embedding himself further within that particular scene and its unhealthy feelings and emotions, the runner begins to direct his mind towards good memories of this friend, shared experiences that were real. As he runs up a steep hill past the university he remembers a fishing holiday in the late 1980s that they experienced prior to going off to university. Our runner imagines himself back in that memory and as he continues on his way, each step makes the memory clearer and more defined. The mood changes and becomes lighter, the negative ruminations of 'he was never supportive to me' and 'I don't know why I bother being his friend sometimes' lift and the anger and resentment eases before disappearing altogether by the time he reaches the crossroads at the top of the hill.

As the adrenaline surges so the runner starts to appreciate his friend in a different way: the time when he helped him with his car when it needed an MOT, the time when he organised a Christmas party and many of their mutual friends turned up, the time when they went to a gig and were mistaken for being part of the band (the management at the venue allowing them to venture backstage and eat some of the food arranged for the actual band). As the song continues to play so the runner is generating positive thoughts and the movie in his mind is one of him shaking hands and hugging his friend at the imaginary book launch. Again, this is fiction, a future projection without reality. However, this is a more positive and helpful fiction, one that has dramatically shifted from the earlier ruminations.

When the same song plays the next time that the runner runs, the association between the friend and the song may be an altogether more enjoyable and useful one. The thought process may be as pleasant, even more pleasant, than it is just now. The runner is aware of the beauty of running and recognises that unconscious processing of biological and physiological components continues in the background every step of the way: control of blood pressure, heart rate, blood pH; blood oxygen levels; rate and depth of breathing; balance and stability as well as a whole lot more. And just as these processes are happening so learning is taking place, and as the mind grinds away in the background, new mental associations, memories, feelings, emotions and behaviours are evolving without conscious effort. For now, the runner is enjoying the moment, the crunch of gravel under his feet, the smell of labour, the steady breath; he lifts his hand to a runner who is running past. Something passes between them, something that is more than air. Another association. Another thought. Another moment.

The above example illustrates how quickly we can shift towards negative thinking patterns and how through these patterns we can 'hypnotise' ourselves into believing something is actually something when it is actually not. So often distorted thinking patterns arise from the unconscious, like zombies in the dead of night, and just like zombies fulfilling their lust for life through feeding on the living, so our thoughts can destroy the sense of self and infect cognitive perceptions and experiences, resulting in cognitive distortions, often brought about by negative schemas, formed during the early stages of life, that are latent and unconscious (Alladin, 2008).

As the runner attaches to the thoughts of his friend *not* being supportive with respect to his writing, so his mind is convincing him that his friend *is not supportive*. But how real is this belief? Perhaps the friend provides support in a way that the runner is not aware of? If one friend provides support, as interpreted in the runner's worldview, does this mean that every other friend must provide support too? Why the need for an attachment to support? Does support have to be reciprocated and if so, why? What are the associations between friends and support?

Widening the angle

Questioning the raft of thoughts generated by the mind, including the emotions and feelings and belief systems governing our perceptions of life, can allow the therapist or client to become open consciously to the things that appear from the unconscious. It allows a shift from a narrow therapeutic focus – where we see, examine, challenge what is directly in front of us – to a wider focus. Using this wider focus, this wider lens, we can see what's in front of us but we can also experience the associations, attachments, thoughts and beliefs in the background, middle-ground, foreground. It is almost as though we have put on a pair of panoramic spectacles allowing us to focus in on particular aspects of our thought processes and behaviours and those of our clients.

James Wong Howe was an influential Chinese American cinematographer who worked on over 130 films during his career, winning Academy Awards for cinematography for *The Rose Tattoo* (1955) and *Hud* (1963). He was also one of the first to use the technique of *deep-focus* cinematography, where foreground, middle-ground and background are all in focus. Deep-focus cinematography allows the significant elements within an image to be placed at different depths and planes, allowing characters and spaces to be given equal importance (Rainsberger, 1981). Now, not only the foreground characters and objects are important, but also the actors, space, objects and action around and behind them. Actions that overlap can become crucial, and the scene can be presented to the viewer as a whole, engaging and clear.

The concept of deep focus cinematography can be applied within the context of developing healthier thoughts within ourselves as therapists, and that of our clients. Focussing on thoughts that are in front of us: 'I'm not good enough', 'He always puts me down', 'Why should I bother, I always fail?' is a necessary operation; however if we wish to deepen our understanding of ourselves and our clients, exploring the spaces and objects and dialogue in the background is vital: the emotions, feelings, belief systems, perceptions. What is causing this thought of 'not being good enough'? How do you know that person is putting you down? What evidence do you have that you always fail? How do you feel about not being good enough? Are there moments in the day when you feel differently? How would you feel if you were successful? In many ways the relationship between therapist and client is no different to an astronomer gazing out at the stars and galaxies only to find that galaxies are much more massive than they ever thought: a hidden universe with invisible matter made up of exotic particles under the influence of strange forces.

As a therapist the focus is not only on what is in front of you: the client, but also the scene around and within you; how the two of you influence each other before, during and after sessions, consciously and unconsciously. Have you ever met someone that suddenly brings up a negative thought within you, for example, of being inadequate in some way? Have you ever met someone who you just don't like the look of and who makes you think angry thoughts? As a therapist, have you ever worked with a client whose issues can elicit unhealthy thinking patterns within you? Forces and particles!

Building awareness of unhelpful thinking patterns in therapists

Jim, a therapist with over five years of experience within clinical practice, has had a good week; many of his clients have moved forwards in terms of therapeutic goals and he has received a considerable amount of positive feedback and praise over the last few days. On Friday morning, Jim sets off to his city-based practice in high spirits; he feels that he has reached a point in his career where he can consider himself a seasoned practitioner, a therapist who can help clients deal with a wide range of issues and is a good listener. When Jim arrives at the office, his secretary hands him a list of clients that he will be seeing during the day. As Jim scans the bookings, his heart sinks as he reads the first name on the list, a client called Ben.

For some reason, Jim feels inadequate and useless at the end of a session with Ben but he really doesn't know why. Ben is a friendly person who is never rude or arrogant in any way, yet there is something about the man that makes Jim question his own capabilities as a therapist. It is as though Ben sends out an invisible signal across the air waves that starts Jim off on a spiral of negative thoughts: 'I can't help this guy', 'No matter what I try to suggest to him it makes no difference', 'I'm not up to the job – he should find someone else'. Jim can also sometimes feel a degree of anger after seeing Ben and again, he doesn't know why.

Because Jim has arrived early there is some time for him to reflect on this scenario. He decides that he will meditate on this cycle of negative thinking and so he sits in his chair and starts to focus on his breathing. He brings up a mental image of Ben in his mind and starts to focus inwards, exploring the negative thoughts and feelings that appear when he begins to imagine that Ben is in the room. As each thought appears so he begins to question each thought: Why is it there? What is its purpose? How does it make him feel? As he becomes more relaxed, he becomes more present with his thoughts and feelings, his attitudes and beliefs surrounding Ben.

Then the eureka moment happens, a light bulb switches on in his mind and Jim understands why he thinks and feels this way about Ben. He remembers one of the early sessions when Ben told him he had left his girlfriend of many years and was dating not one, but two women, neither of whom had any idea that they were being cheated upon. Jim's wife had left him a couple of years ago for another man and it was an unexpected breakup that he had not fully processed yet: he still held some level of resentment and anger towards his wife.

The more Jim meditated on his thoughts, the more he became aware that Ben's behaviour was challenging one of his own core beliefs: that relationships are precious and should always be worked upon, especially in difficult times. Jim saw in Ben, his wife's own 'heartless' behaviour, and this provoked the unconscious spark of anger and worthlessness within him, reinforced with thoughts of inadequacy as a therapist.

Now that Jim was aware of the unconscious triggers for his thinking and feeling, he spent a few minutes meditating on focussed compassion. Perhaps Ben's ex-partner was not very nice to him? Maybe the relationship had run its course and both of them had mutually agreed to separate? Wasn't playing the field a natural reaction after a breakup, especially for the younger generation? By focussing himself in this way, Jim had built an awareness of the unconscious triggers for his negative thinking; he could be more conscious of what Ben said or alluded to in the subsequent session(s) and rather than attaching, he could let these triggers pass. At the end of his short meditation, Jim's mind was focussed and positive towards helping Ben.

Developing healthier thoughts in clients and therapists

The following exercise can be utilised by both therapists and clients in order to change negative and destructive thoughts into healthier thinking patterns:

1. Allow your client to settle back in their chair and focus on their breathing: the in breath, the out breath. They can choose to close their eyes if they wish; this exercise

often works better when the eyes are shut. As they focus on their breathing, ask them to allow any intrusive or negative thought to drift into their mind; once a thought appears, instruct the client to say hello to the thought and to begin getting a sense of its dynamics: the volume of the thought; where it is located in/outside of the mind; the tone of the voice. Is the thought/inner voice female or male? Does it sound like someone that they know, for example, father, mother, friend, wife or a person that they don't get along with at work?

2.   Once the client gets a sense of this thought or inner voice, they can begin to change the dynamics in some way. This can be empowering for the client because they can begin to discover that through changing the aspects of a thought they can reduce its impact. The therapist instructs the client throughout this process, with the client providing verbal (and visual) feedback: 'Imagine you have a dial that controls the volume of the thought. Begin to turn the dial so that the thought becomes louder. How do you feel when the thought is loud? Now imagine turning the dial so the thought becomes softer. How do you feel when the thought becomes quieter? Imagine changing the pitch of the thought – using a dial make the pitch higher so that it sounds like a cartoon voice. How does the thought make you feel now? Make the thought very low in pitch – how do you feel now? Get a sense of where the thought is in your mind – in front of you, behind you, to the left, to the right, above or below you? Get a sense of where it is in your mind and imagine taking the thought and placing it somewhere else. Imagine placing it outside of you, by the chair. How do you feel now in relation to the thought? Imagine placing the thought very far behind you. How do you feel? Keep changing the dynamics of the thought until you are comfortable with it.'

3.   Thoughts can often have associated feelings, images, colours, even sounds and smells so it's useful to expand on this experience in order to lessen the impact of destructive thoughts: 'Get a sense of any feeling that this thought brings up. Get a sense of where this feeling is located in your body. Get a sense of the texture and shape of the feeling. Now begin to change the feeling in some way: move it to a different part of your body, for example, your big toe. If the feeling feels rough and spiky, make it smooth and soft. Change its shape in some way. Make it very small. How does the feeling change when you alter its dynamics? If the thought brings up an image within you, get a sense of where this image is and move it outside of your body, make the image very small and fade any colours away. Make the image the size of a postage stamp. How do you feel now in terms of the image and the thought?'

4.   Once the client has changed the aspects of the negative thought(s) in a way that lessens their impact, they can begin to replace negative thoughts with positive thoughts, again under instruction from the therapist: 'Now imagine fading the negative thought away and bring up a nice thought, something that makes you feel good. Perhaps a thought of something that you've enjoyed doing recently or have enjoyed in the past: a hobby, a holiday, a family trip, birthday party. Get a sense of this thought in your mind now and notice how you feel, notice any positive feelings or sensations that this thought brings. Make this experience as dynamic as you can, turn up any colours, make any colours bright and bold, turn up any sounds and allow any positive feelings to flow through you. . . .'

Through verbal and visual feedback, the therapist works with the client to make the positive experience rich and immersing. The above exercise could be set as homework, with the client instructed to change the dynamics of negative thoughts in the above manner, replacing these with positive thoughts or experiences instead. This shifts the focus of responsibility upon the client and their own internal resources, which can be empowering and illuminating.

A useful way of ending this exercise would be to get the client to imagine themselves in the future at some point where they no longer have negative thoughts or no longer attach to any destructive thoughts. Once more this internal experience can be heightened through turning up colours, sounds and feelings. Future imagining in this way can provide a blueprint for change and can impact directly and positively upon therapeutic goals.

Imagine a future without the thoughts

Once more allow the client to get comfortable in their chair, to close their eyes and focus on their breathing. The therapist guides the client to an imaginary future where the negative thoughts have gone or no longer have impact:

> 'Now just imagine yourself at a point in the future where you no longer have these nega-
> tive thoughts, a point in the future where they no longer have any impact. Get a sense of
> yourself at this point in the future and notice what is different about you. How do you act?
> How do others act towards you? How do you think differently? What positive thoughts do
> you have? If you could listen in to your internal dialogue what things would you be saying
> to yourself that make you more positive? What new things do you do in the future now that
> you're no longer burdened by the negative thoughts?'

The therapist can utilise imagination and verve in order to allow the client to make this experience rich and vivid in their minds. Imagining the future in this way can send powerful unconscious messages to the client that change is possible and that negative thought patterns can be broken.

Case study

Bernard came to therapy plagued with difficult and destructive thoughts and feelings surround-ing his ex-partner; they had split eight years ago and shared joint custody of a child. Although Bernard had felt that he was in a secure loving relationship at the time, his partner had suddenly left, taking the child with her and telling Bernard that she no longer loved him. The split had been so unexpected that Bernard felt that he had never let go of his ex-partner; eight years after the split he could not accept that the relationship was over. Bernard found himself obsessing over his ex-partner, constantly thinking about her to the point that he felt totally incapacitated in life: unable to move on, unable to change his career, unable to socialise and meet new people. He lived like a hermit, coming home from work and never venturing out. During the evenings he would drink a bottle of wine and his thoughts would drift towards his ex-partner. Why didn't she love me anymore? Why did she take the baby and leave? What's her new boyfriend like? Is her boyfriend better than me? Did I love her enough? I miss her company. I miss being with her.

These thoughts would be loud and clear in his mind, unsettling and destructive; so low was his self-esteem that he could no longer bring himself to visit her and collect his child for the weekend. Instead this task was left to his parents, who were supportive and understanding.

The goals for therapy were to lift the obsessive and destructive thinking patterns with regards to his ex-partner, to let go of the emotions and feelings surrounding the breakup and to boost Bernard's self-esteem and confidence so that he could take back control of his life.

During session one, Bernard was taught techniques for mindfulness and self-awareness: breathing in for three and out for four and progressive muscle relaxation. With Bernard in a relaxed state, metaphors for non-attachment to thoughts (such as the 'Cloud Gazer Meditation' in Chapter 1) were introduced and Bernard was instructed to imagine a place where he felt completely calm and relaxed. Bernard eventually settled on a beach in Goa, which he had visited in a gap year during university. Under guidance from the therapist, Bernard was able to make this calm, relaxing place very real in his mind. As part of his homework, Bernard was to focus on his breathing and bring up the beach in Goa whenever the obsessive thoughts over his ex-partner became overpowering.

Bernard reported in session two that he was feeling a bit better; although he hadn't moved on from the destructive thinking patterns and the feelings of jealousy towards her current partner, he was able to bring up relaxing imagery whenever he recognised himself spiralling with unhealthy thoughts and this calmed his mind. He was also able to recognise certain moments during the day when the thoughts were less prevalent, for example, whenever he was occupied with a difficult task at work. Utilising a state of hypnosis, Bernard was instructed to explore these moments where his thoughts were different, where he found himself absorbed in an experience that was altogether better than any negative thoughts and feelings. As Bernard developed his experiential awareness of these specific moments where his thoughts were freer, the unconscious part of his mind could begin to make the connection between recognising old destructive thoughts and subsequently changing the external situation (for example, occupying the mind with a task) and internal experience (for example, being aware of the thoughts related to that task and any positive feelings that arose from these thoughts). Age regression was utilised to help lift the feelings of blame and anger in relation to the split itself and Bernard found it very useful to imagine the moments where his ex-partner had left with the baby as 'small black and white images that were sepia toned and grainy like the Charlie Chaplin movies'.

During the next two sessions, Bernard reported that he still found it difficult to lift the destructive thinking patterns, so a cognitive approach was adopted: the obsessive thoughts were written down by Bernard and challenged through providing new frames of reference. For example, the recurring thinking pattern based around Bernard not being good enough to deserve a relationship was reframed with the understanding that his ex-partner was an unsettled, unhappy person, prone to making rash decisions, and that her track record of several broken relationships over the last few years had proven this to be the case. Bernard was instructed to write down positive thoughts about himself, on pieces of card, and to place these cards around his house so that they were in clear view. He even took cards with positive affirmations with him to work, which he kept in his wallet. He wore a fitness watch around his wrist and was instructed to pull its band with his other hand whenever a negative thought surfaced, to take several deep breaths and to imagine himself doing something pleasant, such as meeting friends for a drink. In this way a cognitive pattern disruption of thinking was introduced along with subtle cues for socialising more and getting out of the house in the evenings.

Sessions five and six involved Bernard bringing the destructive thoughts up in his mind, and under guidance from the therapist, changing the dynamics of these thoughts: volume, pitch and location. Bernard was able to imagine his thoughts placed outside of himself, which negated their impact in relation to any uncomfortable feelings he was experiencing as a result of these thoughts. During these sessions, Bernard became very aware of the triggers for his destructive thinking patterns: seeing his ex-partner's profile on Facebook with pictures of her new boyfriend, old photographs of her that he kept on his mantelpiece, his parents bringing his child over from his ex-partner, parents evening and school plays where the two of them would be present. Utilising mindfulness and progressive muscle relaxation, Bernard was able to imagine himself in these situations with very clear boundaries and focussed on his own sense of self, his own positive characteristics, his own positive thoughts and feelings.

Gradually, the pattern of negative obsessive thinking subsided and Bernard became more focussed on nurturing, in his words, his own 'inner voice' of wisdom and happiness. Under hypnosis, during session seven, the therapist worked on developing this notion of the client's inner voice as a voice that could transcend the clutter of the world around him, the thoughts and feelings, the actions of others; a voice that could guide him towards the things that he wanted to feel about himself: that he was capable and articulate and intelligent; that he could look forward to meeting someone that was right for him; that he didn't want to dwell on the past anymore. Bernard reported experiencing this inner voice as a wise old man with a long grey beard, thereafter referred to as his wise inner counsellor by both Bernard and the therapist.

By session ten, Bernard was in a much better place, gaining enthusiasm for going out with friends a couple of times a week. He had also joined a tennis club and was looking forward to the mixed doubles events, where he could meet women and enjoy their company. Most importantly he had also started to pick up his child from his ex-partner and now felt as though there was 'absolutely nothing there anymore' in relation to the old thoughts and feelings surrounding their relationship. The therapist encouraged him to explore this enhanced version of himself and together they worked on boosting self-esteem and confidence for three more sessions until Bernard suggested that he no longer felt that he needed to come to therapy.

The above example illustrates an integrative approach to therapy that focusses on identifying the sequence of thoughts, feelings and actions that led to the problems that Bernard presented. Not only were specific thoughts examined, but also the context surrounding his thoughts: where did the thoughts arise? What was he doing? Who was he with? Did the thoughts go away, if so, when? Did he experience periods of the day or night when his thinking pattern shifted? Interventions were designed to focus on several specific points of the problem in order to draw away from it. For example, not only was he taken back to the traumatic event, the split itself, in order to shift emotions and feelings that kept him stuck in the past, he was taken back further still in order to examine the relationship with his ex-partner, as well as his ex-partner's relationships with others. Bernard was able to determine that his ex-partner had difficulties maintaining strong relationships throughout her life, including her parents, and with this information, a reframe could be constructed which could lessen the critical self-thinking and beliefs. Cognitive behavioural strategies were adopted in order to challenge the negative thinking while hypnosis was used to instil mindfulness and to help Bernard deal with the triggers for obsessive thinking patterns. By 'attacking' the problem at several points as opposed to a more conservative approach focussing on one area, the interventions led to the client utilising his inner resources in order to change for the better.

Conclusion

This chapter has focussed on thinking, in relation to our clients and ourselves as mental health practitioners. The chapter has demonstrated the importance of considering thinking content and structure, and the need to identify and explore unhelpful, or distorted thinking. We have suggested that often clients will be stuck within their worlds of thought which they believe to be true. Therefore, it is important for us as therapists to try to understand clients' thinking errors and to facilitate them to challenge these and consider new ways of thinking – or even to go beyond thought. This chapter has highlighted the ways in which thoughts can influence the therapeutic relationship between a therapist and a client, and how important it is for therapists to not only consider what clients are saying to them, but also to be picking up on subtle clues from their body language about what their thoughts might be like or about. We have suggested that people can have thoughts around rules for living and that these can impact upon relationships, and how trainee counsellors can find that their own relationships change as they become aware of their own and others' thinking. We have also looked at thinking through an integrative lens and have presented the case study of Bernard, where we have shown that some very interesting and powerful therapeutic work can take place through focussing on thought by drawing upon person-centred, relational, CBT and hypnotherapeutic modalities. We have also suggested some interventions that can really help work with clients' distorted thinking. In the next chapter we turn to exploring the conscious and unconscious mind through an integrative therapeutic lens.

References

Alladin, A. (2008) *Cognitive Hypnotherapy*. Chichester: Wiley.

Berne, E. (1964) *Games that People Play*. London: Penguin Books.

Gerrig, R. & Zimbardo, P. (2009) *Psychology and Life: International Edition*. London: Pearson.

Hadley, J. & Staudacher, C. (2001) *Hypnosis for Change*. Oakland, CA: New Harbinger Publications.

Harris, T. (1973) *I'm Ok, You're Ok*. London: Random House.

Lear, E. (1871) 'The Owl and the Pussycat', http://www.nonsenselit.org/Lear/ns/pussy.html (accessed 20 September 2017).

Rainsberger, T. (1981) *James Wong Howe: Cinematographer*. Lancaster: Gazelle Book Services Ltd.

Rogers, C. (1961) *On Becoming a Person*. London: Constable.

Yapko, M. (2001) *Treating Depression with Hypnosis. Integrating Cognitive-Behavioral and Strategic Approaches*. New York: Routledge.

Chapter 5

Working integratively with our conscious and unconscious minds

The whole is greater than the sum of its parts.

Aristotle, *Metaphysics, Book VIII* (350 BCE)

Introduction

Working therapeutically with people involves working with both conscious and unconscious processes. Clients often come to therapy because they want to understand better what motivates and governs their actions and emotions, and therapy can be an important mechanism through which to shine a light on their conscious and unconscious minds. Some clients may already have experienced being in crisis, where they are harming themselves or experiencing hallucinations or other distressing symptoms. Some of these clients may tell us that they went into crisis when they felt they could no longer cope, that distressing emotions and perceptions had gathered such a momentum that they could no longer contain these safely. Here there is often an interplay between the conscious and unconscious – between clients' thinking selves and those parts of themselves that they are unable to access but somehow help create and sustain their anxiety, depression and other mental health challenges.

The following chapter explores the unconscious and conscious mind and how we can work integratively with an understanding that human beings have both. We look briefly at the structure of the brain and how this links with the conscious and unconscious. We also explore the role of stories, myths and metaphors in therapy and relate this to the interplay between the conscious and unconscious mind. Firstly, we present Maslow's hierarchy of needs from the perspective of our bodies and minds being driven, often unconsciously, by our very human needs. We then tell the story of Paul and Jim in order to examine how we might come to understand the unconscious and conscious mind, the interplay between them and how integrative therapists can and do work with both.

Maslow's hierarchy of needs as a model of unconscious and conscious motivations

Maslow's (1943) proposition is that as humans we are driven by various biological and psychological needs. It is these needs that motivate us to act upon our world. For Maslow there is a kind of order to our needs, beginning from our most basic and biological needs and ascending to more sophisticated and less biologically driven needs. Importantly, these needs can be unconscious and conscious, and so we can be propelled into doing things without really consciously deciding to take action. The following is a breakdown of Maslow's hierarchical model, beginning from the first level and most basic needs to the more sophisticated needs. Whilst Maslow's original model had five levels of need, this was expanded to incorporate further higher levels, leading to an eight-level model:

> **Level One needs: Biological and physiological** – food, air, shelter, intercourse, sleep, warmth etc.
>
> **Level Two needs: Safety** – to be secure, to be protected from violence, for there to be order and stability.
>
> **Level Three needs: Love and belongingness** – to be accepted by others, to experience intimacy, to give and receive love, to feel that we are part of a larger group whether that group is comprised of family, friends, work colleagues and so on.
>
> **Level Four needs: Esteem** – the need to feel valued by others, the need for status, also esteem in relation to oneself, to feel independent, a sense of dignity and achievement.
>
> **Level Five needs: Cognitive** – to have meaning, to explore our environments and ourselves, to have knowledge and understanding.
>
> **Level Six needs: Aesthetic** – a search for beauty, for balance, to appreciate things.
>
> **Level Seven needs: Self-actualisation** – the need to realise our full potential, to continue to experience and grow, to seek self-fulfilment.
>
> **Level Eight needs: Transcendence** – the need to be motivated by values that go beyond the self which can include religious, spiritual and other mystical experiences; to serve others; to pursue various political, religious and other ideologies and belief systems.

The above levels of needs suggest that as a species humans have multiple motivations, and these may be conscious as well as unconscious. As therapists we have been particularly struck by those clients who come telling a story of what has happened to them and being filled with guilt and shame as to what they have done. For example, a client revealed how she had sex with a boy when she was 17 and that she became pregnant and had an abortion. This client carried guilt and shame for the next five years until she came for therapy. It can be enlightening and relieving to clients to see Maslow's hierarchy of needs and to come to a realisation that they are governed by needs that are often beyond their own conscious control. The young woman who became pregnant at 17 and then had an abortion perhaps was driven unconsciously by a number of different needs – her biological, sexual needs, her need for belongingness and love, and a need for esteem. Exploring these needs with the client and raising awareness that these needs are unconscious as well as conscious helped the client to look at herself more compassionately, to let go of much of her guilt and shame. Maslow's hierarchy of human needs can be a useful integrative therapeutic tool in that it highlights and explains what motivates us as humans, and we can use this therapeutically in order to explore with clients what some of their current unconscious and conscious needs might be, which needs are being met, how and by whom; and which needs are still to be met.

If we are being driven both consciously and unconsciously by such diverse and powerful needs as Maslow's hierarchy suggests, then this inevitably means that we can create all sorts of intra and inter personal, and intra and inter group challenges for ourselves. These multiple unconscious and conscious needs make for complex relational dynamics and histories between people. The following is a short fictional story about Paul and Jim, about their unconscious motivations and how these can influence how they talk to one another when they meet for the first time as adults in a prison cell.

Paul and Jim and the great unconscious

Paul rarely looked at himself in the small plastic mirror that hung on his cell wall. Today was different, however, and he stared at himself thinking, 'Am I gonna look like this guy?' Paul was wearing a grey tracksuit and black trainers. Although originally he had been of reasonably slender yet muscular build, during his long ten years in prison Paul had worked out daily in the gym, building up his body so that it resembled a kind of shadowy alter ego of Michelin Man. Paul sat down on his bed and felt a craving for a pot of rice pudding, just like he always did at 7 in the morning. He grabbed hold of a small carton of sweet rice and started eating it slowly from the edges of the carton with a plastic teaspoon, just like he always did.

During his time inside Paul had noticed that he had quite an obsessive side to his character. He was fastidious in folding his clothes into the wardrobe in his cell. He colour coordinated which clothes should touch which, and when making himself a cup of coffee Paul always made sure that he stirred the liquid three times before he began drinking it. He was also very well-manicured because he would spend a certain proportion of each day in his cell filing his nails so that they were smooth and perfectly aligned with the shape of the ends of his fingers. Yet when Paul thought about his now deceased mother, he remembered her for her spontaneity and free spirit, for her wisdom and love. Paul smiled to himself, 'My mum was light and compassion and I dedicate myself to her. She was not subsumed by the matrix.' Paul often thought about the Matrix, which in his mind was the dark side to life, a higher power that could invade people's bodies and their minds making them do very sinister things. He himself had experienced episodes in his life where he was consumed by the Matrix, which ultimately had given him his current lengthy prison sentence.

Keys suddenly turned in the lock of Paul's cell door. 'Your visitor has arrived', explained Mr Webbon, a prison officer who had a lot of respect for Paul given that Paul had once been a mixed martial arts champion. Paul stood up. 'Bring it on', he said and followed Mr Webbon out the door and into the labyrinthine-like corridors of HMP Snelton. Paul was taken to a small room away from the visitors area; somehow his visitor had gained access to the innermost corners of the prison, and Paul was not at all surprised by this, given that his visitor was his biological father, a man who had played quite a senior role in MI5, a man who called himself Jim.

For the first time in his life Paul sat down opposite his father. He sat and looked directly at Jim, saying nothing, doing nothing, just breathing and trying to stay focussed.

> 'Hello Paul' said Jim, 'How have you been?'
> 'Well Jim, if that's your name, not so good. I can't see my daughters, I couldn't go to mum's funeral – don't know if you went to it – and still have 18 months left here and I'm just so bored with being here now.'
> 'I did go to Linda's funeral.'
> 'Lucky you.' Paul could not resist saying this.

Then there was silence between the two men. Jim looked around the room, noticing the prison's various booklets on dealing with drugs, relationships, getting an education. Paul noticed Jim's fastidiously clean and clipped fingernails, he noticed the plastic poppy pinned so carefully to Jim's black woollen coat, and he recognised the thin lips of his father so well because Paul himself had those very same lips. Paul grew cold.

'Your mum was a special lady. I still regret disappearing from her life in the sudden way that I did. Things were different in those days. Defending this country from subversives was my main objective'.

'The Matrix got to you Jim', responded Paul. 'You used my mum and then deserted her, and I have been left figuring out who I am ever since. Now I can see where I get my obsessiveness from, I can see why I delve into the dark side of things, why I have killed to stay alive.'

'You were a beautiful baby Paul, I remember how much dark curly hair you were born with and how big your eyes were.'

At that moment an alarm began to ring.

The above brief story can serve as an illustration of how individuals are governed as much, if not more, by their unconscious as by their conscious minds. We invite readers to consider some of the following questions regarding Paul and Jim:

- Drawing on Maslow's (1943) hierarchy of needs, what needs do you think underpin Paul's comments to his father Jim?
- Drawing on Maslow's hierarchy of needs what needs do you think underpin Jim, what he did and his interaction with Paul in the prison cell?
- What emotions do you think underpin Jim's responses to Paul?

If working therapeutically with Paul, we would be looking to explore with Paul his identity because it seems that Paul is quite confused about who he really is. As Paul had never met his biological father before that day in prison, it seems that Paul was driven by an unconscious need to understand who he is and where he comes from. This links to Maslow's hierarchy of needs, in relation to the need for love and belonging. Paul consciously knows that there are aspects to himself that he finds hard to understand, and so therapy might include examining these aspects, to see if over the longer term Paul might better understand himself and be able to integrate the various aspects of his character, some of which he clearly inherited from his biological father. Paul also indicates in the story above that he has cognitive and transcendental needs. He clearly has committed a violent crime and he has a need to understand why he did this, to find some meaning in this, and in referring to the Matrix this indicates that Paul perhaps has some transcendental needs – he may be on a path of enlightenment, of discovering values that may be driven by a spiritual or mystical framework of understanding. When our unconscious or conscious needs go unmet, they can generate powerful emotions in us. When Paul eventually meets his father, it is clear from this initial exchange that Paul is carrying a lot of anger inside him towards Jim, and Paul may not necessarily be aware of this; this may at the moment be in his unconscious. In fact, one of the reasons why Paul might be in prison is as a result of unprocessed and strong emotions towards his biological father as a result of him being abandoned and unloved. Working therapeutically with Paul might therefore involve raising his awareness of any suppressed emotions in his psyche and how these can then influence his actions and interactions with others. Therapy might also provide a powerful mechanism through which Paul can process some of the anger he carries towards Jim so that he is less affected by anger in the future.

Turning now to Jim, it is clear from the interaction above that Jim feels guilt and shame over having disappeared from the lives of Paul and his mother. Jim rationalises this as him placing national security over and above his other values in life. This might be linked to cognitive needs on Maslow's hierarchy – Jim is searching for a meaning behind why he abandoned Paul and his mother. Interestingly, Jim tries to connect with Paul by telling him what he looked like as a baby and that he had been to Linda's funeral. However, when the guilt and shame become too much for Jim he avoids maintaining emotional and psychological contact with Paul, instead turning to observing what is in the prison cell where they are both sitting. Jim is also at this stage unable to verbally acknowledge his guilt and shame; he does not apologise to or seek forgiveness from Paul. Jim is perhaps terrified of his own inner guilt and shame and as a result remains defended – avoiding talking about how he feels or how hard it is for him to acknowledge the many years spent thinking about Paul, a son that he only saw once before having to abandon his fake identity as a gardener and green activist and returning to a desk job at MI5. Perhaps if Jim were to know that his actions as a young undercover agent were also influenced by his unconscious needs for love and intimacy, he might not feel so guilt-ridden.

It is also likely that Jim was governed by an unconscious need for esteem – to be valued by his managers, by MI5, the organisation that he worked for, and this drove Jim to override the questionable ethics of getting into a sexual relationship whilst being undercover. Jim's need to be seen as an effective undercover agent perhaps helped motivate him to suppress or avoid any discomfort associated with lying to Paul's mother Linda. It might be that this need for esteem was so deep within Jim's unconscious that it set him along a pathway of deceit without him ever fully considering the consequences of his actions. No wonder humans can cause chaos in their own lives, in the lives of others and more generally on planet Earth!

The TTM: An integrative model of change that incorporates the unconscious and conscious

When considering the unconscious and conscious, it is perhaps worthwhile to look at the trans-theoretical model of change (TTM) as developed by Prochaska and Norcross (2003), in order to provide an integrative structure to counselling practice. The TTM is not a theory of counselling but is a multistage model of change that incorporates an understanding of the natural tendencies that people show for effecting self-change. The TTM is an integrative model because it incorporates many different therapeutic systems. The TTM is a framework, a guiding structure for practice and is used to describe, explain and predict the processes of intentional behaviour change. The TTM consists of five stages and levels of change, with ten processes of change and these help therapists to use those interventions that are deemed most effective for any particular stage of change (Prochaska & Norcross, 2003). The TTM treats behaviour change as dynamic, rather than an all or nothing phenomenon. This distinction is considered one of the model's strengths (Marshall & Biddle, 2001).

Prochaska and Norcross (2003) found that particular psychotherapies are more useful during particular stages of change, providing a practical basis for the successful integration of a range of therapeutic approaches. Although the TTM was primarily developed to inform the area of addictions counselling, it has been shown to have significant potential for counselling in general. The TTM's theoretical integration is achieved using a combination of ten processes of change, five stages of change, and five levels of change (Prochaska, DiClemente and Norcross 1992).

The TTM incorporates the unconscious and conscious through the five stages of change as can be seen below:

Pre-contemplation	Client may be unaware or under-aware of their problems, no intention to change in foreseeable future. Resistance to recognising a problem. Not considering altering their behaviour in the foreseeable future.
Contemplation	Client is aware that a problem exists and seriously thinking about overcoming it but have not yet made a commitment to take action. Knowing where you want to go but not being quite ready yet to go there.
Preparation	Ready to start taking action soon – planning and preparation. Combines intention and behavioural criteria. Intending to take action immediately and may report some small behavioural changes.
Action	Individuals modify their behaviour, experiences and/or environment in order to overcome their problems. Involves the most overt behavioural changes – requires considerable commitment of time and energy.
Maintenance	Maintenance is the stage in which people have made specific overt modifications in their lifestyles and are working to prevent relapse; however, they do not apply change processes as frequently as do people in Action.

Thus, the pre-contemplation stage might be considered to be what is in a client's unconscious, whereas the four stages that follow involve a client being consciously aware of some of their challenges. The TTM is dynamic in that a client is likely to be at a number of different stages of change, according to the many different issues that they may be facing. It is also important to point out that the unconscious/conscious is not necessarily a binary split, but might be viewed more as a continuum, so clients have different degrees of awareness of their challenges, with awareness itself as something in constant flux.

The TTM also has five levels of change that can help us and our clients to understand where they are in terms of their issues, thus:

TTM: Levels of Change	
Symptom/Situational	Treating the symptoms/ behaviour only. According to Prochaska & Norcross (2003: 502) 'in the TTM we prefer to intervene initially at the s/s level because change tends to occur more quickly at this more conscious and contemporary level of problems'.
Maladaptive Cognitions	Negative thinking.
Current Interpersonal Conflict	Intimacy and sexuality, communication, hostility, control of others.
Family Systems	Family conflict/beliefs – attachment
Intra-Personal Conflicts	Anxieties and defences, self-esteem problems, personal responsibility, core beliefs, self-concept

Prochaska and Norcross (2003) also highlight various processes of change – the things that we can facilitate with clients in order for them to experience change and growth:

TTM: Processes of Change	
Consciousness Raising	Increasing awareness, making the unconscious conscious, increase information available to clients, includes feedback on the individuals' own experiences and actions (experiential) and education or psycho-education (environmental). Individuals' ways of thinking/ schemas/internal working models can influence the information they choose to accept/assimilate/dismiss/select, and so by raising awareness and helping the client see things in a different way can help to change the way they view things or how they behave.
Cathartic Relief	Expressing (supressed) emotions – provides relief. Often 'unacceptable' emotions such as anger, guilt or anxiety are blocked from direct expression – results in pressure (often anxiety/depression) for some sort of release e.g. indirectly through headaches. Clients need to express emotions – often are consequently better at accepting such emotions as natural without the need to be so severely controlled. Experientially this can be termed 'corrective emotional experiences', where an intense emotional experience produces a psychological correction. Cathartic reactions or 'dramatic relief' can also be evoked by observing emotional scenes/music/literature etc. or during role-play, psycho-drama.
Self Re-Evaluation	Where an individual can modify or re-evaluate the value or meaning behind the problem behaviour (emotionally and cognitively) – may include imagery, dramatic relief. Realising that the healthy behaviour is an important part of who they are and want to be.

(Continued)

(Continued)

TTM: Processes of Change

Environmental Re-Evaluation	Where an individual can modify or re-evaluate how the problem behaviour affects the physical and social environment. Realising how their behaviour affects others and how they could have more positive effects by changing.
Self-Liberation	Where individuals become aware of the potential to choose different alternatives, including the deliberate creation of new alternatives for living. Involves the anxiety in being responsible for which alternative is followed – this is a move toward self-liberation. Social liberation occurs when changes in the environment/society make more alternatives available to individuals.
Counter Conditioning	Changing behaviour to stimuli – involves conditioning to do the healthy opposite of the behaviour – subsisting alternatives. For example, relaxation, assertion, positive self-statements, desensitisation.

Prochaska and Norcross (2003) then highlight how some processes of change are more relevant for certain stages of change than for others. For example, consciousness-raising might be more appropriate for the precontemplation and contemplation stages of change; whereas self re-evaluation might be more relevant for the action stage of change.

The TTM can be a useful integrative model that helps us to have an overview of where a client is in relation to their conscious and unconscious regarding specific issues in their lives. As therapists we have found this model useful. Nonetheless, there are some criticisms of the TTM. Some researchers have suggested that the model cannot work if the client is unmotivated to change. Also, because the relationship between processes and stages of change are only tendencies, there is a risk that practitioners could use TTM in a prescriptive way and cause harm to clients by using the wrong change process at the wrong time (Petrocelli, 2002). Macnee & McCabe (2004) question the applicability of the model to specific populations. The population researched was in Southern Appalachia, where cultural characteristics and the history of economic dependence on tobacco raise questions about whether the TTM is appropriate for unique populations and even non Westernised countries at all. However, Rodgers et al. (2001) found support that the principles of the TTM do apply to diverse populations. Their study examined self-efficacy and processes of change of the TTM with exercise across three populations: high school students, university undergraduate students, and employed adults. The results of the study suggest that the underlying principles of change in the TTM are similar across all populations; arguably, however, these populations are once again from a westernised society.

Case study of the TTM

Mary is a 39-year-old woman who has 3 children – aged 12, 7 and 4. Mary is a single mum, having recently separated from an abusive partner with whom she had two of her children (the middle and youngest ones). Previously, Mary had been in a relationship with another man with whom she had her oldest son. Mary believes that her most recent partner has been emotionally and psychologically abusive towards her through his manipulation and bad tempers and he has also been physically abusive towards her children – these allegations have been pursued by the police and this partner is no longer able to see his children. Mary is currently experiencing high anxiety. She finds it difficult to sit still and relax and feels compelled to keep doing things like the housework. Mary relies on alcohol to relax and can be a binge drinker – she doesn't see herself as being dependent on alcohol. Mary also can get very angry and can at times become angry with her children, although she is not physically abusive towards them. Mary would like to pursue a career, as she always dreamt of being a teacher but fell pregnant just before she was about to start a teacher training programme. Mary has a difficult relationship with both of her parents. She feels that they do not support her, but rather intrude on her personal space. Mary would like to be more assertive with her parents.

If placing Mary on the TTM, the following might reflect where Mary is in terms of levels and stages of change:

	Pre-contemplation	Contemplation	Preparation	Action	Maintenance
Situational High Anxiety Binge drinking	Mary doesn't necessarily perceive herself as having a drink problem.	Mary is aware of how stressed she feels, she just doesn't know what to do about it.			
Maladaptive Cognitions 'I am not a good mum' 'I have to keep myself constantly busy'	Mary is likely to be at pre-contemplation stage here because she is likely not to be aware of her thinking processes.				
Current Interpersonal Conflict Mary is in conflict with an ex-partner.		Mary is aware of some of the interpersonal conflicts in her life.			
Family Systems Mary has a challenging relationship with both her parents.			Mary wants to take action but doesn't know how. Hence she is at preparation stage – preparing to learn how to re-establish boundaries with her parents.		
Intra-Personal Conflicts Mary perhaps feels conflicted in relation to being a mum but also feeling that she wants a career for herself.	Mary is not necessarily aware of the conflict in her in terms of wanting to have a career as well as wanting to be a good mum.				

It can be helpful to plot a client according to the TTM's levels and stages of change. This can also be shared with clients. In this way the TTM can provide a strong framework within which to work. It can also be helpful to plot a client according to the TTM's levels and stages of change at different points throughout therapy – perhaps at the start, middle and end. In this way it is possible for us and our clients to see where there has been movement – for example, from contemplation to action stages of change. It is also important to note that there is no 'correct' version of the TTM in relation to a client – that as therapists we will perceive our clients in unique ways and so whilst one therapist might view Mary as being in contemplation stage regarding a particular issue in her life, another therapist might see her as being at pre-contemplation stage. The point is that the TTM can provide a good focus for therapy and a mechanism through which to discuss change and growth with our clients. We can also use the TTM to think about processes of change that work most effectively with our clients, according to which stage and level of change they are at. For example, techniques that can raise a client's conscious awareness of some of their challenges are most appropriate for the pre-contemplation and contemplation stages of change. Consciousness raising can include suggesting books or articles that clients can read (psychoeducation) and/or various techniques that encourage our clients to explore their feelings, behaviours, perceptions and so on. For example, CBT based approaches can use Socratic questioning, which involves using open-ended and exploratory questions, in order to help a client to become more aware of themselves. In the case of Mary, Socratic questioning could be used in relation to situational, maladaptive cognition, current interpersonal and intrapersonal conflicts. In this way we would be helping Mary to raise her own awareness of, and understanding about, the various TTM related levels of change in her life.

Carl Jung and the unconscious

Carl Jung (1953) was a student of Sigmund Freud, who developed his own approach to the unconscious. Jung (1953) made a distinction between the personal and collective unconscious. The personal unconscious is similar to Freud's in that it comprises of repressed memories and forgotten information. For Jung, however, the personal unconscious is more easily accessible through exploring complexes, a complex being a collection of emotions, attitudes, cognitions and memories that focus on one single concept. The collective unconscious for Jung (1953) comprises of shared memories from our ancestral and evolutionary past. As Jung (1953: 188) argued, 'The form of the world into which [a person] is born is already inborn in him, as a virtual image.' We are born into this World already with memories that are imprinted in our minds – for example, a fear of the dark or of spiders. For Jung archetypes are images and thoughts that have meanings shared across different cultures that can be found in literature, art or religious systems. These archetypes are in our unconscious, and as such influence our thoughts and behaviours. This brief discussion would suggest the importance again of considering the unconscious, the conscious and the interplay between the two.

Left side right side and the metaphor of conscious and unconscious

As Citrenbaum, King and Cohen (1985) suggest, psychologists often refer to the left side and right side of the brain metaphorically as the 'conscious' and the 'unconscious' mind respectively. So let us stick with this metaphor and ask ourselves *two* questions:

1   What exactly are the differences between the conscious and unconscious mind?
2   How can we apply our knowledge of these elements within integrative therapy in order to
     facilitate positive change within clients?

Differences between the left and right hemispheres begin with control of the body: the left
hemisphere of the brain is responsible for controlling the right side of the body, while the right
hemisphere controls the left side of the body (Buzan, 1988). Split-brain research by Roger
Sperry elucidated the different activities of the two sides of the brain (Trevarthern, 1990),
resulting in a 1981 Nobel Prize in Physiology and Medicine shared with neurophysiologists
David Hubel and Torsten Wiesel. Sperry's experiments facilitated discoveries within the functioning of the human brain. The left, or dominant, hemisphere is concerned with analytical and
logical processes, reasoning and logic. This side of the brain controls, for example, skills such
as reading and writing, language and speech, as well as maths; it likes verbal instruction and
accepted information. The right side of the brain functions by using sensory information such
as visual imagery, colour perception, emotional recall, creativity and fantasy. Skills that the
right hemisphere 'enjoys' include music and art appreciation, dance, perception and sculpture
(Thomas-Cottingham, 2010).

Making the invisible visible

The unconscious, or right hemisphere, does not use language in order to function so how can
we get a sense of it? How can we grasp something that is, in fact, unconscious or hidden or elu-
sive? Instead of trying to describe it within the context of conscious actions such as language,
let us undertake a simple experiment that highlights differences between left brain–right brain
functioning:

Say the Colour *not* the Word
     Look at the word below and say the <u>COLOUR</u>, not the word:

ORANGE

Your right brain tries to say the colour (which is black) but your left brain is determined to read
the word (which is orange). The difference in awareness, or *experience* of the *reality* of the
word ORANGE – whatever the reality may be to the individual – causes a conflict of interest
between the two hemispheres and this results in a double-take, or delayed reaction, in order to
answer the puzzle correctly (Stroop, 1935).

Building awareness of unconscious processes

As you are reading the words in this chapter, so you can begin to appreciate all the background
work that the unconscious mind does within the Autonomic Nervous System, helping control
processes such as breathing, heartbeat, blood pH and digestion: processes that keep us healthy
and living and safe, throughout the day and night.

Now start to focus on your own heartbeat. Notice how fast or slow it is, how loudly or softly
your heart beats. Perhaps your heart is beating so softly that you find it difficult to perceive?
Maybe it is beating heavily and rapidly, in which case, we understand and sympathise with the
excitement you are feeling as you read this book! Awareness of the heartbeat, a few seconds

ago buried within the unconscious, is now subject to conscious awareness. This in turn provides a shift in how we experience ourselves within the moment. Shifting the focus of our experience in this way underlines our continual transition between conscious and unconscious awareness.

The interplay between the conscious and unconscious

Let us now examine some examples of experiences where conscious and unconscious processes build our awareness and shape our reality:

Beware of the cat

How often have we driven a car and not remembered the journey at all, the process of driving left literally in the hands (and feet and eyes) of the unconscious? And suddenly a cat runs out in front of our vehicle and right then and there we are back in the car and not in the supermarket planning what food we are going to buy. We are consciously slamming our foot on the brake, consciously sounding the horn, consciously turning the steering wheel in order to drive around the cat, consciously checking in our mirror that the traffic behind is not too close. A shift of awareness has occurred with respect to operating the car. After a few minutes, we forget about the cat and begin once again to plan our evening meal. The experience of driving in relation to the rest of the journey is centred around a critical question: will it be lasagne or a vegetable curry?

The self-conscious meeting

It is Tom's first day in his new job as an insurance salesman; the team that he works for meets every Monday morning in order to go through sales targets and discuss business growth opportunities within a saturated market. This is fine with Tom, who does not mind meetings and feels comfortable with people. He sits down at a table and notices that out of the seven people gathered, two are female and the rest, including his manager Simon, are male. One of the females, a woman in her late twenties with blonde hair, catches his eye and for a split second something passes between them, undefined and buried. Tom is not really conscious of this as he is focussed on doing well in the meeting. Because he is new he is not expecting any questions, but if someone should ask him something Tom is confident that he will reply well. After all, he used to captain the university football team and if he can handle that sort of pressure he can certainly thrive in an office environment!

Tom's manager introduces him to the rest of the group; Tom smiles warmly and adjusts the collar of his shirt slightly. He does this without noticing that he is doing it. Consciously he nods approval towards his manager. Everything is going fine and Tom laughs when the rest of the group laugh, nods his head when the rest of the group nod theirs; he sips his coffee in tandem with his manager and is aware that he is doing this. Nothing wrong with unconsciously sending a message to his boss that Tom respects his actions by copying them. Then a few minutes later the blonde girl fixes him with her eyes and asks him a question about insurance policies. Tom knows the answer to the question. It is an easy question that he has answered many times before. Yet the unconscious part of him starts to appear, like a white dove from a magician's hat. Suddenly he feels a sensation of heat weaving its way up his neck. Even before he registers this consciously and any thoughts begin to stir, the heat spreads into his cheeks and they start to smart. He can feel himself reddening, his ears tingling. Now the conscious thoughts begin to appear: Oh no, what's happening!? I feel so embarrassed! I'm blushing in front of all these people! Stop it!

The thoughts add a new layer of discomfort to Tom's current experience and he begins to stutter a response to the question, trying to engage in eye contact with the blonde woman, but finding that his blushing has made him very self-*conscious*. Surely she thinks him a fool! And his boss must be wondering why on earth they ever hired such a weak character! Finally he manages to answer the question and the blonde woman nods her head. His boss nods his and takes a sip of coffee. Tom leaves the coffee alone as his hands are shaking slightly. Or are they shaking a lot? His conscious experience now is fixated upon his hands, which he has placed on his thighs, out of the way of everyone's stares. The meeting ends and Tom is once again feeling comfortable; during the week his experience of the meeting fades away and Tom forgets about it. Until the next Monday morning that is, when Tom finds himself shaving. He stares at the reflection in the mirror. Will *it* happen again?

The one

Hayley is out with her friends, enjoying an evening at a wine bar. A man walks into the bar and Hayley notices him: he is good-looking with black hair, blue eyes and a muscular body. As she casts her eyes over him, Hayley begins to feel a very strong desire for him: a warm feeling that spreads through her body. Her heart starts to beat rapidly and there is a shift in the pit of her stomach: she begins to feel a very strong sexual desire for the man. Is this what 'love at first sight' feels like? Hayley feels drawn to him, like a magnet, and as he orders a drink at the bar she begins to imagine tearing his clothes off and jumping into bed with him.

This example emphasises the interplay between the conscious and unconscious mind in building a perception of reality that is unique to Hayley. At a surface level of perception she is very conscious of how the man looks: his eyes, his hair, his physique, the nice clothes that he wears. Yet why is she experiencing such powerful physical and emotional feelings as well as sexual thoughts? After all, she has never spoken to him before so how could she possibly know what his personality is like? There are many other good-looking males in the bar so why is she drawn to this particular man in such an irresistible manner? Why is he so special?

We have already mentioned Hayley's conscious observations of the man. Yet to start to build a 'picture' of her reality we need to consider the unconscious processes that are building her internal experience of this event. Unconsciously, Hayley's brain is building associations between the man and her own memories, experiences, knowledge and belief systems. Perhaps the man's lips remind her of the first kiss that she ever experienced? Maybe his hair takes her back to a previous relationship when she was deeply in love? Perhaps his eyes remind Hayley of her first true love? Unconscious associations such as these are creating Hayley's reality, while on the surface level it feels to Hayley as though she has simply fallen in love.

Stan and his story of survival

Stan was a small child during the Second World War. Late one night, German soldiers appeared at his family's home in Warsaw, Poland, and took Stan, his mother, sister and grandparents to a concentration camp in the south of the country. All night, while the train rumbled along the tracks, Stan cried for his father, who was fighting the war with the Polish army. Stan spent two years within the camp, witnessing horrors and deprivation that no human should ever experience. His mother, sister and grandparents all lost their battle with life and, after the war

had ended, Stan found himself an orphan in the UK where he subsequently discovered that his father had been killed when his plane was shot down across the Channel. Miraculously, Stan managed to build a life for himself in his new country, studying and eventually marrying. Stan was a man of few words. Sometimes his silences at home would go on for several weeks at a time: in the evenings after work he would often stare with sad eyes through the living-room window overlooking the garden. As they grew older, his kids would recognise his forlorn, solemn expression and ask their father whether he was okay. Stan would smile wanly, 'I'm okay, just thinking about a problem at work.' At other times he would put his mood down to worries about redundancy or what someone had said at one of the dances in the local Polish Club. Throughout Stan's long life the silences and distant stares remained.

The above example illustrates the interplay of two stories in Stan's life: the conscious story of Stan's explanation of his low moods and the unconscious story of danger, death, fear and loss that a young boy experienced during the war. Whether he was *conscious* of his prosaic explanations of behaviours and feelings we cannot be sure: he may have provided these responses in order to protect his children from his past. On the other hand, he may also have believed that the reasons he gave for his behaviour were truly real. Attributing our behaviours, feelings and emotions to one particular origin, when clearly there is another, more unconscious origin at play, is a common human characteristic, illustrating the influence of the unconscious mind upon the conscious platform, where we live out our lives.

The unconscious can have a powerful, almost hypnotic influence upon our lives; the British rock critic and musician Nick Kent (2010) described his addiction to heroin as a battle between conscious and unconscious processes. He was consciously aware of 'stepping over a dangerous line' whenever he took heroin but the unconscious would keep replaying 'the ecstasy of the moment when heroin first revealed its full power within you', resulting in the inevitable: heroin addiction for much of the 1970s. Earlier in this chapter we suggested that the unconscious mind functions in order to keep us healthy and safe and this is generally a correct assumption. However it would be useful to include the caveat that it does so in the way that it *knows best*, and as Heller and Steele (2007) suggest, subject to the framework of its reality and reality of the conscious mind. In short, it makes use of what it thinks are the best options available at that time, or *allowable* at that time. Kent had originally started using heroin as a way of coping with a relationship breakdown, describing it as 'an enchanted island' where all emotional feelings ceased. Through replaying the island over and over again, the unconscious may have been trying to provide Kent with the serenity and solace that he needed in order to cope with loss, but with devastating consequences. It may have offered him the forbidden apple, without realising that it was poisoned.

The conscious–unconscious bridge and symptomology

As therapists, it is useful to imagine the bridge between the conscious and unconscious and to consider what would happen if this bridge were blocked at the *conscious* end, in such a way that the unconscious could no longer easily communicate with the conscious. As Heller and Steele (2007) suggest, this could result in physical or emotional symptoms that result from the denial or ignorance of unconscious messages. Heller and Steele provide a simple example of just such a process. He considers the case of a tension headache and the unconscious factors involved:

> Imagine yourself working hard; so engrossed you are in your task that you have spent a much longer time on this than you realise. Nevertheless you keep going, intent on finishing

what you started. Your mind and body are tired but you are not consciously aware of this; however the unconscious part of you is *very aware* and understands that you need to *stop what you are doing and take a rest*. It begins to communicate kinaesthetically, tightening up the muscles in the back of your neck and down your back, your shoulders tightening up as result of the added strain on your body. You become aware of the muscular discomfort but you choose to ignore it. The task must be done. And so the unconscious, in a bid to protect you from overtiredness, starts to ramp up its communication: muscles tighten up even more until your whole body feels tense and overwhelmed and the result is a full blown headache where your head throbs persistently, your eyes cannot focus easily and you cannot think properly. Now finally the unconscious has achieved its goal: you take a rest, closing your eyes and regretting that you didn't take one earlier!

The man whose heart stopped beating

A few years ago a client came into therapy with a fear that his heart would stop beating at any moment. Added to his anxiety was a pain around his heart region, a dull throbbing sensation that was 'constantly with him'. After working with changing the dynamics of the pain and externalising it through the use of his imagination, the client was able to lessen the discomfort. Age regression in a relaxed state was utilised in order to take the client back to the source of the fear and he clearly pictured himself with his father, a forthright bully, jabbing him in the chest and yelling: 'You useless lump of lard! God knows I'll be dead by the time you achieve anything!' The client's father would often abuse him in this way; during age regression the client was able to imagine the discomfort that his father's finger caused when it prodded him. After his father had died suddenly, the client built up a successful business and that was when the pain in his chest suddenly became constant. During therapy, the client was instructed to bring up the part causing the pain in order to find out what its intentions were. In a relaxed state, the client was able to make this happen and discovered that the pain was his father's finger jabbing him in the chest as though a reminder from beyond the grave: *God knows I'll be dead by the time you achieve anything.* With the understanding that the unconscious was reminding him to be a good little boy and do what his father said, and that because of the unconscious prompts he had built up a very conscious fear of his heart stopping, the client was able to tell that part that he had 'done well enough and wouldn't be bullied anymore'. Eventually the part accepted this reframe and began working with him in order to help him feel better. Gradually over a period of several sessions, the pain eased and then disappeared entirely along with the fear of his heart stopping.

Myths, stories and therapeutic metaphors

The above examples illustrate the stories and metaphors surrounding our lives; the myths governing emotions, feelings and behaviours based around our belief systems. Now that we have a greater *conscious* awareness of the differences between conscious and unconscious aspects of the mind we can begin to apply our knowledge of these 'metaphors', stories and myths in a therapeutic context.

Psychiatrist Milton Erickson recognised that most of our lives were determined unconsciously (Rosen, 2010) though not in an unchangeable way; each time we read something inspiring, for example, both our conscious and unconscious are affected: a memory of the inspirational character or story or situation can be stored and 'played back' or presented to the conscious by the unconscious at a later time when we need inspiration: perhaps when faced with a task that needs completing or a problem that needs a solution. A fiction writer may ruminate on a particular way to end a chapter. He or she will go through various scenarios consciously only to find that none of them are quite right. Then a few days later they may wake up in the middle of the night with the perfect ending, something quite unexpected! The unconscious has been searching the vast library of memories and experiences we store for a solution, which it delivers to the conscious mind.

Erickson developed approaches in therapy that often *did not* utilise insight regarding a particular problem; in fact he discovered that insight could be detrimental to facilitating positive growth. Instead Erickson worked on changing a behaviour or attitude on an unconscious level (Citrenbaum, King & Cohen, 1985). Many times he would reply to a question with a story; often he would tell stories filled with messages for intuitive understanding and learning on an unconscious level (Rosen, 2010). Through stories the client could discover the solution within themselves; 'unconscious learnings' removed from conscious thoughts and issues. When told in an intriguing, amusing and interesting way, stories can present a pathway for positive change, introducing fresh ideas and concepts to the individual that bypasses conscious resistance (Rosen, 2010). Identifying with the meaning of a story can introduce a subtle change in approach to a behaviour or feeling, emotion or thought.

The power of myth

Since the evolution of human consciousness and social cultures, stories and myths have been used for spreading values and ethics within societies. A myth is defined in the *Oxford English Dictionary* as: 'A traditional story especially one concerning the early history of a people or explaining a natural or social phenomenon, and typically involving supernatural beings or events.'

Ancient humans respected animals but also had to hunt them for food, clothing and shelter. Hunting myths developed as a way of lessening the guilt of the kill: a balance was forged between living organisms and the spirits of dead animals (Davis, 2010). In this way, our distant ancestors were able to justify the fact that they had to kill entities that they deeply revered: an early example of *reframing* through the power of myth. Tribes gathered around campfires and explained traumatic events through stories and myths involving archetypes and legends. So the loss of a good hunting dog due to a rock fall or some other natural disaster could be rationalised by referring to gods and supernatural beings in order to create a story around this happening, based upon the belief systems within the tribe. How different from modern existence where 'freak' accidents are almost always attributed to 'bad luck' or 'chance'? Terms such as these seem realistic in our empirical world, when compared to a story built around celestial gods for instance, but offer no real comfort or solution or ending. How exactly do we define *chance* in existence? Does knowing a tragedy happens as a result of *bad luck* provide closure and make us feel better?

Rollo May (1993) suggests that a myth is a way of 'making sense in a senseless world', a way of nurturing positive mental health and an awareness of our ancestral past. Myths are the 'beams within a house' providing the structure of the house so that we can live in it. Without the notion of myths surrounding our existence we lose a sense of who we are and the true purpose and essence of our lives. May (1993) attributes the large number of suicides in young people in the USA over the last few decades to a loss of our myths in the western world: the loss of personal identity. The American writer, Alex Haley's quest to discover who he really was, led to the creation of the book *Roots*, which took his own myth of identity back to his ancestor in Africa, a man called Kunta Kinte. As May (1993) suggests, more Americans watched the *Roots* mini-series when it was first released than any other programme in the history of American TV. Clearly the concept of rootlessness and loss of identity resonated with the public.

Man's search for story

Storytelling is an inherent characteristic of humans; it is what stands us out from other organisms in the world. We create fiction in every moment of our lives: our own unique perceptions of an event, a moment in time, a particular experience or happening: the fiction of wealth and happiness; the fiction of permanency; the fiction of a happy ending. We find ourselves searching for a story, a meaning or an insight. We visit the cinema, read a book, listen to a song and watch the news. We want to know what happens at the end. Often we live our own lives out through metaphors: the man with the slumped shoulders who thinks 'things are always on top of me'. We experience ourselves through imagery and symbolism and attach meaning to these: the story of the impoverished boy born in Mississippi who moved to Memphis and became the most famous singer in the world before succumbing to drug abuse and a premature ending is passed down from generation to generation. Millions relate to Elvis without ever having met him.

Within a therapeutic frame, stories can allow a client's existence to be opened up to positive experiences. For example, an individual with premature ejaculation can experience having a successful sexual experience with their wife or partner. The metaphor of a gardener 'taking more time' to explore the leaves and petals, the different colours of plants in his garden as he 'extends the time for pleasure' can be constructed and made sense of unconsciously by the client. In this way a 'story' is created that offers the possibility of success and a sense of accomplishment. The accomplishment of learning to walk, learning to talk, learning to grow a plant or build a wall can provide excellent starting points for therapeutic gain. Erickson understood the need to highlight achievement and accomplishment in his stories, garnering the rich metaphorical content of stories to change attitudes and behaviours. He worked with the natural curiosity of our species, trusting our ability to find answers through insight and internal search of unconscious expressions such as dreams and symbols. Therapeutic stories can bypass conscious resistance and lead to sudden enlightenment. When presented through hypnosis, normal conversation or a deeply relaxed state, ideas through stories and metaphors can be absorbed unconsciously, catalysing new insights, behaviours and conceptual understandings.

Characteristics of therapeutic metaphors and stories

When creating therapeutic stories and metaphors it is useful to consider the following:

1   The metaphor or story should contain something that is useful to the client from a therapeutic standpoint, addressing a goal or issue or outcome that they need help with.

2   The metaphor or story should consist of a beginning, a middle and an end, built around a theme, for example, coping with loss, overcoming a fear, gaining a positive outlook, dealing with guilt or shame. The story can relate directly to the theme or can be written in such a way that it *parallels* the theme in some way, allowing the client to unconsciously draw conclusions and 'fill in the blanks' with their own internal search for answers and solutions. Creating therapeutic stories for children can bring into play characters such as superheroes, animals and characters from fairy tales and legend.

3   The metaphor or story should be interesting and engrossing so that the client is curious about what happens next. Creating suspense and mystery captures the listener's attention and imagination.

4   There should be a conclusion at the end of the story, implying the achievement of a particular goal or desirable outcome. For example, our hero discovers that they can let go of traumas from the past and get on with their life. The client can unconsciously begin to search for ways in which they can overcome their own issue or problem and achieve their own goal or outcome.

5   The story or metaphor should be specific to the client's worldview so it is important to gather as much information as you can about a presenting problem, issue or difficulty.

Creating therapeutic metaphors and stories

Gathering as much information as you can about your client and their difficulty is the first stage of creating a strong metaphor or story: the more information you have at your disposal, the more the metaphor or story relates to their experience of the world and the more powerful its impact.

During this stage it is useful to ask the following questions:

*   What people are central to the client's life?
*   What are the interrelationships between the client and these people?
*   What hobbies and interests does the client have?
*   What does the client do for a living?
*   How does the problem manifest itself?
*   Are there times during which the problem lessens or disappears? If so, what is different about these periods?
*   Has there ever been a time when the problem did not exist? If so, when was this and what was different about that time?
*   If I (the therapist) had your problem, what things would I be experiencing? How would I think? How would I feel (emotions)? Would there be any physical symptoms?
*   How would the client feel without the problem? How would they know that the problem had gone? Would friends or family notice anything different if the problem were no longer there?
*   Has the client tried ways of getting rid of the problem in the past? What did they try?
*   Are there barriers stopping the client from making changes in their life? If so, what are these barriers?

Constructing metaphors and stories can be time consuming so it is recommended that a set of standard metaphors are used which can be adapted for individual clients. Below are three examples of standard metaphors and the themes addressed; all these metaphors have many parallels and can be adapted to different situations and contexts. Italics refer to phrases or words that the therapist delivers in a slightly different tone or speed of voice in order to emphasise them.

Standard metaphors for editing and adapting

Learning to walk

This metaphor focusses upon learning a new skill: consciously at first and later performing it unconsciously. It invites the client to explore performing actions without conscious thought or intention.

> And you know [client's name], you've been *learning new things* since the day that you were born, although many of these things you've forgotten about ever having learned them. After all, you learned how to walk and you learned how to talk but can you really remember anything about these processes and how you learned them? Yet learn them you did. And walking, it's such a miraculous thing if you think about it. Did you know we're the only mammals that can *stand on our own two feet* with our backs completely upright? And that the process of learning to walk starts long before we actually *get down to it* when we start to lift our heads as we lie on our tummies and this builds the strength in our back muscles, the strength needed to *begin to explore new ways* of using our limbs and to just start crawling around and after a while we begin to take our first tentative steps, falling down a lot, but *picking ourselves up again and trying harder*, keeping our balance that little bit longer, and *the more that we put into this process the more we discover about ourselves*, that we really can walk and we fall less and our balance improves until *it just happens by itself* and our walking shows *improvement every day* and then you reach a point where *you don't have to think about doing it*, we walk naturally and freely without giving it a thought, and you can begin to wonder how this *opens up your world* and the *new things you discover* as walking becomes a part of your everyday life.

Allowing anxiety to pass

This short metaphor focusses on unconsciously letting go of anxiety; it can be adapted for a wide range of fears and phobias as well as Generalised Anxiety Disorder. It can be included easily within a story.

> And [client's name] I'd like you to imagine yourself standing on top of a hill. Below you in the distance there is a large lake. You notice that there is a storm around you and the wind is blowing so that the water on the lake is rough and choppy. There is rain in the air but *you remain calm and relaxed*, safe in the knowledge that you have *prepared well*: you have wrapped up in a warm coat that shields you from the wind; you have an umbrella which protects you from the rain, and so you are *quite happy and safe in that situation*. And sure enough, as you look down at the water in the lake so *the storm begins to fade* and the wind dies down so that the water becomes *very calm and still* while the rain disappears and before long you're left with a bright sun and blue sky, the

warmth from the sun warming you from the top of your head to the tips of your toes, as *you feel so very good now*.

Clearing a house

This is a versatile metaphor which can be adapted for weight loss (in this example), getting rid of the past, increasing self-esteem and boosting motivation.

> And one thing [client's name] I've thought about recently is clearing out my house and it's something that I've put off *until now* and I know what you're thinking: we all tend to put this task off because *clearing it all out* takes a certain level of motivation don't you think? And when I started to think about motivation I began to realise that I am actually quite motivated to *do a lot of things in a day*. After all, we're motivated to get out of bed and dress, to brush our teeth and make some food are we not? And people often find that they're motivated to find a job, buy a car, talk to friends and so when I thought about this, clearing out the house didn't seem such a chore anymore so if *you put your mind to it you can achieve it*. Now imagine this scenario, imagine that you're clearing out your house: imagine yourself armed with a bin liner, going from room to room and *getting rid of the excess*, spend a while in each room just *removing any unwanted items* and *feel the weight lift off you* as you do this. Imagine carrying the full bin liner out to your car and then taking a fresh bin liner and going into another room; imagine your house *feeling lighter* with all that *excess removed* and so you go from room to room *getting rid of the rest* of your unwanted items and once you have done this you can look at yourself in the mirror and think that that was a job well done and so you can smile at yourself and *feel better* now that you *have achieved your goal* of getting rid of all those unwanted items and the house feels so much *lighter* don't you think as you imagine taking the bin liners filled with the excess stuff to the waste bins at the local *dump*.

Metaphors and stories can be integrated within conversations between the therapist and client so you don't have to rely upon utilising hypnosis. As soon as you start to tell an interesting story, be aware of the client and how they react to it: the chances are that their eyes will start to glaze over or become still and their expression change in some way, perhaps a nod of the head or a raise of an eyebrow. Their posture and breathing may change as they relax and sink into their chair. These are signs that they are entering an altered state of consciousness and awareness as a result of listening to your story: unconsciously they are searching within in order to make sense of what you are talking about.

Alternatively, stories and metaphors can be delivered in a state of hypnosis or by going through a progressive muscle relaxation before delivery.

Exercise

Working in pairs, with one person the client and the other playing the role of therapist, the therapist constructs a metaphor based on the issue/problem of the client and a favourable outcome(s). Roles are then reversed and the process repeated. Practise delivering key phrases with a different vocal attribute such as a change in tone or speed. Record your voice and see if you can recognise the key phrases in terms of a change in your voice. Get feedback from others with regards to how you could improve the delivery of your metaphor or story.

Conclusion

This chapter has focussed upon the importance of the conscious and unconscious mind when working with clients. A number of different psychological models have been presented as a way of working with the conscious and unconscious. We have demonstrated that humans are governed as much by their conscious as unconscious minds, and having an understanding and awareness of this is crucial in terms of being an effective counselling practitioner. This chapter has integrated person-centred, CBT, relational and hypnotherapeutic modalities when discussing the conscious and unconscious. In particular the TTM has been presented and discussed as an example of an integrative model of therapeutic change that incorporates the conscious and unconscious. The TTM, whilst having certain drawbacks, as discussed in this chapter, nonetheless can be a useful model for practice. We have also shown the importance of therapeutic stories, myths and metaphors and have suggested some standard metaphors that therapists can adapt to use with their clients. The next chapter focusses on loss and bereavement, where perhaps the use of metaphors and stories can be particularly important within a therapeutic context.

References

Aristotle (350 BCE) *Metaphysics, Book VIII*, 1045a.8–10, https://www.goodreads.com/quotes/20103-the-whole-is-greater-than-the-sum-of-its-parts (accessed 29 January 2019).

Buzan, T. (1988) *Make the Most of Your Mind*. London: Pan Books.

Citrenbaum, C., King, M. & Cohen, W. (1985) *Modern Clinical Hypnosis for Habit Control*. New York: Norton.

Davis, W. (2010) *Shadows in the Sun*. Washington, DC: Island Press.

Heller, S. & Steele, T. (2007) Monsters & Magical Sticks. Tempe, AZ: New Falcon Publications.

Jung, C. (1953) *Psychology and Alchemy*, https://www.jungiananalysts.org.uk/wp-content/uploads/2018/07/C.-G.-Jung-Collected-Works-Volume-12-Psychology-and-Alchemy.pdf (accessed 22 January 2019).

Kent, N. (2010) *Apathy for the Devil*. London: Faber and Faber.

Macnee, C. & McCabe, S. (2004) 'The transtheoretical model of behavior change and smokers in southern Appalachia', *Nursing Research*, vol. 53, no. 4, pp. 243–250.

Marshall, S. & Biddle, S. (2001) 'The transtheoretical model of behavior change: A meta-analysis of applications to physical activity and exercise', *Annals of Behavioral Medicine*, vol. 23, no. 4, pp. 229–246.

Maslow, A. (1943) 'A Theory of Human Motivation'. *Psychological Review*, vol. 50, pp. 370–396.

May, R. (1993) *The Cry for Myth*. London: Souvenir Press.

Oxford English Living Dictionary, https://en.oxforddictionaries.com/definition/myth (accessed 2 November 2018).

Petrocelli, J. (2002) 'Processes and stages of change: Counselling with the TTM of change', *Journal of Counselling & Development*, vol. 80, no.1, pp. 22–30.

Prochaska, J., & DiClemente, C. (1983) 'Stages and processes of self-change of smoking: Toward an integrative model of change', *Journal of Consulting and Clinical Psychology*, vol. 51, no. 3, pp. 390–395.

Prochaska J.O. & DiClemente, C. (1984) *The Transtheoretical Approach: Crossing Traditional Boundaries of Therapy*. Homewood, IL: Dow Jones Irwin.

Prochaska, J. & Norcross, J. (2003) *Systems of Psychotherapy: A Transtheoretical Analysis*, 5th edition. London: Thomson Learning.

Prochaska, J.C, DiClemente, C. & Norcross, J. (1992) 'In search of how people change: Applications to addictive behaviors', *American Psychologist*, vol. 47, no. 7, pp. 1002–1114.

Rodgers, W., Courneya, K., & Bayduza, A. (2001) 'Examination of the transtheoretical model and exercise in 3 populations', *American Journal of Health Behavior*, vol. 25, no. 1, pp. 33–41.

Rosen, S. (2010) *My Voice Will Go with You: The Teaching Tales of Milton H. Erickson.* New York: W. W. Norton & Company.

Thomas-Cottingham, A. (2010) *Psychology Made Simple.* New York: Three Rivers Press.

Stroop, J. R. (1935) 'Studies of interference in serial verbal reactions', *Journal of Experimental Psychology*, vol. 18, pp. 643–662.

Trevarthern, C. (1990) *Brain Circuits and Functions of the Mind.* Cambridge: Cambridge University Press.

Chapter 6

Working integratively with bereavement and loss

My grief lies all within/ And these external manners of laments/ Are merely shadows to the unseen grief/ That swells with silence in the tortured soul.

William Shakespeare, *Richard II*, Act 4, Scene 1, ll. 295–298

Introduction

Perhaps the most significant challenge that we face as humans is experiencing loss and bereavement. The capitalist and consumerist-based cultures that dominate western societies inevitably place loss and bereavement on the margins, out of sight out of mind seems to be a dominant theme here. We are taught from a very early age that accumulation is a major goal for our lives. Hence we set ourselves objectives – accumulating assets, money, careers, family – and find that when we lose some of the things that we have accumulated we can struggle to cope. Loss can bring about rage, denial, hopelessness, guilt, alongside many other difficult and severe emotions. Clients that we see often come for therapy when they find themselves struggling to cope with their losses and grief. As therapists we have found that a significant aspect to our work is therapeutically holding clients whilst they explore, process and begin to understand their loss. This is why we have dedicated an entire chapter to bereavement and loss.

Traditionally, within therapy books the view that loss and bereavement are natural is taken, and the perspective that therefore there is little in terms of interventions that we can provide clients with is taken. However, more recently a number of authors have suggested ways in which interventions can be helpful for clients experiencing loss and bereavement. This is our perspective also – that whilst loss and bereavement are natural aspects to being alive, there are nonetheless ways in which therapists can intervene in order to help empower their clients through this most torturous experiencing. We therefore present integrative interventions to demonstrate what we as therapists can do.

This chapter looks at what loss and bereavement are, through academic work but also through the use of stories, because we believe that we learn best through sense-making and story-telling. We also then explore PCT, CBT, relational and hypnotherapeutic modalities for the insights these bring to loss and bereavement. We provide a broad range of integrative techniques for working with clients who are experiencing loss and/or bereavement, techniques that we can also apply to ourselves as therapists.

The old man in the cave

There was once a very old man living 20 feet beneath the Earth's crust. This old man's hair was like a flowing glacier, forever growing, inching forwards so that it was now gently touching his hips. The man's beard was so long that he had to tie it into a knot just so that he would not trip over it. Riazzin was the old man's name, but having spent so long on his own Riazzin had forgotten what his name sounded like. To occupy his days, Riazzin would walk along the network of tunnels connecting one cave to another. Each cave had its own distinct character. Riazzin would spend many hours walking between the crystal-bedecked cave where he slept and relaxed, and the water-filled cave about 500 metres away, which had a hole in its ceiling allowing some light to get through. This enabled old man Riazzin to grow some basic vegetables, which meant that he never had to venture up into the outside world. Slowly over the years Riazzin had fused with his surroundings – he could almost feel his shadows merging with the walls of the tunnels and caves that surrounded him. Riazzin had made himself at home here and felt a strange sense of belongingness in the cold and damp environment.

One day Riazzin stepped into the cave where he could access his water and food supply to find a brightly coloured parakeet sitting on a ledge, looking down on him and squawking. Riazzin was shocked. 'How did this bird get here?' he asked himself, 'How is it possible that any bird survived the destruction and chaos beyond the cave walls?' Riazzin blinked and opened his eyes again to make sure that he was not simply imagining this bird, but lo and behold the bird was still sitting there. Riazzin smiled at the parakeet and at that moment the parakeet noisily flew up above through the air hole into the wider world outside. Riazzin continued with his daily routine, not paying much attention to what he had seen – he was at peace with his decision to have stayed so long down here in his cave dwelling.

Then the next day Riazzin once again entered the cave that he called his pantry because that was where his food and water could be found. Riazzin took a deep breath as he noticed an orange lying on the ground in front of him. 'This is not possible' thought Riazzin, 'the only things that grow down here are potatoes and turnips'. Riazzin stooped down to pick up this exquisite bright orange fruit, held it in his hand and smelled its pungent citrus aroma. Riazzin had not seen an orange in over twenty years. Then he shook his head and threw the orange against the wall, saying 'I must not eat this because if I get a taste for this wondrous citrus fruit I will no longer enjoy eating my potatoes and turnips.' For the rest of the day Riazzin felt strangely unsettled, as if his senses were somehow beginning to awaken to a powerful longing for other things, for the companionship of other things and even people. That night Riazzin slept badly, having dreamt about his old life up above ground where he used to have a farm with his wife and children. Then the war came, his home was destroyed and his family murdered, forcing Riazzin to flee below into this dark network of caves.

Riazzin awoke feeling upset. He did what he usually did – walked over to his pantry-like cave and there, lying amongst this season's turnips, Riazzin found a silver necklace. He picked it up and held it in his hand, 'Could someone have survived all those years of conflict?' Riazzin asked himself. Then a strong wind blew from above and from the air hole a piece of paper gently floated down to the cave, directly to where Riazzin was standing. He held out his hand and the piece of paper gently landed there. Riazzin looked at the black print – faded, with a date of 1990,

which was twenty years ago. Riazzin read the script on the piece of paper and could not believe his eyes. THE WAR HAS ENDED PLEASE COME OUT OF HIDING. Riazzin had to read this message again, and he took another look at the date – this message was printed twenty years ago. Riazzin was flabbergasted – the war that he thought was still taking place up above ground had ended a long time ago without Riazzin realising this. At that moment Riazzin excitedly ran back to his sleeping quarters, put on all the clothes that he owned and he began climbing his way up out of the caves that had been his home for so many years. On exiting the cave Riazzin found that he was standing on farmland and could see children happily playing in the fields, with men and women talking merrily and eating and drinking their harvest. 'The war really has ended', thought Riazzin to himself as he made his way excitedly to his newly found community.

Analysis of Riazzin's story

Exploring the story of Riazzin from a psychotherapeutic perspective, we can make connections between Riazzin and the process of traumatic loss and bereavement. A conflict in Riazzin's homeland had resulted in the sudden and tragic deaths of his wife and his children, and Riazzin had to run away and find for himself a safe place within which to hibernate. Hibernation here is a key word to describe Riazzin's psychological, emotional and physical process because Riazzin had been so overwhelmed by his losses that he could no longer function normally in the outside world. Riazzin had to find a space for himself where he could slow his life down, take external pressures away from himself, and where he did not have to explain to other people what he was going through. Whilst this state of hibernation benefitted Riazzin, it might be argued that when certain events came into his life Riazzin chose to ignore them – the parakeet, orange, necklace – and to continue to live in his solitary world. However, Riazzin then had a huge wake-up call with the message telling him that the war had ended and it was this ultimately that shook him into action, to go outside and re-connect with other people and wider society.

Overwhelming loss and its associated grief can mean that clients that we see do experience this state of hibernation. They may be tearful, fearful, they may struggle to undertake everyday activities that once they would have done without any thought. Clients may talk about no longer going to work, no longer getting any pleasure from pastimes that they used to enjoy, and they may tell us that they struggle to concentrate and to focus on things. Clients may also tell us that they are unable to talk to friends and family because their grief is just too overwhelming for them and they are unable to talk about their experiences. Therapy can therefore be a safe space – Riazzin's cave – where clients are able to come and talk about their hibernation, and we as therapists can normalise clients' experiences of loss and bereavement. We can do this by expressing the overwhelming nature of loss and bereavement, that symptoms that clients are experiencing are perfectly normal given the circumstances. We can also share with clients models of loss and grief that can help them gain a wider understanding of what they are going through. It is also important to help support clients to start new beginnings, no matter how small these may be. It is helpful to work with clients towards processing their grief whilst at the same time encouraging them to look at things they might be able to do now for themselves. In this way, unlike Riazzin, our clients can come out of hibernation at a time that is right for them rather than staying within this state longer than they need to because they lack confidence or lack a person supporting them to develop and grow. The dual process model of grief by Stroebe and Schut (1999) is worth exploring here, which captures this sense of processing one's losses whilst at the same time learning to live our lives with loss.

The dual process model of grief

The dual process model of grieving by Stroebe and Schut (1999) suggests that one important dimension to loss is that of processing one's grief. Mourning can be emotionally, psychologically and physically draining and can involve uncontrollable shaking, crying, even wailing. It is important to provide the space and time for mourning because otherwise if we repress our grief it can build up inside us, leading to severe depression. The other important dimension to grieving is that of learning to cope with one's life after loss, to build activities that can bring pleasure or some relief from one's mourning, or even just sorting the things out that need to be sorted as a result of our bereavement. We can move from one dimension to the other regularly, and so it might be worth explaining to clients that they don't need to feel guilty or ashamed that they are not constantly thinking about, and mourning, their loss, rather, that it is okay to dip in and out of mourning as a natural way of grieving. It can also be worth drawing upon Worden's (2008) contribution to dealing with loss. According to Worden (2008) there are four key tasks of grieving: to accept the reality of the loss, to work through the pain of grief, to adjust to an environment in which the deceased is missing, and to emotionally relocate the deceased and move on with life. Another key thinker and practitioner in relation to mourning and loss is Elizabeth Kubler-Ross, who wrote an incredibly influential book in 1969 about what we can learn about death and dying from those who are terminally ill. From this work Kubler-Ross (1969) developed a model of grief which relates to how terminally ill people can experience their loss of life, alongside how people grieve the loss of a loved one. According to Elizabeth Kubler-Ross (1969) there are five stages to grief: denial, anger, bargaining, depression and acceptance. A person doesn't have to follow each stage and, moreover, these stages are not linear and so don't have to necessarily be experienced in any order. It is worth knowing about this model because it can be used to normalise clients' symptoms – it can be very empowering to know that how you are feeling is not something dysfunctional or bad about you but rather is a natural aspect to loss and mourning.

Another key thinker and practitioner worth including in this chapter is Irvin Yalom, an existential therapist concerned with how humans struggle with their existence. According to Yalom (1989), death, meaninglessness, existential isolation and freedom lie at the core of human concerns:

> the inevitability of death for each of us and for those we love; the freedom to make of our lives as we will; our ultimate aloneness; and finally the absence of any meaning or sense to our life. However grim these givens may seem they contain the seeds of wisdom and redemption.
>
> (Yalom, 1989: 4)

For Yalom (1980), drawing on the work of Choron (1964), within humans there can be fear and anxiety about what happens after death; the event of the dying; and ceasing to be. However, it is also important to consider the wider cultural context to death and dying because different cultures relate to these key aspects of living and dying differently and can therefore influence how a particular individual may experience death, dying and loss. Apparently in Japan there is a belief that one's dead relatives are close to hand and act as guides and as a result, people are less concerned by death (Rees, 2015). Within Muslim countries and Muslim communities, there can be a belief that Allah guides people's lives and that moreover, the dead are 'making a journey to their true home' (Crabtree et al., 2008: 149). Again, this religio-socio-cultural context perhaps means that a person of Islamic faith can draw on their religion to provide understanding and healing in relation to bereavement and loss.

Working with bereavement and/or loss can be challenging for a therapist because there are no solutions to this natural part of life. Also, we may find ourselves re-living or re-visiting our own bereavements and/or losses as a result of what our clients have said to us. We have met therapists who say that they enjoy supporting people experiencing loss and/or bereavement due to the aspects to grief that are explored, aspects which are often not talked about in wider society. Thus, clients may talk about their belief systems, their decisions about cremation or burial and then the practical aspects in terms of arranging funerals, deciding what to do with a loved one's ashes, organising a service that celebrates a person's life and so on. We have also met therapists who do not offer bereavement counselling as a result of having experienced their own traumatic and significant losses. Thus, for some therapists working with bereavement can trigger too many things for them and as a result in order to keep themselves safe they do not work with grief. Before working with a client around loss/grief it is therefore important to consider one's own experiences of loss, one's own belief systems around death and dying, and to have appropriate supervision and therapy in place in case a client should trigger difficult emotions.

The following are some interventions that can be used when working with loss and bereavement.

Letter writing

Letter writing is a powerful therapeutic tool that can be used across wide-ranging therapeutic modalities. Letter writing can be an important process through which a client can understand better their perceptions and their feelings, and can act as an important cathartic release. A letter can also be used in order for a client to better understand the relationship that they had which they have now lost. For this activity we ask our clients whether they would like to write a letter to themselves, to the person(s) they have lost, or to a significant other person that is still in their life. We tell the client that this is a letter that will not be sent anywhere, but rather will be brought to the counselling session. Clients can be encouraged to read out their letters during therapy, or they may give us the letter and ask us to read this out. Our role as therapists is to facilitate exploration of the contents of the letter, so that the client gains a better sense of what parts of the letter are particularly significant, what the key issues are in relation to their loss/bereavement and relationships. Explore the language that the client has used, look at how supportive or critical this letter is, explore how the client felt when writing the letter and how they feel now upon reading it or presenting it to the therapist. Also explore whether the client wants to keep the letter or whether they wish to destroy it and if the latter is the case how do they want to destroy the letter. Explore with the client whether they would like to get a special envelope to put the letter in. It can also be important to explore how a client is feeling regarding not being able to send this letter, particularly if written to a loved one that they have lost.

Anniversaries/significant dates

Anniversaries of death can be particularly traumatic and painful for loved ones. It can therefore be important to work with a client to explore what they might want to do on any important dates concerning their dead loved one. Some clients may want to visit a graveside, others may want to distract themselves from the pain by going to watch a film or going shopping. Others may decide that they would like to spend the day with family and friends. Providing space for the client to explore what they would like to do is therefore a key aspect of supporting a person through loss and mourning.

Talking about and engaging with the dead loved one

It can be helpful to ask the client to talk about the person that they lost. What was this person like? What did they enjoy doing? What was the client's relationship like with the person they have lost? Sometimes clients can be full of guilt because they feel that they did not do enough for the person who has died. However, upon exploring their relationship some clients can come to an understanding that actually the deceased person was not easy, that they had a challenging relationship, potentially even abusive relationship, and this can lessen their guilt. Some clients may experience rage or anger towards the person who has passed away and this may be because that person treated them badly, or it can also be rage or anger at the person having deserted them, leaving them to cope with everyday life on their own. Techniques that can help process anger can therefore also be beneficial. Letter writing can be one technique, another technique can be encouraging the client to express their anger during a therapy session, for example, through chair work or just allowing them to talk and express their emotions. Some clients will also talk about how they continue to have a relationship with the deceased – either talking to them or even experiencing their presence.

Long live Elvis Presley, the King

There was once an old woman living in Memphis, Tennessee. Her name was Martha and she lived within walking distance of a beautiful mansion where Elvis Presley, the King of Rock and Roll had lived. Martha had adored Elvis. She had been his cook and maid at Graceland for about twenty years. Each day Elvis would request Martha to make his favourite food and she loved spoiling him, making him his peanut butter and banana sandwiches just like his mother used to. Martha enjoyed taking Elvis's favourite food to him and then watching him gain so much pleasure from every bite that he took. Despite being the richest man on Earth, Elvis enjoyed simple home pleasures and simply home cooked food. He had been born poor and his personal tastes had remained unchanged regardless of his worldly success. Whenever Martha brought Elvis a favourite meal, they would exchange a few words, there was a deep affection between them, like mother and son.

Then one day Elvis began to feel a pain in his left shoulder. This was a nagging pain that would not go away. The pain then spread to his legs and Elvis began to struggle to walk such was the agony he experienced. Within a month Elvis had become completely housebound, unable to physically move and then suddenly he took his last gasping breath and died. When Martha entered Elvis's bedroom she was shocked to find his dead body, of a pale yellow colour, his face thin and unmoving. Martha ran up to Elvis and clung to his body weeping; she was inconsolable with grief.

In the aftermath of Elvis's death, Martha found that she was completely disorientated, even lost. She found herself walking the paths of Tennessee without any direction, and what seemed so familiar and vibrant to her was now grey and fog-like. Nobody could make contact with Martha and friends found that when they tried to offer her words of comfort she would simply stare at them, tears rolling down her cheeks. Martha went on like this for many months, and the months turned into years. Then one night Martha fell asleep and dreamed the best and most amazing dream of her life. Elvis had come to visit her. She had dreamt of Elvis arriving outside her home in a large bus. Elvis invited Martha onboard and pointed out the beautiful garlands that he had decorated the bus with. Martha was particularly impressed by the row of creamy lilacs that were hanging along the front of the bus, and the flourish of red roses in between them – Elvis would often say to Martha that he liked having a splash of colour in things. Then the bus sped off at breakneck speed. Elvis was having fun, more fun than he had ever had in his life. He was excited and happy, whizzing along the roads and Martha was not afraid – she felt completely safe and yet also exhilarated by being on this bus with Elvis.

Eventually, the bus came to a stop and Elvis got out of the bus. 'It is time Martha', he said. 'Time for what?' she asked. 'Time for me to go', he replied. At that point Elvis took Martha's hand and escorted her back to her house, which now seemed so vibrant and joyful. Elvis then got back onto his bus and drove away. At that moment Martha opened her eyes. It took her a while to realise that she was truly back in her home, lying in her bed. From that dream onwards Martha felt differently about the death of her beloved Elvis. She sensed that he was having a fantastic time in the universe that he was inhabiting; she sensed that he was untroubled by the painful experiences of his childhood, that he had shed all the problems that had engulfed him in his life, to become this wonderful and light celestial being. Martha felt soothed and found that she now began to enjoy life again, understanding that Elvis had not abandoned her but rather had left planet Earth to experience a more wondrous adventure. It seems that the powerful dream that Martha had experienced enabled her to move on through her grief. As therapists it is not for us to judge or decide whether there is a material reality to Martha's experience; rather, the focus on the therapeutic lens is the sense-making of our clients. Some clients may really struggle in the aftermath of a significant loss and/or bereavement and so it is to the integration of person-centred, CBT and relational modalities that we now turn in order to think theoretically about grief work with clients.

Taking an integrative, theoretical approach to loss and bereavement

From a person-centred perspective, it is important to remain with the client, to make psychological contact with them, to understand their experiences and perceptions concerning the losses in their lives. Every individual client will have unique experiences of grief, and so it is important for a person-centred approach to lie at the core when working with clients. Importantly, loss and/or bereavement can impact upon a person's self-concept. The perception of how they are viewed by others can be impacted by loss. For example, it can be a huge thing for a parent to lose their only child, because they may say to themselves that other people no longer view them as a parent, even though they still feel like one. It may also be that an individual values themselves according to those values associated with their self-concept and so any impact on the self-concept may lead to anxiety, shame, humiliation, anger and other difficult emotions regarding how they view themselves. It may also be that loss and/or bereavement may change a person – change their true self. As such, a person-centred approach in therapy can be very effective in that we can help a client to explore aspects of their 'true self' that they believe have changed, and to explore what new meanings and values they may have developed as a result of their grief. CBT based approaches can also be integrated with a person-centred stance. A loss/bereavement can produce in a person negative automatic thoughts (NATS), and these NATS can severely impact on their daily life. For example, a person whose daughter has died may develop a NAT of 'I cannot leave my house'. After exploring this with a client, it may be that other thoughts underpin this, thoughts such as 'I was a bad mother because I let my daughter die', 'I am being judged by others'. It can be important to focus on the thinking content and process with clients in the aftermath of a loss and/or bereavement because we can help our clients explore these, challenge them and replace them with more helpful thoughts and thinking patterns. A person's core beliefs can be altered by loss and/or bereavement and so techniques like using a downward arrow technique can help us uncover a client's negative core beliefs, in order to help that client challenge these. Relational modalities might place the focus upon past experiences of loss and/or bereavement. It can be therapeutic for a client to explore any significant losses that they had when growing up, to see whether these might be impacting on how they are experiencing their current loss. If a client experienced a significant bereavement early on in their life and felt a sense of abandonment, then they might take this into their adult life and be terrified of being abandoned. This means that when faced with a loss and/or grief this can re-trigger earlier experiences of loss and thus be particularly significant for the client. It is important also to consider the attachment style of the client and how this may impact on how they cope with their loss. Individuals with a predominantly preoccupied attachment style may be completely overwhelmed by their loss because they may have overly depended on the person or animal or thing that they have lost, a kind of co-dependency. People with a preoccupied attachment style may also quickly seek out and find another person, animal or object to replace what previously they had relied upon. Individuals with a predominantly avoidant attachment style are perhaps less likely to provide space in their lives to experience the powerful emotions of their grief, and this may be detrimental to them in the long term. Individuals with a largely secure attachment style are perhaps the most resilient to loss and/or bereavement. However, it is important to note that cumulative loss/bereavement can be overwhelming even for those individuals with a secure base. Experiencing a series of losses over a reasonably short space of time can overwhelm a person and so it is not uncommon for people with secure attachment styles to seek out bereavement counselling. We now turn to hypnotherapeutic modalities to explore what insights these provide to loss and/or bereavement.

Hypnotherapeutic modalities in loss and bereavement

The story of Riazzin and the cave gives us a sense of the emotional paralysis that the old man experienced as a result of loss. Perhaps he felt guilty about letting his family die? Maybe he felt responsible for their deaths? Could he have protected them better? Should he not have taken a dagger to the blackened hearts of his assailants? Surely he must realise the danger and take action! He has to kill them now! As he spent the days and nights in hibernation, so the events surrounding the murder of his family may have replayed over and over in his mind, creating a state of immobilisation, both unrelenting and savage, obscuring any chance of redemption and freedom.

Within Riazzin's world the war could not end until he transcended immobilisation and gained acceptance of the emotions of loss: the guilt, anger, regret and sadness that accompany a devastated soul. Clients come to therapy because they are stuck in some way and cannot move on. This immobility, whether physical, mental or spiritual, can be due to denying or resisting difficult emotions; in the context of loss and bereavement this denial and resistance can prolong the grief and cause undue suffering. Our role as therapist is to listen carefully and be open so that we gain a true sense of the loss that our client is experiencing (this can only be experienced through presence); once we resonate with the client we can begin to help them accept and let go of the emotions in order for healing to take place.

The separation reaction: Physical symptoms and emotional recovery

Separation and loss can bring about emotional turmoil, physical and psychological pain, as well as debilitating grief. The depressed, anxious and angry thoughts generated by the mind during and after loss can manifest difficult physical symptoms as our body reacts to our disturbed mental state. Clients who suffer loss and bereavement often complain of not being able to sleep, of suffering from panic attacks, feeling down and de-motivated, of eating too little or too much. They can experience feeling disconnected from the outside world; this withdrawal can be so acute that nothing may feel real anymore: this in turn can manifest into severe anxiety and incapacitating fear.

Being fully present with our client allows us to delve into the thinking, feeling, experiencing of the being sat in the chair on the opposite side of the coffee table. As May (1994) suggests, our self-world relationship is thrown off balance by any genuine encounter with a human. Does the client make us feel anxious when they describe their loss? Do we feel anger when he talks about the events leading to separation? Do we feel depressed? Do we open out even further to the client in order to learn something deeper about ourselves? Or do we put the boundaries back in place and avoid further discomfort?

May's (1994) concept that all encounters with humans are potentially creative is one of profound therapeutic freedom. As a result of the encounter, both therapist and client are changed, however large or small this change is. This can be particularly poignant within loss and bereavement, where there can be wild oscillations of grief emotions experienced by the client and indeed, where there can be periods of emptiness and silence too. Just like the concept of sympathetic vibration, where striking a particular string on a guitar causes the corresponding string on another guitar in close proximity to vibrate sympathetically (as a result of the oscillations in the air), so we too, as therapists, vibrate and resonate and oscillate through the cycles of emotions and grief and suffering experienced by our clients – if we are open.

The emotional turmoil and physical symptoms together form a *separation reaction*, as proposed by Hadley and Staudacher (2001) who suggest five stages of emotional adjustments for recovery:

The five stages of recovery from loss

Coping – loss can be sudden and unexpected: the loss of a loved one, loss of a job or a relationship. Immediately after this loss we can enter a state of self-preservation where our thoughts are directed towards immediate needs such as finances, food, shelter, sleep, caring for the children.

Realisation – after a period during which some level of stability is achieved, the full impact of the loss confronts us, unleashing powerful grief emotions such as anger, fear, anxiety and depression.

Immobilisation – a state of emotional standstill where we feel 'stuck': unable to let go of the loss in order to move on. This stage is often accompanied with feelings of powerlessness and victimisation. There can also be the need to revisit and remedy events that resulted in the loss in order to overcome feelings of guilt and regret.

Acceptance – a stage where we begin to accept our feelings surrounding loss: sadness, fear, anxiety, abandonment and anger. The emotional suffering begins to diminish as we start to open up and share our feelings with others. Acceptance provides the conduit for healing beyond pain and suffering.

Letting go – the final stage of recovery based on the concept of forgiveness: we forgive those that have hurt us; we also forgive ourselves, and past actions, focussing on existing in the present moment and building for the future.

Although many people experience the sequence of stages listed in the order above, Hadley and Staudacher (2001) suggest that the stages can be experienced in almost any order. According to Hadley and Staudacher (2001), the stages of *Realisation* and *Immobilisation* are often the most repeated. In terms of realisation of loss, acceptance of emotional suffering and letting go, there are similarities between this model and the four tasks of grieving proposed by Worden (2008). Adams et al. (1976), as cited in Weston et al. (1998), propose a model of changes in self-esteem that result from dramatic life transitions: immobilisation as a result of shock, acceptance of reality after a period of denial and depression, followed by a search for meaning - making sense of the change – and ultimately acceptance of transition and integration of changes; these closely parallel the five stages of recovery in Hadley and Staudacher's (2001) model.

Facilitating recovery from loss and bereavement with hypnotherapy and cognitive techniques

Letting go of obsessive memories of loss

A client may find herself within the *Immobilisation* stage of grief, replaying the events or situations that led to loss over and over in her mind. This obsessive pattern of thinking can indicate the masking of difficult emotions and feelings that need to be acknowledged and let go of in order for the next stage of recovery to begin. A useful procedure for clearing repetitive imaginings or experiences of an event or memory of loss is to relax the client using a combination of progressive muscle relaxation and a deepener – which enhances the experience of relaxation – and then begin the process of changing the dynamics of the event or memory. Within a calm, relaxed state the client can begin to imagine the event or memory playing out on a movie screen with a version of herself sitting a safe distance away from the movie screen. This allows dissociation from any memory that proves too discomfiting. Through the use of an imaginary remote control the client can change the dynamics of events and memories of loss. She can fast forward and fast rewind through them, she can turn them black and white and make them grainy like the old movies. She can imagine each memory as very small, perhaps the size of a thumbnail or a postage stamp. She can acknowledge masked emotions such as anger, fear, depression and begin to process and let go of these feelings. Before this process, it is useful to work with the client and build mental states of calmness, safety and inner peace before and after each event or memory. These can be real or imagined, for example, a memory of relaxation or a perfect holiday, and allow the client to access these states after subsequent forwarding and rewinding of memories of loss, reducing their emotional impact. Altering the dynamics in this way can help lift the negative emotions and feelings surrounding particular events and memories, facilitating progression from realisation and immobilisation towards acceptance and letting go.

Once the dynamics have been changed and the client reports that she can think about an event or memory of loss without experiencing the usual upset, a new set of events and memories can be elicited. Under guidance from the therapist, the client can imagine the memory or event in a way that she would have liked to have happened in reality. For example, the client can imagine herself dealing with things in a different way: saying the things that she wanted to say, acknowledging the difficult emotions experienced at the time of loss, hugging a loved one before they died, letting her husband know what she really thought about their separation. The client can imagine floating into this new version of the old situation and the experience can be heightened using visual, auditory, olfactory and kinaesthetic modalities. During these activities it is useful for the therapist to help the client associate her new experiences of previous festering thoughts with feelings of calmness, relaxation, relief and inner peace.

It is useful to note that clients are all unique individuals and the above techniques may provide the necessary emotional release after one session, or the process may need to be repeated over several sessions, or as each new event or memory of loss appears between appointments.

Breaking the cycle of repetitive thoughts surrounding loss

Philip lost his father to illness and two years later he feels that he has not been able to move on. Surrounding his loss are repetitive thoughts that keep him stuck and immobilised; thoughts such as 'I was a big let-down as a son', 'I didn't even manage to see him when he took his last breath', 'I can't forgive myself for what happened with dad'. Philip blames himself for his father's death and cannot seem to shift his destructive thinking. Rather than realising and accepting the complex emotions and feelings surrounding the loss of his father, Philip is trapped in a single emotion: a *depressed state* as a result of his thinking. Instead of focussing on the many emotions of loss – fear, anxiety, depression, guilt, regret – he focusses solely upon one: depression. A 'many emotion' issue has been reduced to a 'one emotion' issue, a form of avoidance or denial. As Philip clings to the above thoughts, he cannot break free from his depression.

In a situation like this, helping Philip work through his thoughts *cognitively* can begin to lessen their impact and reframe their meaning. Instructing Philip to write down negative thoughts and to challenge these thoughts with positive affirmations can begin to release his emotions. For example, the thought 'I was a big let-down as a son' could be replaced with 'I always did the best I could for my dad. He would be proud of me.' Philip would benefit from writing his positive affirmations on cards and placing these in places where he can regularly focus upon them. This primes the mind to accept that change is possible and that positive thoughts can allow him to feel better about himself and the loss of his father.

Utilising hypnosis, Philip can experience himself living out the positive affirmations that he has created. He can begin to acknowledge and let go of all the emotions he has suppressed, opening up the possibility of a positive future that he can focus upon.

Imagining a future after loss has been processed

Sometimes a client is so immobilised by the emotions associated with loss and bereavement they may feel that they will always be this way: depressed, anxious, fearful. On more than one occasion within the authors' practice, clients have referred to this feeling along the lines of 'being in a long dark tunnel with no light at the other end'. Helping the client break out of his internal world into a future where the loss has been accepted and processed can start the process of change. It is somewhat like reading the final chapter of a book and working backwards in order to find out the events that led to the denouement. Through hypnosis, a client is guided through a visual, auditory and kinaesthetic experience of himself at a point in his life where he has let go of his loss. During this experience, the therapist asks questions designed to pique the natural curiosity of the client: What is different about that future version of yourself? How do you act without the loss? How do others act towards you? How do you know that the loss is behind you? What things are you doing in the future? How are you feeling there? Instinctively, the client can begin to find the answers to these questions through his imagination, while unconsciously the mind works towards achieving his future.

Metaphors and stories for overcoming loss

Therapist: So how do you know that you feel this loss?
Client: It's like, you know, a dark shadow. Always there, following me wherever I go.
Therapist: How does that shadow make you feel?
Client: Down, I feel down. All the time. It haunts me.
Therapist: What exactly haunts you? The shadow?
Client: Mmm, yes the shadow and the fact that I couldn't be myself when we separated.
Therapist: You mean you and your wife?
Client: Yes, I couldn't say what I wanted to say. I should have told her, should have told her how I was feeling.
Therapist: How were you feeling?
Client: Angry! Fucking angry! She took everything: the house, the boys. I was scared of losing the boys. I am scared. But I was pleasant and careful, for the boys. I always am but I hate it!
Therapist: How would you know that this shadow had gone? What would be different?
Client: I could be myself. I wouldn't be so nice to her; I'd be more confident and assertive I guess. I wouldn't be scared all the time!

That's right . . . you know [client's name] . . . the things we've discussed today remind me of a story I was told when I was a young boy . . . I can't remember who told me the story but it's stayed with me all these years . . . I guess it makes me *feel positive* . . . all the best stories have happy endings don't you think? . . . and meanings that resonate with us in some way . . . you know sometimes things are so obvious that you don't notice them . . . I suppose it's like wearing a pair of glasses and after a while forgetting that you've got them on . . . sometimes I can't remember what I've had for lunch until I've walked past the deli counter and spotted all the nice meats and cheeses . . . anyway I'm going on a bit . . . the story . . . yes it was about a ghost in an old mansion . . . but this isn't a typical ghost story . . . for this ghost was scared of its own shadow . . . imagine that! . . . a ghost that was terrified of its own shadow lived in an attic in a big mansion . . . a family lived in the mansion and the ghost would have so liked to see what the family were up to during their daily lives . . . but the other ghosts had shunned this particular ghost . . . had forced it up into the attic where it spent the days fearing the coming of night . . . for that was when the shadow would appear . . . a big dark thing whenever the silvery moon came out . . . the ghost was terrified of this shadow . . . which followed the ghost wherever it floated in the large attic . . . the ghost was terrified that he would never be able to see the family downstairs . . . the other ghosts in the mansion sometimes paid a visit to the ghost . . . laughing and teasing the ghost as it hid itself in one of the drawers of an old discarded dusty cabinet . . . angry at the other ghosts, the ghost would sometimes take a peek out of one of the drawers . . . but as soon as it saw the shadow loom across the floor the ghost would float back into the drawer . . . then one night a wise old owl appeared by the attic window and began tapping on the glass with its beak . . . although frightened the ghost floated over to the window and opened it . . . the owl's eyes gazed compassionately at the ghost . . . who had noticed the shadow below it and had begun shaking . . . 'you know, I've been flying past this window every day for years and noticed you stuck in that cabinet there scared of the shadow . . . *your shadow*' . . . 'my shadow?' the ghost replied nervously . . . 'yes, your shadow' the owl replied . . . 'I'll prove it to you', the owl continued and flew into the attic, flicking the light switch with its beak . . . the room suddenly filled with light and the ghost looked down and the shadow had gone . . . 'you see you've been scared of this shadow all this time and now you can see that it was you that you were scared of!' the owl declared . . . something changed within the ghost there and then . . . he would no longer be scared anymore . . . in fact he would *let all the fear go* and explore the mansion with his head held high . . . thanking the owl the ghost floated from room to room . . . much to the surprise of the other ghosts who began to react differently to the *new confident manner* in which the ghost handled itself . . . the ghost thought he would still be angry at the other ghosts for teasing him but found that *all the anger had gone* . . . somehow knowing that the shadow was harmless made the ghost *let go of the anger and frustration* and instead of anger the ghost felt a kindness to the other ghosts . . . after all it wasn't their fault that he had been scared of his own shadow . . . and the really interesting thing that the ghost found out was that the family who lived in the mansion always knew that the ghost was hiding upstairs in the attic . . . and that when he came down for the first time . . . they felt his presence and were *happy and content* to be with him . . . from then on the ghost spent many a happy time with the family . . . and as time went on he found that he was no longer a ghost . . . that he no longer noticed the shadow anymore . . . and that he was *part of the family now* . . . he could *act himself and be himself* and everything was fine . . . he said the things that he wanted to say . . . and did the things that he wanted to do . . . and the family responded in a way that he never thought possible . . . and this made him *even more confident and happy* . . . [pause 1 minute] . . . I don't know why that story has stayed with me [insert client's name] but there's something comforting about it don't you think?

Example script: Saying the things that you want to say

The following script can be used under hypnosis or in a relaxed state. It is designed for clients who feel that they can benefit from saying the things that they wanted to say to someone or something that they have lost. The script can and should be adapted for the loss of a loved one or pet through death; a relationship breakdown; leaving home; a geographical move and when helping children overcome loss and bereavement. The script focusses on imagining a beautiful flower garden with a wooden bench where the client can sit and chat with the person/animal/object concerned. A metaphor for change and new possibilities is presented with reference to

the rich myriad of flowers and their different blooming patterns. Certain words or phrases have been italicised to signify vocal emphasis. Within the flower garden, the client can begin the process of letting go of negative emotions such as guilt, regret and anger that often accompany unprocessed loss. There is also an opportunity for clients to give themselves permission to cry, something that many people deny themselves as they avoid the difficult emotions of grief and bereavement.

The flower garden

Now that you're so relaxed and comfortable . . . every word that I say relaxing you more and more . . . so you can begin to appreciate how in this quiet relaxed state . . . your unconscious mind . . . that part of your mind that takes care of you night and day . . . taking time to help you in any way that it can . . . that unconscious part of you can begin to really listen and learn . . . from this wonderful experience of drifting inwards . . . every breath that you take relaxing you more as you drift deeper and deeper within your inner being . . . as you begin to imagine yourself opening a door now . . . a large wooden door that leads into the most beautiful garden in the world . . . imagine yourself opening the door now and walking into the garden . . . a flower garden . . . filled with beautiful flowers of different shapes and sizes . . . different scents and aromas . . . some tall with large golden-rayed petals . . . others with willowy stems and flowers that form a sea of blue . . . poppies and shrubs . . . ferns and holly . . . imagine walking through this wonderful garden . . . breathing in the soft scents . . . the wonderful fragrances that hang in the air . . . and as you explore the flower garden, you begin to realise how the garden is *constantly changing . . . constantly growing . . . constantly evolving* and how different are its flowers from season to season . . . you can *discover this for yourself* . . . how some flowers bloom all summer long while others rise only in spring . . . how the festival of colour and fragrance changes throughout the year . . . and as you consider all this . . . so you can begin to realise that *nothing stays the same* . . . in this garden . . . in our world . . . that time glides onwards and like the flowers in the the flower garden, our *emotions change . . .* our *feelings change . . .* our *thoughts and memories change . . . reactions change . . .* and as you make your way through the garden . . . so you notice that in front of you . . . a short distance away . . . in a little clearing of grass there is a wooden bench . . . begin to make your way towards the bench . . . and imagine sitting down on that quiet relaxing bench . . . the flowers dancing and swaying in the soft breeze that kisses the air . . . take in a nice relaxing breath and notice that you have left some room on that bench . . . room for a person that you would like to chat with . . . someone that is in the flower garden . . . someone that you want to say something to . . . perhaps something that you didn't have a chance to say before . . . it could be something that you didn't have the time to tell them perhaps . . . something that you want to get off your chest . . . and before that person appears on the bench next to you . . . imagine the breeze sweeping away any guilt or shame . . . sadness or regret . . . imagine any *negative feelings or emotions lifting from you now* . . . [short pause] . . . any anger or frustration . . . floating away from you now . . . because the person that you want to chat with doesn't want you to feel like this anymore . . . they want you to be happy . . . so imagine the breeze lifting away any remaining negativity and take another relaxing breath . . . as you open your heart . . . as you open your heart . . . and the compassion within you flows like a bright white healing light . . . and that person appears on the bench next to you . . . as you get a sense of that person . . . so you can begin to let them know how you feel about them . . . how you feel about the loss . . . let them know all this . . . tell them what you wanted to say before . . . [short pause] . . . and notice how *much better you feel* as you share with them all the things that you have kept inside . . . and if there is a tear then that is good . . . this is perfectly natural . . . let the tears flow . . . for they will moisten the earth and nourish the flowers . . . tell the person next to you all the things you wanted to say . . . let them know . . . take your time . . . relaxing with every breath that you take . . . and every word that I say relaxing you more and more . . . as you chat on that bench . . . [short pause] . . . enjoying some quiet time on that bench . . . and once you have finished saying what you needed to say . . . then you can rejoice . . . a heavy weight has been lifted from you . . . imagine this weight lifting off your shoulders now . . . feel yourself relax . . . as you imagine *saying goodbye now* . . . and as you imagine this so the person next to you begins to float away from the bench . . . and into the wonderful flowers of the garden . . . and take a deep breath as you enjoy peaceful relaxation on that bench . . . allowing your heart to open up to joy and happiness . . . to wonder and positivity . . . knowing that you can always pay a visit to the person in the flower garden whenever you wish . . . enjoy these feelings for a while longer as I quieten down in the background . . . [pause two minutes].

Then re-awaken with a count-up.

Example script: Saying goodbye to a loved one

This script is designed for clients who have a spiritual worldview and believe in the existence of the soul after death.

The magical palace

That's it . . . and now you can relaxed more deeply . . . just enjoying now the peaceful relaxed state that the wonderful experience of hypnosis brings . . . and the really interesting thing about this useful state of relaxation . . . is that your unconscious mind can begin to discover new possibilities . . . fresh learnings . . . that can start the process of letting go and moving on . . . and you don't have to make any effort to make this happen . . . it can happen all by itself without any conscious awareness on your part at all . . . as you begin to go deeper now . . . every word that I say . . . allowing you to drift deeper within yourself . . . within that part of you that is the very essence of you . . . the very essence of your being . . . so take some quiet time to find your inner self . . . the spirit within you . . . the spirit of you . . . the spirit around you . . . [short pause] . . . as you begin to imagine a magical palace where your inner self can go and roam free . . . a place where you can communicate with the spirits of others now departed . . . a place where you can set your loved one on their journey . . . imagine a magical palace manifesting now . . . around you . . . within you . . . through you . . . a beautiful magical palace with spiral staircases and domed ceilings . . . imagine exploring the vast rooms filled with exquisite furniture . . . content in the knowledge that you are relaxing more and more deeply as you do . . . now there is a room at the back of the palace with large patio windows leading onto a beautiful terrace filled with flowers . . . imagine opening the patio doors and walking onto that terrace now . . . and notice at the far end of the terrace there is a gate leading to a wondrous garden . . . a garden where souls reside before they move on to heaven . . . go to the gate now and open it . . . and as you do so the soul of the person . . . the loved one that has departed . . . begins to manifest around you . . . you may get a sense of the presence of the soul of your loved one now . . . perhaps it forms the very image of the person . . . perhaps you sense a colour or a feeling . . . just go along with whatever comes into your experience . . . as you imagine hugging your loved one . . . who has great love and compassion for you . . . as you embrace . . . say the things that you want to say . . . [short pause] . . . get a sense of what your loved one wants to say . . . [short pause] . . . if there are any feelings that need letting go . . . let go of them now . . . [short pause] . . . knowing that your loved one is starting a new journey . . . safe in the knowledge that they are going to a place of serenity and happiness and peace . . . as you feel the love and compassion flow through every pore of your mind and body . . . enjoying some quiet time together . . . and it's fine to cry . . . that's perfectly natural and okay . . . for you will find that your tears are the tears of joy . . . of deep compassion and love . . . as you lead your loved one through the gate and say the final goodbye . . . imagine your loved one floating into heaven with all the other souls there lovingly guiding your loved one every step of the way . . . and once your loved one has gone you can come back onto the terrace . . . for there are plenty of things that you need to experience in your own life . . . and you can close that gate when you are ready as I quieten down and you enjoy the peaceful relaxation . . . [pause two minutes].

Then re-awaken with a count-up.

Ideomotor signals

Taking the 'Magical Palace' example above, and prior to any hypnotic induction, you can instruct your client to provide ideomotor signals to let you know when they have said all they needed to say to their loved one and when they are ready to close the gate. Ideomotor signals are non-verbal forms of communication, for example, raising a finger or nodding a head. They are useful in situations where deep hypnosis could be broken with the client speaking.

The importance of a . . . pause

Pauses are included in many sections in the example stories and scripts in this chapter. In certain situations it is useful for the client to spend some time reflecting on what they wish to say to a loved one, or when experiencing difficult emotions and feelings as they go through the process of acceptance of grief and letting go of loss. Taking a step back as a therapist and letting the client get on with what they need to do can be a rewarding exercise for the client to discover internal resources for positive change. Pauses are useful inclusions at the end of a metaphor, story, hypnotic induction or in a general discussion between client and therapist, whenever you wish the client to internally search for answers and solutions to a problem within themselves; often this occurs unconsciously, especially if you have told a story with many layers and hidden meanings. It is these meanings and layers and their relationship with the clients own issues and goals and unique worldview that form the basis of a 'treasure hunt' for a solution. A well-timed pause can bring a solution to a mystery, can lead to digging for treasure and unearthing a pot of gold.

Conclusion

This chapter demonstrates that there are many ways of working integratively with loss and/or bereavement. Hypnotherapeutic modalities provide the opportunity to help clients to explore their complex and conflicting emotions in the aftermath of loss/bereavement with the potential to re-imagine their experiences and to engage with their losses in more empowering ways. Person-centred, relational and CBT based modalities also provide some interesting insights into the therapeutic challenges when working with loss and/or bereavement. We have found that a useful way of integrating these different modalities in relation to client work is to use the trans-theoretical model of change (TTM), as introduced in the previous chapter. This can help guide us to introduce different interventions according to which stage and level of change the client is at for any given loss/bereavement. The TTM offers a way of integrating all the techniques that we have discussed in this chapter.

References

Adams, J.D., Hayes, J. & Hopson, B. (1976) *Transition: Understanding and Managing Personal Change*. London: Martin Robertson.

Choron, J. (1964) *Modern Man and Mortality*. New York: Macmillan.

Crabtree, S., Husain, F. & Spalek, B. (2008) *Islam and Social Work*. Bristol: Policy Press.

Hadley, J. & Staudacher, C. (2001) *Hypnosis for Change*. Oakland, CA: New Harbinger Publications.

Kubler-Ross, E. (1969) *On Death and Dying: What the Dying Have to Teach Doctors, Nurses, Clergy and Their Own Family*. New York: Philip & Schuster.

May, W. (1994) *The Discovery of Being*. New York: Norton.

Rees, G. (2015) 'Japan a Resilient Nation?' European Society for Traumatic Stress Studies, https://www.estss.org/japan-a-resilient-nation/ (accessed 15 July 2015).

Shakespeare, W. (2011) *The Oxford Shakespeare: Richard II*. Edited by Anthony B. Dawson and Paul Yachnin. Oxford: OUP.

Stroebe, M. S. & Schut, H. (1999) 'The Dual Process Model of coping with bereavement: Rationale and description', *Death Studies*, vol. 23, pp. 197–224.

Weston, R., Martin, T. & Anderson, Y. (1998) *Loss and Bereavement*. Oxford: Blackwell Science.

Worden, W. (2008) *Grief Counselling and Grief Therapy*, 4th edition. London: Routledge.

Yalom, I. D. (1980) *Existential Psychotherapy*. New York, NY: Basic Books.

Chapter 7

Working integratively with anxiety

Clients often seek to pinpoint the source of their anxiety with the aim of eradicating it. Through exploring potential triggers, past and present, and enabling clients to devise ways of managing their anxiety, it becomes more tolerable.

Catherine Fitzpatrick, Integrative Psychodynamic Therapist

Introduction

Anxiety is a complex phenomenon. We agree with Rollo May that anxiety is part of being a human being and as such anxiety is not something to be 'fixed'. However, it is the responses to anxiety that require our attention, for this is where people can become stuck and suffer. This chapter approaches anxiety as an intricate aspect of being human. As such, unlike many psychological and therapy books, we do not look into explaining different anxiety-related conditions or diagnoses. Rather, we approach anxiety holistically, exploring anxiety in relation to the binary of being/non-being. This includes a focus upon, and exploration of, creativity, story-telling and meaning making, as part of a person-centred approach to anxiety. We also then focus on some CBT, relational and hypnotherapeutic aspects to working with anxiety. We demonstrate how we integrate these modalities when working with anxiety through presenting two case studies where we highlight the key integrative concepts as set out in chapters one to five of this book: presence, emotional processing, attachment, thinking, and our conscious/unconscious minds. The learning inherent within this chapter is not only intended for use when working with clients, but is also part of self-growth and the development of self-awareness within ourselves, as therapists or other kinds of mental health practitioners. We firstly begin with a short description of the life of a citizen inhabiting a planet called Planet Alpha, as an illustration of some of the challenges that anxiety brings in the 21st century.

Planet Alpha

Citizen 2020 entered the canteen, tray in hand. She looked at her phone: 'five minutes then go', she told herself. Then she breathed a sigh of relief because she remembered that she had set her mobile to ring an alarm in exactly five minutes' time, lest she forget. Citizen 2020 queued for some soup and a piece of bread, too afraid to talk to any of her colleagues, afraid that she would go over her five permitted minutes of lunch. She sat down and spoon fed herself the pulverised green liquid, tearing the bread into the bowl in order to soften it to aid her digestion. Her mobile phone began bleeping. Citizen 2020 stood up and walked briskly out of the canteen.

Citizen 20/20 strode over to the Knowledge Centre, just like she did every day, and spent the next 8 hours there revising for her forthcoming exams. Indeed, Citizen 2020 could not remember a time when she did not have any exams to prepare for, when she did not spend up to 14 hours a day studying. She knew that one day she would become an Adult, and that the Knowledge Centre would then be replaced with the Work Centre, but until that time arrived this was her daily life. She had heard it whispered that her people had once inhabited a planet called Create, a planet that was lush and mesmerising, where people spoke about who they were, their origins, their dreams and their nightmares. However, Citizen 2020 and her comrades had no collective memory of this time, and now that they inhabited Planet Alpha there were no myths or stories here to tell, only targets and indicators to strive for, one big tick box exercise. And constant agitation. Nobody spoke about this but they all knew they had it because agitation seeped through in the abrupt way that people spoke to each other, in the shortness of breath and brusque body movements.

Suddenly, Citizen 2020 began to unravel. Her most recent exam results had come back and she had not achieved her cherished goal of A star plus. Citizen 2020 could not make any meaning out of simply getting an average grade, for this was not in her set of performance indicators. Little by little the agitation engulfed her, like an icy cold waterfall inside her very heart, bringing forth panic, terror, physical and emotional pain. Citizen 2020 had no understanding of where she had come from, of who she was; her values had merged with the values of Planet Alpha. Citizen 2020 had no anchor within herself so she could not challenge the way that her exam results made her feel, and as a result she disintegrated. Planet Alpha citizens discovered Citizen 2020's motionless body, and there was nothing they could do for there was no storybook within which to rebuild her.

Whilst the above short story might seem a little 'out of this World' and unreal, it is based upon the numerous young people that we have seen in our private and professional practices. Our society is very goal-driven, and young people from a very early age are being pushed to learning a mass of information that they are then examined on. It seems that their own sense-making of who they are, their stories, their intuition and wisdom are being sacrificed at the altar of 'progress', ''technological advancement' and neo-liberal capitalism. As a result, we are seeing many young people (and indeed many older people!) coming to therapy with deep-rooted, neurotic, anxiety.

Normal and neurotic anxiety, existence and non-existence

A therapist friend of ours often says that humans are the only species that constantly have to learn how, and what it means, to be human. The phrase human being suggests that being human is complex, under constant construction and negotiation. Human beings have the capacity to think about what it is to be human, what it is to exist, and to also contemplate non-existence. Perhaps the basis of 'normal anxiety' lies in the challenges inherent within the being/non-being binary of being human. Anxiety might therefore be viewed as natural, for existence and the idea of non-existence are inherently anxiety-provoking. For May (1977), anxiety is not a problem in that a natural amount of anxiety is normal to being a human. What is an issue is where the anxiety becomes pathological, harmful, unhealthy. It is therefore useful to distinguish between normal and neurotic anxiety. Normal anxiety is that reaction which:

Is not disproportionate to the objective threat.

Does not involve repression or other mechanisms of intrapsychic conflict.

Does not require neurotic defense mechanisms for its management.

Can be confronted constructively on the level of conscious awareness or can be relieved if the objective situation is altered.

(May, 1977: 193)

On the other hand, neurotic anxiety is:

A reaction to threat which is disproportionate to the objective danger, involves repression (dissociation) and other forms of intrapsychic conflict and as a corollary is managed by means of various forms of retrenchment of activity and awareness, such as inhibitions, the development of symptoms, and the varied neurotic defense mechanisms.

(May, 1977: 198)

Neurotic anxiety perhaps is a broad umbrella term for a very large number of anxiety disorders, including social anxiety disorder, generalised anxiety disorder, substance-induced anxiety disorder, panic disorder, agoraphobia and other phobias . We are not going into any detail about any specific disorders because information about these can be easily accessed, for instance, from the Diagnostic and Statistical Manual of Mental Disorders (DMS-5)(American Psychiatric Association, 2013). Instead we are focussing on a general overview of anxiety in relation to person-centred, CBT, relational and hypnotherapeutic modalities, before then considering how we work integratively with these. We begin with a focus on our approach to anxiety through a person-centred modality, where the importance of story, creativity and meaning-making is stressed.

Person-centredness and anxiety: The importance of story, creativity and meaning

Although we tend to take 'being' as something straightforward within wider society, 'being' is complex and challenging. Everyday existence takes great courage for we simply do not know what future outcomes there may be in our lives and in the lives of people that we love and cherish. It takes courage simply to be, to exist, knowing that one day this particular form of existence will be no more. Anxiety is therefore part and parcel of our existence and creatively facing our lives can be a healthy way to deal with normal anxiety (May, 1977). We argue here that an important aspect of creative existence is story-telling. If the process of being is a creative endeavour and inherently anxiety-provoking in relation to being and non-being, we argue that human beings have evolved to be storytellers. Through the act of story-making, we can make sense of our lives, of the lives of others, the challenges and victories, and we can create myths around our existence and non-existence. For centuries, story-telling has been inherent to all human beings across all cultures and contexts.

In his book *The Actor and the Target* Declan Donnellan suggests that in order for us to believe something about ourselves, we need to make others believe it first (Donnellan 2002). One implication here is something like: I discover myself through the telling of my story. The concept of discovering the truth about ourselves through stories is epitomised in Harold Bloom's observation about Shakespeare. Bloom suggests that Shakespeare was so advanced in his ability to comprehend and reveal the human condition that *The Complete Works* should be re-titled *The Book of Reality.* In Hamlet's 'To be or not to be' soliloquy, the protagonist attempts to discover a truth by talking to the audience. His focus is being and non-being, and the stasis he is experiencing, frozen between a mind that imagines death as a nightmare, and a body that knows life to be one. The soliloquy does not appear to resolve the paradox, Hamlet has therefore more to see and say. The story, as is our search for self-knowledge, is continuous. Hamlet's journey ends with a request to Horatio to continue his myth. With his dying breath, Hamlet makes the instruction: 'Tell my story' (Shakespeare, *Hamlet*, 5.2.333, referenced in Burton, 2018).

The gradual erosion of story-making within post-industrialised societies has led to reduced spaces where we are able to make sense of our life challenges, an important cultural resource has been lost. There might be many opportunities to post messages onto social media and send texts and emails to our friends and colleagues, but these are often very short, created out of agitation rather than a state of presence. In *The World Beyond Your Head* Crawford (2015) argues that distractability has become a cultural problem in post-industrialised societies, partly as a result of technological developments that have led to our attention constantly being bombarded by information and electronic stimulation, alongside our ethically void style of existence. For Crawford (2015: 5), 'Our changing technological environment generates a need for ever more stimulation. The content of the stimulation almost becomes irrelevant. Our distractability seems to indicate that we are agnostic on the question of what is worth paying attention to – that is, what to value.' We are expected to convey meaning through very brief interactions with each other, rather than taking time to create reflective accounts of our lives that are open to exploration and growth. Perhaps psychotherapy is one space within which individuals can still continue to build stories about what it is to be human, and through this space understand how it is that we can experience neurotic anxiety and what we might be able to do about this.

The moon child

She climbed out of bed, a mere three years in age, for she was drawn to the beauty of the large shining planet that was gracing her bedroom with pure white, vibrating light. She sat on her bed and stared at the beauty of what was outside her window in the vast expanse of the night sky, a sky rich with luminous beings. She knew that her existence was somehow linked to the shiny planet out in the sky, and she sat in awe and wonder. She experienced herself as outside of her body, her existence as a part of something vast and unlimited by time, her existence being at the core of creation itself. When she was 7 years old this child found herself worrying about the possibility of her forthcoming death, 'If I don't awake in the morning it means I will have died'. She remembered what had happened earlier that day, how she had placed the stem of a wild flower in her mouth to keep it alive, to keep it watered, how her mother had scolded her, 'Don't do that because it might be poisonous and you might die'. The child didn't know whether she had been poisoned or not and she was afraid. But then the blue moon outside her window caught her attention and the child instinctively knew that there was nothing to be afraid of, that the anxiety that she had been feeling was not her own but that of her mother's. From that point on she knew that she was a moon child – both finite and infinite.

Alexa, which anxiety do I suffer from?

Treating anxiety as part of the human condition, something that is there from the beginning of existence to its very end, opens up a freedom of possibilities within therapeutic approaches. We avoid, as much as possible, labeling and diagnosis of anxiety into the various disorders: Panic Disorder, Post Traumatic Stress Disorder, Acute Stress Disorder, Generalised Anxiety Disorder and so on. Attaching diagnostic labels to the individuals' unique experience of anxiety can reinforce discomfort and suffering. An individual that labels himself, or is diagnosed as having Panic Disorder, can become so absorbed in symptomatology that he forgets or ignores the instances and situations where he *doesn't* experience a panic attack. This diminished or protracted sense of self, so absorbing to the individual, can limit internal potentialities and resources for overcoming the anxiety.

However, the fact remains that clients come into therapy with labels: 'I have generalised anxiety disorder' or 'I suffer from post-traumatic stress disorder'. Information is readily available through the Internet and physicians happily diagnose anxiety into disorders before prescribing medication. In these situations, trying to convince a client that they may not have the particular disorder they refer to serves no purpose other than to weaken the therapeutic alliance between client and therapist. The client may begin to think that the therapist is falsifying the client's understanding of their anxiety. As Erickson (1998:8) suggests, approaches to fear and anxiety must focus on the client recognizing that you as the therapist 'agree with them and that they agree with you.' Erickson (1998:205) further suggests that 'one of the reasons patients enter therapy is to receive an acceptance of their particular problem from the therapist.' In cases of severe anxiety, with the almost total dissolution of self, this acceptance is a way of holding onto fragmented existence. If we are so very anxious that we cannot relate to ourselves or the world in any way other than through suffering, having a therapist nodding her head and saying that she understands how we feel can be a comforting, and ultimately human, experience.

So we enter the anxious world of our client and utilise their labels as a reframing potential:

> 'Well, it's great that you have such an awareness of the panic attack cycle within your disorder James, because that means that there are plenty of opportunities where this cycle can be broken in order for you to begin to experience life without the panic attacks. . . .'

This statement reframes the cycle of panic from a symbol of reinforced continuity with no beginning or end, into a symbol that shows weakness at certain points; we are taught from an early age that weakness often results in loss so the unconscious message is: *your panic cycle is weak and you will lose it*. Utilise the suppositions within the client's own understanding of their anxiety in order to prime potentialities within therapeutic interventions. Again Erickson (1998:10) suggests that 'You never ask the patient to falsify his own understanding; instead you give him other understandings that nullify, that contradict, that absorb and hold his focus, so that he cannot give all his attention to what is distressing him.'

Reframing and anxiety

Reframing the triggers of anxiety can alter the perceptions of a situation in such a way that the anxiety can dissolve. Let us consider the example of a male client in his mid-thirties who came into therapy with an anxiety of speaking to large groups of people. Whenever faced with this prospect, the client was so riddled with catastrophic thinking and the fear of appearing stupid in front of his audience that he would find it difficult to sleep during the several nights leading up to his performance. As he stood in front of his audience, he would often experience uncomfortable physical symptoms that included shortness of breath, sweating and shaking in his hands. As the physical symptoms appeared, he would find it difficult to get his words out and would often stutter through a presentation.

However, whenever he was in front of a small group, *specifically seven people or fewer*, then there was no anxiety at all. This was the most important aspect of the client's story in relation to his anxiety. Once the therapist knew this, the suggestion was made that everything that we experience *is a sum of its parts*, for example, an ant forms one small cog in a colony, an atom interacts with another atom to form a molecule, a drop of water sticks to another drop of water and eventually we have an ocean. Each of these examples, communicated in the form of short stories, were accepted by the client because they held an inherent truth. A final suggestion was made: the next time he was to give a presentation in front of a large group the client was to imagine the group in front of him as the sum of smaller parts, *no part being more than seven people in size*. Mental rehearsal exercises were introduced where the client imagined his future audience in groups of seven: he was instructed to make the first seven people who sat in front of him one small group; the person who sat after the seventh person would then form a new group of seven and so on. He also imagined people sitting around tables in groups of seven. The client reported that he felt much more relaxed and confident the next time that he gave a presentation in front of a large group. Several weeks after this positive experience the anxiety had gone and a new story of being and presenting in front of a large audience had evolved.

Indira and the spider's web

On a large patch of sand in front of her uncle's hut, a girl called Indira would often play during the afternoons, hitting a ball made from rabbit skin into the sky with a bamboo stick. One day, several days ago, she hit the ball so well that it lifted beyond the row of huts that made up the village and bounced down the hill. Indira dropped her stick and chased after the ball, which had landed next to a bunch of prickly cactus plants beneath a tall palm tree. As she knelt down to pick up the ball she noticed a spider that was spinning a web close by. The edges of the web were held between some thick cactus leaves and Indira became entranced as the spider, precariously balancing on a thread of silk, continued its journey around the web. Before long someone had called out her name and she rose from the sandy gravel and made her way up the hill. That night it was cold and the stars had gathered amongst the grinning moon. Indira found herself dreaming about the spider and its web. In the morning she would show her uncle the web. Sure enough, when the first hint of day had snuck in through her window she got up and went to her uncle's house. Her uncle, already up and tending to the chickens, lifted her into his arms. 'What a pleasure to see you Indi!' he declared smiling. 'Uncle, I'd like to show you something,' the girl said seriously and the two of them descended down the hill, hand in hand. 'Look at this web uncle, I found it yesterday.' Indira pointed towards the spider's web, illuminated by the fading stars. 'My, that is a handsome web!' The uncle got down on one knee. 'Look at the beads of moisture on each strand,' he indicated with his hand. The girl bent down and sure enough, hundreds of beads hung on the silken threads like tiny jewels. 'How was the spider able to build such a thing?' Indira asked, following the spider with her eyes as it disappeared under a nearby cactus plant. 'Ah, now that's a secret between the spider and the

universe. But if you look closely you can see the reflection of each star in every bead there on that web,' her uncle pointed with his finger. Indira looked at each bead and saw the stars reflected in each bead. 'Everything in our world is interconnected Indi.' He turned and ran back up the hill, returning with some burning cane. He held the flames up to the web. 'Look, see the flames in each of the beads now.' Indira's eyes opened. 'I can uncle, I can see the flame in each bead!' Her uncle smiled. He snuffed out the torch and they stared at the tiny reflections of starlight in the beads once more. 'You see, every reflection of every star in the sky is held in each tiny little bead,' the uncle said. 'So if I shook the web all the beads would fall!' Indira smiled at her uncle. 'Yes they would,' he said. 'And if I shook the cactus leaves then the web would break up and fall!' Her eyes were large. Her uncle raised an eyebrow. 'Yes but why ever would you wish to destroy something so complex and beautiful?'

The above story, based on an ancient Buddhist metaphor, signifies the complexities of anxiety, the spider's web conveying the interconnectedness of the different strands of its experience, whether subjective, cognitive, physiological or behavioural. From a holistic viewpoint, the beliefs, thoughts, irrational fears, physical and emotional disturbances are the sum of the whole state of anxiety. A ripple in one part spreads to other parts of the web, distorting in shape; so too the protean nature of anxiety which can change moment by moment.

If the strands of the web represent the anxiety itself, then each bead of moisture can be thought of as an opportunity for therapeutic intervention. Changing just one element or facet of the experience of anxiety, such as a subtle reframe of a fear trigger or cognitive restructuring of an anxiety-provoking event, can profoundly affect the system as a whole. Removing a strand in a critical place can weaken the web significantly.

As long as the therapist is fully *present* with the client, there are many opportunities within the construct of anxiety in order to facilitate change. The role of the therapist is similar to a quarter back in American football, an offensive playmaker that needs to be very aware of what is going on around him in order to instigate a penetrative pass. A deep awareness of our client's suffering and discomfort can allow the synthesis of interventions based upon the integrative components of *presence, emotional processing, attachment, thinking and conscious/ unconscious concept of mind* presented in this book. It is as though each of these is a running back, a center or wide receiver that we can throw the ball towards, each component connected to every other within the frame of integrative practice.

Opportunities exist for direct and indirect interventions and suggestions, stories and metaphors that can be absorbed and processed at an instinctive level. No too anxieties are ever truly the same and a 'one size fits all' approach should be avoided so that the individual is not forced into the procrustean bed of a therapeutic theory or modality.

CBT approaches to anxiety

CBT approaches to anxiety will focus on cognitions and behaviours. In terms of cognitions, distorted thinking that helps create and sustain emotions and behaviours relating to anxiety are explored, and clients are helped to identify triggers for these thoughts, the content of such thoughts and then to challenge unhelpful thoughts to create more helpful ones. We can distinguish between negative automatic thoughts (NATS), underlying assumptions and core beliefs, as demonstrated in Chapter 5 on thinking (Wilding & Milne, 2008; Briers, 2009; Greenberger & Padesky, 2015). In order to get from a NAT through to an underlying assumption and core belief, therapists can use a downward arrow technique whereby the therapist keeps asking the client, 'What would be bad about that ?' and 'What would that mean?' (Wells, 2011). For example, a client who has social anxiety might have the following NAT when thinking about going to a dinner party: 'I will have nothing to say'. The therapist might ask, 'What would be bad about that?' and the client might reply, 'People will think I am stupid.' The therapist then might say, 'You seem to have the assumption that if you have nothing to say then people will think you are stupid. How much do you believe this?' The client might then respond with, '85%.' The therapist might then focus on the core belief that the client has identified and ask, 'How much do you believe that you are stupid?' The client might say that in these social situations they believe that they are stupid. In this way a therapist moves between NATS (I will have nothing to say), underlying assumptions (if I have nothing to say it means people will think I am stupid) and core beliefs (I am stupid). In this way the therapist helps the client to have a better understanding of their distorted thinking when it comes to social situations, and to challenge this with more helpful thinking.

Behaviourally the therapist might encourage the client to test out their underlying assumptions by taking part in activities that they normally avoid because they are so anxiety-provoking. Graded exposure can be used whereby the client is encouraged to break down into stages the things that they find fearful, to slowly expose themselves to these situations and to explore the use of coping strategies. Thought records are very useful here, in that clients can document the anxiety-provoking situations, they can make a note of their thoughts and emotions and behaviours and also can record the intensity of these (marking out of 10 or 100). In this way the client can come to see that they can be active in their own recovery, they can draw on thinking and other techniques to cope with anxiety-provoking situations to reduce how much anxiety they feel. CBT approaches also tend to involve different models for different anxiety conditions. For example, Wells (2011) presents models for obsessive compulsive disorder, for generalised anxiety disorder, panic disorder, health anxiety and social phobia. Such models can help therapists to work with anxiety disorders in that they can help to gain a better understanding of what is happening for the client and to work out strategies to deal with this. This chapter does not go into any detailed explanation of CBT based models of anxiety as these can be easily accessed in books specialising in CBT.

Relational modalities and anxiety

Anxiety might be looked at through the lens of childhood experiences with significant others. Thus, it can be useful to explore with clients who their main caregivers were and how they experienced this care, and whether any significant relationships were ruptured. It may be that clients have not experienced unconditional love from their caregivers, but rather love based on conditions of worth. In this case, where the client feels they cannot achieve those conditions this can create anxiety within the client – anxiety of perhaps being rejected by others or being a disappointment to others. It can be helpful to explore these dynamics with clients so that they are able to identify some of the ways in which their experiences of relationships in childhood help create and/or sustain their anxiety. The process of identification can be extremely liberating for clients as they begin to see that they are not necessarily prone to anxiety because of their own fault but rather that there is an historical relational context to the anxieties that they experience and since the bases of these come from childhood they are not easily rid of. We can also encourage our clients to have a more supportive caring relationship towards themselves. Clients with neurotic anxiety can often be extremely self-critical, which adds to their anxiety. By facilitating exploration of what a supportive relationship to oneself might look and feel like this can help shift clients' focus so that their self-criticism is not as intense and they begin to experience a supportive self which can help alleviate their neurotic anxiety. Exploring healthy emotional and psychological boundaries can also be helpful when working relationally with anxiety. Clients who have neurotic anxiety often see themselves as responsible for how other people behave and feel, and so by facilitating exploration of who is ultimately responsible for feelings and behaviours can be beneficial. If a client starts to perceive that how other people react is not down to them then they can start to feel less anxious about other people's reactions around them. This can help with neurotic anxiety like social anxiety or generalised anxiety. The following is a relational-based intervention you might try with clients:

> Think of the significant people in your life. How supportive do you find these people? What emotions do they trigger in you? When you think about asserting your emotional needs what thoughts come to mind for each individual you have identified? If you can, think back to a time when you first started thinking this way in relation to these individuals. What would you now like to say to each person in turn and how would you like them to respond? If a person does not respond in a way that you want them to, what coping strategies do you have/can you think of doing in order to help you tolerate any emotional distress that is generated in you ? (Note that coping strategies can be wide-ranging, including mindfulness, a thought diary, speaking with a supportive friend/family member, relaxation-based activities etc.).

Hypnotherapy and anxiety

Phobic responses, irrational fears, 'free floating' anxiety and obsessive compulsions are examples of common anxiety states where hypnotherapeutic modalities can be utilised. According to Nejad and Volny (2008) hypnotherapy can be used to treat anxiety disorders through positive influences on a person's thoughts, emotions, feelings and perceptions of, for example, an anxiety event. The process of hypnosis itself often follows a simple sequence of events: progressive muscle relaxation, relaxation deepener and mental elicitation of place of comfort within the client, direct and indirect suggestions (including metaphors and story-telling) for anxiety relief, ego-strengthening for building confidence and self-esteem (this reinforces the will and belief of the client to change), post-hypnotic suggestions for eliciting coping mechanisms at the onset of fear triggers and reawakening into full consciousness.

A system or process can seem rigid, yet if we delve deeper than the technique itself, integrating presence, emotional processing, attachment, thinking and the conscious/unconscious concept of mind presented in earlier chapters, each stage of hypnosis forms a microcosm for creative intervention within the macrocosm of anxiety.

For example, a client who presents the issue of anxiety may be on medication, in which case it is worth probing the effects of the drug upon the individual. Should the medication elicit feelings of relaxation, it may prove useful to recreate these feelings during progressive muscle relaxation in order to help induce relaxation, or during post-hypnotic suggestions to facilitate and impress upon the client the association of relaxation and the experience of an oncoming anxiety or fear trigger.

An analysis stage can be introduced within the hypnotic cycle: irrational fear inducing thoughts are brought to awareness and subsequently challenged; corresponding emotions and feelings associated with the fear or anxiety can be processed in order to break attachments while the cause of the anxiety can be dealt with at both the conscious cognitive level and the *feeling* instinctive unconscious.

The anxiety or fear provoking situation or event can be experienced in a dissociative manner, the client visualizing the event taking place on an imaginary screen (Spiegel, 1989). This prevents any reinforcement of trauma and discomfort as well as providing the metaphor of separation from fear or anxiety. For example, the therapist guides the client through a visualisation exercise where the client imagines herself sitting in front of a TV screen. The client is instructed to allow any causative events or memories associated with her anxiety to appear on the screen. Since the client is dissociated from the trauma or horror of these memories, there exists the potential to gain rich understandings and fresh perspectives of the experience of her anxiety. Uncomfortable emotions and feelings can be processed and reframed; coping mechanisms, for example, diaphragmatic breathing and replacing catastrophic thinking with positive statements can be rehearsed in situations which in the past would have triggered a panic response. Through *presence*, the client can be taught to accept her feelings, however distressing, and the physical sensations and fearful thoughts that often accompany an episode of anxiety. Acceptance provides opportunities for reframing her anxiety, providing a conduit for letting go. The relaxed state of hypnosis allows the unconscious mind to process new *learnings* without conscious criticism and resistance.

Anxiety states

According to Dally and Watkins (1986) an anxiety state can be defined as a repeated or persistent feeling of discomfort and stress, manifesting without a rational cause. Within the context of hypnotherapeutic modalities it is useful to understand how anxiety states develop and the role of the subconscious mind in helping suppress anxiety through the paradoxical *elicitation of fear*. Let us begin by focussing upon phobias and irrational fears. Often traumatic or unpleasant memories are repressed within the unconscious mind as a way of protecting the individual from experiencing these events over and over again. The traumatic emotions and feelings attached to these memories are buried along with the actual memory itself. In order to prevent the emotions and feelings from surfacing consciously, the subconscious mind turns the anxiety into fear (Allen, 2004). This provides a *substitute for the anxiety itself, shifting the focus of attention towards the fear*, which can often be irrational and excessive to the point of eliciting panic symptomology. The pattern of irrational fear and associated panic response forms a phobic reaction.

In order to alleviate the irrational fear and get rid of the phobia a combination of hypnosis and *age regression* can be utilised. The memory associated with the anxiety that resulted in the irrational fear developing can be recalled, providing opportunities for creating new interpretations and understandings surrounding this experience. The anxiety provoking event(s) can thus be reframed and new associations created; any inner conflict involving the initial anxiety can be resolved. The irrational fear becomes redundant and, as Allen (2004) states, the phobia disappears.

A phobic response or irrational fear can evolve over a period of many years, mutating into complex avoidance strategies and beliefs surrounding this fear. These complexities can make it difficult for anyone experiencing this type of anxiety to have the confidence and belief that they can let it go. For example, an agoraphobic may initially avoid situations such as walking down the garden path and onto the street outside; over time they can limit themselves to stepping out no further than beyond the edge of the doorstep. They may eventually find themselves avoiding a corridor or hallway in a house until the only place that they feel safe is in a single room in the house, then so many feet away from a window and so on. Obsessive compulsions can evolve too: checking a single radiator for leaks can evolve into checking the radiators in the entire house; a client can present OCD as a complex system or set of rituals that become ever more limiting; more checking, greater repetition, more anxiety. So how do we instill the belief that freedom from anxiety is possible?

A combination of hypnosis and *age progression* can present the possibility of relief from these types of disorders; a future can be imagined without the phobia, irrational fear, obsessive behavior or anxiety. The experience of freedom can be heightened through mental rehearsal techniques. For example, a useful intervention for obsessive compulsive behavior is to induce hypnosis within the client and get them to imagine the sequence of events based around their behavior. As the client develops a greater awareness of their behavior, as opposed to *doing it automatically*, the therapist can ask questions in order to determine a deeper understanding of the obsessive compulsion: what thoughts lead to checking the radiators for leaks? Which radiator is checked first? How is the radiator checked? Are the taps checked before or after the radiators? What is the anxiety or fear behind the behaviour?

As the client becomes more conscious of the thoughts, feelings and actions surrounding the compulsive behavior so a new sequence of events can be experienced through age progression. A client can imagine himself going through the ritual at some future point *in a completely different order or sequence of events*, interrupting the pattern enveloping the compulsion.

In the case of obsessive compulsive behavior, the conscious fear and unconscious anxiety surrounding the experience of *not checking* or *not going through a ritual* can be determined and addressed through hypnosis. This process of self-discovery is often conducted in a dissociative manner: for example, a client experiences a version of himself on a movie screen *not performing* the compulsive behavior, the ritual. This experience can lead to an awareness of anxiety provoking thoughts, providing opportunities for releasing attachment to the underlying anxiety through acceptance and understanding of its manifestation. Interpretations and appraisal of the emotions surrounding the obsessive behaviour, for example having the need to check radiators after a previous experience of flooding, can be acknowledged and reframed in order to overcome the anxiety and resolve the fear.

Utilisation of anxiety characteristics

From a therapeutic perspective, utilisation of the client's awareness of their difficulties can prove rewarding. A client may present their anxiety, obsessive behavior, irrational fear or phobia as a *part* of their Being: '*Part* of me needs to check the radiators . . .', 'I want to fight the fear but then I get a voice telling me to ignore *that part*. . . .' The experience of anxiety and fear as a *part* within someone provides an example of its characteristic, its signature: how it is appears and is experienced within the individual. Addressing the part responsible for the fear or anxiety, utilizing a hypnotic state, can provide clues to its origin and meaning, and begins the process of breaking it up. For example, a therapist may invite the client, while under hypnosis, to bring up the part responsible for the anxiety in order to determine its purpose and suggest the possibility of alternative ways of behaving or responding to situations that prove more beneficial. This is an example of reframing utilizing the metaphor of *part* built around the pre-supposition that humans are complex psychological organisms made up of many parts that can conflict with each other.

No two written signatures are the same and this is no different within the context of the characteristics of anxiety states. When asked to describe their anxiety or fear, an individual may utilise a vast range of descriptors including images, pictures, shapes, objects, colours, feelings, emotions: 'I know when the anxiety starts to happen; I get a feeling of dread just here above my heart; this starts first thing in the morning when I wake up. If I close my eyes and imagine the anxiety, it's like a fuzzy grey cloud inside me.'

Within the above signature there are opportunities for therapeutic intervention. Utilizing hypnosis, the client can heighten her awareness of the fuzzy grey cloud and begin to imagine where it is located in the body. The therapist can instruct the client to move the grey cloud to another part of the body, for example, the big toe. In this way, the metaphor of taking control of her anxiety can be introduced unconsciously while being experienced consciously. The fuzzy grey cloud can be lifted out of the body, for example, by imagining it floating away and becoming replaced by a bright sun and blue sky. Again this provides a metaphor for externalizing the anxiety as well as an indirect suggestion that anxiety is not a permanent state; that it can change into something more pleasant.

In a similar way the experience and perception of feelings such as dread can be explored and reframed through imagination: a representation of dread as a colour can be changed into a different colour that lessens the discomfort; a shape or object of dread can be altered into a different shape or object, for example, a heavy lead weight can be turned into a floating balloon. The client can experience this as a guided visualisation. These ideas can be presented through direct and indirect suggestions as well as post-hypnotic suggestions:

> 'And during the next few days you may begin to find yourself thinking about that dread as an altogether different feeling and experience, something light and easy; in fact you might already be thinking about a balloon floating away from you as I say these words, and whenever any dread comes along you can remember the balloon and remember how comfortable and relaxed you are feeling right now as you let go of the things that you don't need and instead focus upon this lightness and positivity. . . . '

Metaphors and stories for anxiety disruption

The sound of silence

In 1952, American composer John Cage produced *4'33''*, a composition structured into three movements. At the first performance, pianist David Tudor sat down in front of the piano and, raising its lid, sat in silence for a period of thirty seconds. He closed the lid and re-opened it once more, sitting in silence for two minutes and thirty-three seconds. Then he closed and lifted the lid for the final movement, sitting in silence for one minute and forty seconds. He closed the lid and departed the stage (Pritchett, 2009). A composition of nothingness had evolved where the sounds of the audience and the experience and awareness of sitting quietly in silence created the performance and story. Influenced by the meditative insight of Zen Buddhism, Cage understood the impact of silence structured within the vessel of time, a concept he dealt with during his *Lecture on Nothing*:

> This space of time is organized. We need not fear these silences, - we may love them. This is a composed talk, for I am making it just as I make a piece of music. It is like a glass of milk. We need the glass and we need the milk. Or again it is like an empty glass into which at any moment anything may be poured. As we go along, (who knows?), an idea may occur in this talk. I have no idea whether one will or not. If one does, let it.
>
> (Cage, 1961, pp. 109–110)

Cage illustrates the concept of silence and time leading to creation using the metaphor of a glass filled – or not filled – with milk. Exploration of the concepts of silence, stillness and awareness – as presented within the chapter on *presence* – through metaphors and story-telling, can allow therapeutic ideas to transcend beyond the conscious barrier. Individuals may suffer anxiety to such an extent that a panic response can manifest during a mindfulness exercise, such as a meditation on breathing and muscle relaxation. It is as though the freedom of letting go and experiencing different physiological and psychological responses serves as an alarm for the shifting state of anxiety, eliciting the fear of experiencing something new and leading to discomfort.

Instead of trying another round of meditation and muscle relaxation, which can prove to be futile, creating a metaphor around an object may provide a useful focal point for the client instead. For example, a glass can be filled with still water and the individual instructed to focus upon the glass while being aware of the silence in the room. This relieves the pressure of trying too hard to relax and can in certain cases elicit a state of altered perception, similar to a light trance in hypnosis. Some crushed peppercorns can be added and the water swirled in the glass. As the individual gazes at the swirling water so the therapist can make her aware of the spiral of thoughts that embody her experience of anxiety. The concept of attachment and non-attachment to anxiety provoking thoughts can be introduced, and as the water stills and the peppercorns float serenely to the bottom of the glass, again experienced within the vessel of silence, so the idea of stillness of thoughts and resulting relief can be suggested. In a world where billionaires send cars blaring out music on rockets into the darkness of space, it can be useful just to have your client sit silently and stare at an empty glass for a few minutes.

Metaphors and stories from previous chapters

Stories such as 'The Boy in the Sweet Shop' in Chapter 3 can be revised in order to highlight attachment to anxiety provoking thoughts while the 'Allowing Anxiety to Pass' metaphor in Chapter 5 provides powerful imagery and indirect suggestions for anxiety relief. As a useful exercise, it is worthwhile revisiting both of these and adapting them to suit specific cases of anxiety that you encounter as a therapist. It can also be a useful exercise to create stories and metaphors for your own experience of anxiety and how you visualise letting it go.

Humour and anxiety relief

Humour and drama can be utilised within the scope of therapeutic metaphors and stories surrounding anxiety relief and delivered under hypnosis. A client once imagined her anxiety as a giant green chicken with small wings and claws on its hands and feet. A story was created involving a girl and a cartoon version of the green chicken: each day the girl and the green chicken played tug-of-war and each day the chicken would pull her closer and closer to itself. Then one day the girl decided that she wouldn't be bullied by the chicken anymore and so she let go of the rope and watched as the chicken fell backwards and landed on its bottom. The girl walked away leaving the chicken rolling around on the floor.

The above story was recorded as a self-hypnosis audio. After two weeks of listening to the audio the client reported that her anxiety, while not disappearing completely, had reduced significantly.

Case Studies in working integratively with anxiety

Case study 1: Martha

Martha is a 28-year-old woman who has accessed therapy privately. Her presenting symptoms are that she feels that she experiences high anxiety. She describes her anxiety as her experiencing a palpitating heart, clammy hands, shallow quick breaths. Martha also talks about how sometimes she can experience a panic attack and feels that she might die. Martha finds it hard to sit still, she finds it difficult sleeping and also finds that she cannot stop thinking – she is constantly planning what she has to do. Martha is seeking therapy because she would like to feel calmer. The physical aspects to her anxiety are getting her down. Martha would also like to be less obsessed with creating lists in her daily life of things to do and she would like to be able to relax more. Martha currently lives with a 30-year-old boyfriend and has no children. Martha is keen to have weekly therapy sessions and she is prepared to come to therapy for as long as it takes for her to start feeling better.

When working integratively with Martha, the therapist in this case drew upon the five integrative concepts outlined previously in this book – *presence, emotional processing, attachment, thinking,* and our *conscious/unconscious* minds. The following is a summarised account of the therapist's work with Martha, focussing on these integrative concepts. It is important to note that whilst these concepts will be discussed chronologically, in practice they are not linear, rather, the therapist will focus on different concepts at different times within therapy, and will often focus on more than one concept during every therapy session.

When working with clients who experience high anxiety it is important to work with *presence*. *Presence* enables the client to build techniques that enable their bodies and their minds to slowly calm down. Through tuning into, and practising, *presence* clients can help their bodies and their minds to learn new, healthier, habits that basically slow down perceived time enabling them to be grounded in the moment rather than anxious about the future or their past. When working with Martha, the therapist engaged in some psychoeducation about the impacts of anxiety on our bodies and our minds. This can help to normalise the client's symptoms so that they are more understanding of what they are experiencing. The therapist also spoke to Martha about the notion of *presence* and how certain activities can be drawn on to help calm down our bodies and our minds so that we feel less anxious and more grounded. Martha seemed quite keen to learn new techniques that would enable her to experience *presence* and so the therapist introduced Martha to relaxed breathing, to mindfulness exercises and to some of the other techniques as set out in Chapter 1 of this book when discussing *presence*. Martha was motivated to change and so she earnestly practised these techniques on a daily basis. She found that the techniques really helped in calming down her body and her mind, although she continued to experience high anxiety and intrusive thoughts regularly. Martha found that she could tolerate her anxiety better through the use of *presence*, and she also found herself less stuck on producing endless lists of tasks to do.

As already discussed in this chapter, anxiety is a complex phenomenon and so a multidimensional approach is often required. Coming to our next integrative, *emotional processing,* the therapist explored any uncomfortable feelings that Martha was experiencing on a regular basis. Through open dialogue and good counselling skills, the therapist found that Martha's key emotions were fear and shame – Martha could at times feel very fearful, with her heart pounding and her body shaking, and she would also then feel ashamed of this fear response. The therapist asked Martha to visualise what these emotions looked like to her. For Martha, she imagined fear to be a box, a Pandora's box, within which were hidden dangers. The therapist explored with Martha what hidden dangers there were in this box, and encouraged Martha to take these fears out one by one, explore them and consider coping strategies for the things that she feared. Martha imagined her shame to be a bright red colour, and so the therapist asked Martha whether she could tone down this intense colour to something paler, as a way of managing the intensity of this emotion. Martha found this helpful. Martha was also asked about whether she could remember when she first felt so fearful and so ashamed. After considering this, Martha accessed a distinct memory of when she was 7 years old and her father left their home, abandoning them. Martha remembered her mum shaking from the stress and the fear, and Martha believed that she had taken on her mum's fear at this very early stage in her life. The shame came from a later memory at school when she accidentally had stood on a worm and a dinner lady had told her off for this. Understanding the early possible roots of her emotions helped Martha understand them and their power over her. She came to see that when experiencing fear or shame, what was being triggered were previous intense experiences of fear and shame in her childhood.

In relation to working with the integrative concept of *attachment*, the therapist explored with Martha her early relationships with her mother and father – she had no siblings. Martha had experienced rejection from her father and had not had any regular contact with him after he left her mother. Martha's mother was also emotionally unavailable to Martha because she was using alcohol as a way of managing her emotional distress. Martha could see how her experiences of these relationships laid the seeds of her own predominant attachment style – preoccupied – and Martha was encouraged in therapy to explore how a preoccupied attachment style might link to her anxiety. Martha started to see that she was desperate for other people's approval and this created a lot of anxiety in her to please others. Martha also could see how her preoccupied attachment style linked to her feelings of shame because when things did not turn out as she had planned, Martha would often blame herself and then feel embarrassed in front of others.

With respect to *thinking*, Martha was encouraged to keep a thought record to note situations that triggered her anxiety, to note what automatic thoughts she had in these situations. Martha began to discover that she had negative automatic thoughts which were not necessarily true, which fed into her anxiety – thoughts like 'I can't cope'. The therapist used CBT techniques in order to help Martha discover her underlying assumptions and unhealthy core beliefs, and Martha was encouraged to challenge these and to create more helpful ways of thinking. Martha found this really helpful in reducing her anxiety. Finally, therapeutic work with Martha's *conscious and unconscious* drew upon the TTM (as presented in Chapter 5). The therapist guided Martha through the levels of change as identified in the TTM and to explore which stage of change Martha was at concerning which level. Martha found this activity helpful as she could see that she was at different stages of change concerning the different aspects of her life – her situational issues, family issues, internal conflicts and so forth. Martha also found Maslow's hierarchy of needs a useful intervention as this helped her to see how her behaviours can be motivated by unconscious as much as by conscious processes. For example, Martha came to see that her need to feel loved was undermined by her anxiety around being rejected and as a result Martha would find herself depending on other people too much and being anxious about whether or not they liked her. Over time Martha became more understanding towards herself so that rather than trying to fight her anxiety she was able to explore it and develop coping strategies. After 14 sessions Martha felt ready to end therapy, her anxiety being significantly reduced.

Case study questions

How, and in what ways, are person-centred, CBT and relational modalities relevant in this case study?

In what ways do you think that an integrative approach empowered Martha to understand and then reduce her anxiety?

What interventions would you use with Martha and can you link these with the integrative concepts of presence, emotional processing, attachment, thinking, and our conscious/ unconscious minds?

Case study 2: Gillian

Gillian, a woman in her late thirties, came into therapy with an anxiety of going to the toilet and the obsessive fear that she couldn't cope in situations where toilets were absent or difficult to get to. Her toilet anxiety had developed over two years and had reached a point where she could no longer go to a gig or a sporting event where there were lots of people: in her world-view large crowds meant that it was difficult to get to a toilet in time. Whenever she found herself in situations where there was no toilet in close proximity she would experience physical shaking and nervousness to the point of almost 'blacking out'. She would start to feel the need to want to go to the toilet and this would cause her to panic. This cycle of anxiety resulted in social events becoming increasingly uncomfortable experiences, Gillian finding herself going to the toilet several times in quick succession. After discussing her fear during the consultation, Gillian determined that her anxiety was 'the fear of peeing myself in front of others'. The integrative concepts of *presence, emotional processing, attachment, thinking and the unconscious/ conscious aspects of the mind* were utilised within the course of therapy, outlined in a summary of the sessions below:

The first two sessions focussed upon the fear of Gillian peeing herself in front of other people and the anxiety of going to the toilet. Integrating the concept of *presence* as a starting point Gillian learned techniques that included diaphragmatic breathing, muscle relaxation and a metaphor based upon the cloud gazer meditation (see Chapter 1) was introduced, utilizing hypnosis in order to emphasise mindfulness and its impact upon self-awareness and relaxation. Gillian was guided through a series of memories where she had experienced her fear of going to the toilet, and in a relaxed dissociative manner, she observed herself on a TV screen in each of these situations. Through the integration of *presence*, Gillian was able to identify thoughts that precipitated the anxiety and the physical sensations of needing to go to the toilet as well as the emotions within her during these instances. Utilizing Baker's 'Model of Emotion' within the concept of *emotional processing*, Gillian was able to reinterpret many of her emotions as the anticipation or excitement of being at a gig or in a restaurant. This allowed the introduction of therapeutic interventions based around the *unconscious/conscious mind*: Gillian was able to reframe her experiences through mentally visualizing herself in situations feeling excited as opposed to anxious. A short hypnosis was included within both of these sessions that reinforced unconscious control of the bladder and learning new habits that reduced the bladder's *overenthusiasm*. By the third session, some four weeks after the initial session, Gillian reported that she no longer had the feeling of wanting to go to the toilet in social situations, while the fear of her bladder relaxing in the presence of others had disappeared. Her confidence had increased, and the session was focussed upon building her awareness of her confidence in dealing with future social situations: she had planned a trip to Milan and wanted to enjoy the experience.

However, something very interesting occurred during her trip to Milan which Gillian reported during her fourth session of therapy. While in Milan, the toilet anxiety and bladder insecurity had returned, although not as acutely as previously. Also, Gillian reported losing her confidence and feeling sad and lonely on her own. For the first time during therapy Gillian opened up with reference to a *relationship split that had occurred two years ago* at the same time that her toilet anxiety had started. For three years Gillian had pursued a long-distance relationship with an Italian man who lived in Milan and she had made plans to move to Italy and get married. While staying in Milan, her partner had unexpectedly ended the relationship. Gillian now felt that this episode provided the catalyst for all her difficulties.

Age regression under hypnosis was utilised during this session and Gillian was taken back to the relationship breakdown in Milan in a dissociative way in order to determine the true cause of her anxiety: *the anxiety that was masked by the fear of going to the toilet*. Gillian responded with the conclusion that she couldn't accept that the relationship had ended because she thought that they were perfect for each other. This was her real anxiety, underpinned with the obsessive thought: 'I've lost the perfect person for me.' A CBT approach was utilised during this and the following session, integrating the element of *thinking* within the therapeutic cycle. Gillian was able to consciously challenge the above thoughts as well as others based upon the notion that she would never meet anyone as good again and that she was not confident to meet new people. She was able to reframe these thoughts with positive affirmations that challenged their notion.

Session five focussed upon the integrative practice of *attachment*: Gillian was guided through a meditation that focussed upon her attachment to the thoughts that led to her anxiety; she was able to rationalise that she was not the sum of her thoughts and this allowed her to experience the pleasantness of letting go of the troublesome thoughts surrounding the relationship breakdown. Gillian took a recording of the meditation home and was instructed to listen to it daily.

Sessions six and seven were focussed upon *emotional processing*, both through the conscious lens of CBT and *unconsciously* utilizing metaphors and stories that introduced ideas such as letting go of the past, focussing on the present moment as well as looking forward to the possibility of meeting someone new. A state of hypnosis was induced when presenting the metaphors and stories, and positive experiences heightened through guided mental visualisations.

By session eight Gillian reported feeling more positive; she had begun to let the relationship go and was no longer anxious of going to the toilet. Boosting Gillian's self-esteem formed the focal point of this session and session nine. At the end of session nine, Gillian felt that her anxiety regarding the end of her relationship had been dealt with and that she no longer needed to come to therapy.

Case study questions

Based upon Gillian's experience of toilet anxiety, what types of metaphors or stories could you construct in order to facilitate unconscious processing of her fears?

How could you challenge Gillian's self-limiting thoughts of relationships that formed the obsessive core of her anxiety through integrative interventions ?

What types of interventions could you use in order to help Gillian overcome her relationship loss and how could you link these to the concepts of presence, emotional processing, attachment, thinking, and the unconscious/conscious mind?

Conclusion

This chapter has explored anxiety through an integrative lens, drawing upon person-centred, CBT, relational and hypnotherapeutic modalities. We have tried to convey the complexities to anxiety and have made links to existential questions. We have used stories to help demonstrate some of the challenges around working with clients who have anxiety, and we have distinguished between normal and neurotic anxiety. We have also presented case studies that demonstrate how we work with clients integratively – by using presence, emotional processing, attachment, thinking, and our conscious/unconscious minds. We hope that readers have gained a sense of the uniqueness of experiencing anxiety for each and every individual, and that we have provided some useful tools through which we can work with clients. Interestingly, clients with anxiety can often also present with low mood and/or depression. Hence the next chapter, Chapter 8, looks at depression through an integrative lens.

References

Allen, R.P. (2004) *Scripts and Strategies in Hypnotherapy: The Complete Works*. Carmarthen: Crown House Publishing.

American Psychiatric Association (2013). *Diagnostic and Statistical Manual of Mental* Disorders, 5th edition. Washington, DC: American Psychiatric Association.

Briers, S. (2009) *Brilliant CBT*. Harlow: Pearson Education.

Burton, E. (2018). 'A philosophical reading of *Hamlet*'. Unpublished doctoral dissertation. Leicester: De Montfort University.

Cage, J. (1961) *Silence: Lectures and Writings*. Middletown, CT: Wesleyan University Press.

Crawford, M. (2015) *The World Beyond Your Head*. London: Penguin.

Dally, P. & Watkins, M. J. (1986) *Psychology and Psychiatry: An Integrated Approach*. London: Hodder and Stoughton.

Donnellan, D. (2002). *The Actor and the Target*. London: Nick Hern Books.

Erickson, M.H. (1998) *Life Reframing in Hypnosis. The Seminars, Workshops, and Lectures of Milton H. Erickson*. London: Free Association Books.

Greenberger, D. & Padesky, C. (2015) *Mind over Mood*, 2nd edition. London: The Guilford Press.

May, R. (1977) *The Meaning of Anxiety*. New York: Norton & Company.

Nejad, L. & Volny, K. (2008) *Treating Stress and Anxiety. A Practitioner's Guide to Evidence-Based Approaches*. Carmarthen: Crown House Publishing.

Pritchett, J. (2009) 'What silence taught John Cage: The story of 4′ 33″ – The piano in my life' [online]. Available at: http://rosewhitemusic.com/piano/writings/silence-taught-john-cage/#ftn16 (accessed 8 February 2018).

Spiegel, D. (1989) 'Hypnosis in the treatment of victims of sexual abuse', *Psychiatric Clinics of North America*, vol. 12, pp. 295–305.

Wells, A. (2011) *Cognitive Therapy of Anxiety Disorders*. Chichester: John Wiley and Sons.

Wilding, C. & Milne, A. (2008) *Teach yourself CBT*. London: Hodder Education.

Chapter 8

Working integratively with depression

It's like being in a very deep, dark, hole; but you also get comfort in that it's a place you know and want to stay there.

Danielle Boshoff, 'Diagnosis Bipolar II' (personal journal)

Introduction

As clinicians we would argue that depression has been one of the most challenging of human experiences for us to work with. Therapeutic practitioners can often feel overwhelmed themselves when faced with supporting clients who are experiencing significant depressive symptoms. It can become very difficult seeing a client regularly without necessarily seeing them move out of any depressive state that they may be experiencing. Working with depression inevitably is not particularly solutions-focussed and so the satisfaction that we would ordinarily receive from clients as we see them change, grow and work with their mental health challenges is not necessarily experienced when working with clients who are experiencing low moods and/or clinically diagnosed depressive disorders.

At the same time, however, working with clients experiencing depression can be incredibly creative, and we argue that through an integrative lens we are empowered as practitioners to maximise creative responses to working with depression. In this chapter we briefly look at the complex manifestations of depression, and then consider depression through person-centred, CBT, relational and hypnotherapeutic modalities. We also use stories and metaphors to help illustrate our integrative approach because it can be extremely helpful when working with clients experiencing depression and/or low mood to use stories and metaphors. We also present case studies of clients with depression that we have supported and we make links with the integrative concepts that we explored earlier on in this book: presence, emotional processing, attachment, thinking, and our conscious/unconscious minds. Firstly, we begin with a story.

The girl with a ghost

It was a cold wintry day and Luella was walking to college, taking the same route that she would take every day. The pavements were covered in cuttingly bright white snow and a bitter cold wind from the East was blowing, so that Luella's coat and hood were flapping around like caged crows. 'Maybe it would be easier if I just walked out in front of a bus' – this thought appeared in Luella's consciousness. 'Then I wouldn't have to keep struggling.' Luella had woken up that morning wanting to stay in bed. Every part of her young and agile body had screamed out at her, 'don't move'. It had actually been Luella's mother who had got her out of bed and helped get her ready for college, just like she had always done. During these moments with her mum, Luella would tell her mum, 'I'm fine, just tired', never revealing the deep, hidden and unbearable inner emptiness that Luella experienced.

Luella crossed the main road keeping herself safe and as she approached the periphery of the small park that was on the edge of her college Luella noticed a grey, goulish, figure hovering above a park bench. Luella knew who this was, her ghost, a ghost that she had named Winston. Winston was your classic, stereotypical ghost – a kind of floating blob, no legs or feet but he did have two arms with hands, a head and two eyes and a mouth, no nose. The only communication that Winston would make with Luella is that he would raise his left hand when he saw her, and so as Luella passed Winston she could see him holding up his hand; for some reason this day Luella noticed that Winston was smiling ominously at her – or had she just imagined this? Winston was, essentially, Luella's chronic depression.

When visiting her therapist that day Luella described this ghost-like creature, his silent yet frightening presence. Luella's therapist encouraged her to draw Winston, and then she encouraged Luella to think about ways in which she would like to deal with Winston. Luella picked up a red pen and began to draw a wall, brick by brick, around Winston. Luella also used a blue pen to shrink Winston down in size. Luella also decided that sometimes she would like to be kind to Winston, and so she drew him a magic rug which meant that he would be able to fly around the planet without using his own inorganic energy. Luella believed that Winston would also enjoy the thick alpaca material that the rug was made from. Luella left the therapy session that day feeling that she might, just might, tolerate Winston better, and in this way experience less self-harming and/or suicidal thoughts.

The fellow who drove his Ferrari into a black hole

Steven was a successful businessman who had sold his company in his early fifties. Retired for several years, he came to therapy with the presenting problem of constant pain in the back of his head. MRI scans had revealed no physical abnormalities; this led Steven to consider that his problem may have a psychological origin. At the start of his therapy, Steven reported unrelenting tiredness as a result of constant pain and poor sleeping habits: he would often wake up very early in the morning and find it difficult to get back to sleep. For years he had worked 18-hour days in order to build up his company, often resorting to completing paperwork late into the evening while he was lying in bed. Sometimes he would wake up in the middle of the night and ruminate over a problem that needed solving at work. As he recalled these years he came to the conclusion that the sleep deprivation had begun as his business grew exponentially and he had never addressed the problem due to lack of time. He also felt that he hadn't spent enough time with his wife or son.

During subsequent treatment for pain management, Steven mentioned that he had been depressed for many years. Reflecting upon his life, Steven concluded that his depression began many years ago when he was running his business, but again, he did not have the resources to deal with it at the time. He talked about the 'dark black days' that he had experienced over the last two decades and how he was stuck in a 'big black hole.' Steven felt that he was held by the past, that it gripped him with 'an iron fist.' His mother had suffered depression while his father had never recognised Steven's achievements within his career. One particular memory that stood out for Steven was when he bought a Ferrari and drove it to his father's house for the very first time, excited about showing it off. Upon seeing the car, Steven's father responded with 'What did you buy that for?' Before Steven could reply his father went back into the house closing the door behind him.

Because of his father's influence Steven never felt good about himself; he could not seem to move forward. With each subsequent session Steven opened up more and more and he was able to consider the different roles that he had played throughout his life: the role of husband, father, businessman, son. He had reached a point in his life whereby, rather than planning for the future and having goals, he would find himself ruminating upon the negative memories and past associations experienced with his parents. His depression brought on the feeling of guilt: guilt that he wasn't there for his mother when she had died unexpectedly.

Gradually, as Steven focussed on mindfulness, muscle relaxation and dissociative techniques for pain management, the pain in the back of his head diminished and the focus of therapy shifted towards his depression. The therapist focussed upon shifting Steven's awareness towards the roles he had played throughout his life and Steven came to the conclusion that his biggest role, that of successful businessman, was also his most superficial one. He had played the role of *successful businessman* in order to live up to his father's expectations. Steven understood that these expectations would never be achieved but had played the role nonetheless. He had a family to look after and bills to pay. Steven realised that, for the last two decades, he had lost a sense of self. Because he hadn't expressed his true self for such a long time, his own identity had become fuzzy and formless. He described it like an out of focus photograph with faded sepia tones and filled with lens flare.

Another characteristic of Steven's depression was his inability to cope with change of any nature. He wanted to sell his house, downsize and live by the sea but the thought of this paralyzed him with fear. He found it difficult to get up in the mornings, especially when chores needed doing. Sometimes he considered suicide as an option. Other moments were spent in bed staring at the ceiling.

Helping Steven through his depression took many sessions over a long period of time, employing a broad range of interventions encompassing:

*   Mindfulness and breathing techniques
*   Mental rehearsal exercises for shifting the dynamics of depression
*   Acceptance of the uncertainty of existence
*   Awareness of 'black or white' thinking and cognitive distortions
*   Storytelling and metaphors to challenge the concept of absolute truth attached to thoughts and beliefs
*   Exercises for teaching discrimination between thoughts and situations surrounding depression

The above strategies evolved around Steven's unique experience of depression. Steven imagined filling the black hole with all the items he had bought over the years in order to impress his father. He imagined driving the Ferrari into the black hole. He imagined throwing all the expensive clothing that he had bought but never worn into the hole. The feeling of having to prove himself to his father lessened through time. Steven sold his Ferrari and replaced it with a far more modest model of car. This felt like a 'huge weight off my shoulders'. He imagined filling the black hole with negative thoughts and ruminations that would in the past have led to depression and a sense of hopelessness. Being able to distance himself from his thoughts and to discriminate between thoughts made him feel happier and more empowered. He was able

to recognise that he was not the sum of his thoughts and that a thought such as 'I am not good enough' can be re-evaluated, challenged and replaced with a positive thought associated with, for example, a pleasant memory from the past.

Steven began to practise positive mental visualisation techniques on a daily basis, focussing on goal setting and imagining his life without depression. Past memories, when Steven had felt better, were evoked and experienced. He began to keep a self-care diary where he had written ten very simple things that he could do in a day and which could afford him some joy: going for a walk, having a coffee, reading a newspaper. Each day he would endeavour to tick two or three items off the list as he undertook these pleasant activities.

After several months he reported feeling a sense of motivation to achieve things. He began to look forwards, signing up to a language course. His large house was put up for sale and he visited smaller seaside properties advertised in estate agents. He started to feel hopeful about the future, and although occasionally experiencing low moods and periods of anxiety, was able to recognise and discriminate between thoughts that in the past he would have considered to be absolute truths, for example, 'I'm not good enough' or 'I'll never be able to prove to my dad that I'm successful'. This shift in the ability to discriminate and accept the unpredictability and uncertainty of life allowed Steven to lift the guilt of not being fully present with his mum when she died.

Towards the end of therapy, Steven had sold his house and bought a dream home by the sea. As he opened the door and stepped out of the therapist's office for the last time, Steven turned and smiled. 'Don't waste your life building a monster of a business that you have to feed with money.' The therapist took his advice.

Depression: Causes and symptoms

The above examples illustrate the rich tapestry of experiences associated with depressive states. Here are stories of chronic fatigue and hopelessness, despondency and desolation. There are ghosts and black holes, emptiness and iron fists. There are curtains drawn and bottles of whisky sunk. There are roles and characters unfulfilled and superficial. *Who am I? What is my purpose?* There are distortions of the concept of self. There is silence and the notion of sudden ending. Somewhere in the gloom, fear lurks ready to strut. There is lack of meaning. There is remorse. There is isolation. There is punishment and self-harming, guilt and shame. There is non-emotion and non-feeling, self-destruction and the inability to construct. There is death. There is the need for death.

Causes for depression can be broadly categorised within biological, psychological and social aspects and if we cast a deeper eye at a person's existence then age, environment and lifestyle are added complications within this experience. As a therapist it is useful to be open to causative factors, an awareness that may provide some guidance for understanding our clients' symptoms. Yet it is also equally important to take a step back from the painting and observe it from such a place that the brushstrokes and textures form the essence of the scene. Causes are part of the story but not all of it. Just as language develops organically through time so the experience of depression can mutate and evolve from causative events or situations, and as therapists we have to be open to evolution. Within our integrative approach, the concept of *presence* is essential in building a strong therapeutic alliance. In Luella's case, *presence* allowed for the creation of metaphors that reframed and disempowered her own unique experience of suffering as a hovering ghost. With depression, changes from session to session may be infinitesimally small (or indeed if we consider the view from the other end of the street, monumentally large) and presence provides us with the awareness and flexibility to deal with the ebbs and flows of our client's experience.

Depression can be associated with tiredness, despondency, lack of energy and motivation, and as Steven explained, 'a loss of mojo'. Luella referred to her own inertia as an 'unbearable inner emptiness'. Sleep deprivation and insomnia can result in fatigue and ultimately manifestation of depressive states. Depressed clients may report poor sleeping habits and, even after a good night's sleep, of feeling exhausted when their eyes open. Once rumination beds in it can be very difficult to switch off the mind, especially a mind filled with worry and hopelessness, and many clients report overthinking and going over thoughts again and again as primary causes for insomnia. Hypersomnia, when an individual may experience trouble with staying awake during the day, can also be a presenting problem.

But it can be the roles we play out in our lives themselves that cause the very exhaustion and mental and physical shutdown that Steven described in his symptoms. Acting out a character that we know we are *not* results in conflict. Yet each day the curtain opens to bright lights and applause. Actor and comedian Jim Carrey describes his own battle with identity, and ultimately depression, when he refers to his past life as 'They're all characters that I played, including Jim Carrey' ('Jim Carrey – What it all means – One of the most eye opening speeches', 2017). Carrey reframes the sense of depression as *deep-rest*; the mind and body, exhausted through playing an unfulfilled character across a lifetime, shut down and rest. The lights are dimmed, the curtains close and the weary actor drags his feet across the spit and sawdust, disappearing from the stage in silence.

Like different coloured strands of yarn swept into a ball, so existence and complexity weave together to form the fabric of humanity. In the western world we fill our lives with clutter. There is a tendency to pack in as much as we can but ultimately most of what we do, or the things that happen to us, does not have inherent meaning. Macbeth alludes to the insubstantial fleeting perception of the existence of man when he declares: 'Out, out brief candle! Life's but a walking shadow, a poor player that struts and frets his hour upon the stage, and then is heard no more.

It is a tale told by an idiot, full of sound and fury, signifying nothing' (Shakespeare, *Macbeth*, 5.5.18–27). The very nature of life and the inexplicability of happenings challenge our need to attach beliefs to things. Humans need to believe. Believing fuels our belief systems. The Shaman believes in power animals and spirit guides, Christians in resurrection and forgiveness of sins, Buddhists in the Four Noble Truths. We tell stories and we believe the stories. We think thoughts and we believe the thoughts. It is the thoughts surrounding our belief systems that keep us within the grip of depression: 'The world is a bad place', 'I'll never be a good teacher', 'Finding a job is impossible'. For most of his adult life Steven thought that he wasn't good enough; his thoughts created an existence where he could never do enough to show his father that he was capable. This would still be the case even if Steven had a million successful companies under his wing. Challenging Steven's worldview and the baggage he carried from his thoughts, and more importantly, changing the perception of his thoughts from absolute truths into less rigid beliefs or even non-beliefs, formed an intrinsic part of his convalescence.

The inability to build a future is a theme that resonates often with depressive states. Sometimes it may not be possible even to plan a future of getting out of bed and feeding oneself; no doubt Luella would attest to this. But the unexpected can happen in therapy and change is only a second away, even less. Think of a bird with a broken wing hiding under the shadows of a huge skyscraper, frightened and hungry. A kindly person one day may stumble upon the bird and take it home. The bird is given water and food and warmth and eventually the wing mends and the bird is set free. After a few moments of puzzled posturing the bird remembers that it can fly. The wings flap and the body lifts and it soars past the shadows of the skyscraper, above and beyond it, before being swallowed up by the blue. Remembering can profoundly affect depressive states: a client can be taken to moments in their past when they didn't feel the way that they do now and they can learn from this experience. Learning from the past can provide motivation for the future.

There exist a lifetime of tales locked behind the eyes of someone that stares through you, lost inside themselves. Perhaps it is the story of a boy and a father. One day the mother suggests that the father take his son fishing and so the father says 'Come on son, let's go fishing.' And off they go but the father leaves the boy sitting on the edge of the harbour while he takes the boat out and fishes all day on his own. Another time the mother suggests that the father take the boy to town and so the father says 'Come on son, let's go into town.' And off they go but after a while the boy is separated from his father. He finds himself inside the foyer of an old Savoy Cinema, feeling anxious and alone. He waits in the foyer but his father does not appear, and so he grows more anxious. Eventually an usherette finds the boy, and he tells her that he is lost. The usherette holds the boy's hand and leads him out of the cinema. The boy sees his father on the opposite side of the road but his father does not seem to be looking for him. In fact his father seems to be quite happy on his own. The boy grows into a man who struggles with anxiety and depression: if he isn't depressed, he is anxious, and if he is depressed, he isn't anxious. He finds himself disconnected and distant with friends, with his wife and children. He finds himself searching for who he is. He stares at you as though you don't exist.

Person-centred approaches to depression

Given the complexities to depression, and factoring in the uniqueness of every human being, person-centredness is the foundational basis to supporting clients. Unpicking diagnoses, symptoms, experiences, perceptions, meaning – person-centred approaches allow us to do this and much more. Trainee therapists are often taught to approach working with depression through a CBT based lens, especially as there is a strong research evidence base supporting CBT based approaches to depression. We argue that whilst CBT approaches can be an important element when supporting clients who are experiencing depressive symptoms, CBT should not be the foundation to our practice, rather we advocate for person-centredness as being the foundation. This means that it is important not to immediately be suggesting tasks and activities that a depressed client can undertake during the week. This is because a client may simply not yet be in an emotionally and psychologically resilient enough state in order to be task/activity oriented. Rather, we argue that it is crucial to explore with the client the subtle and not-so-subtle ways in which they are experiencing depression. As therapists we need to be able to understand as best as we can the depth, intensity and severity of the different physiological, emotional, behavioural and psychological symptoms that clients are dealing with. We can facilitate any meaning that clients construct for themselves regarding their depressive symptoms, and we can help clients to explore and sometimes question the usefulness of some of these meanings. As therapists it is important ourselves to be mindful of whether we have ever ourselves experienced severe/moderate or low levels of low mood and/or depression and the significance or not of this personal experience when it comes to trying to understand the physio-psycho-emotional spaces that our clients are experiencing. We have seen too many clients who say to us that previous counselling experiences were not particularly effective for them because they felt too rushed into engaging in activities when simply getting out of bed was a massive challenge for them. Therefore, we argue that person-centred approaches are the foundations of working integratively with clients who have depression and/or low mood.

As demonstrated in previous chapters, person-centred approaches involve cultivating presence so that the therapist is able to enter freely into relational depth with a client. This is a way of being within the therapeutic relationship (Mearns & Thorne, 1988). This enables the therapist to empathise with the client, to moment by moment be in relation with the client, and through providing the core conditions (Rogers, 1961) enabling the client to explore what it is that they are experiencing – in this case what is their own unique experiencing of depression, and if applicable allowing the client to construct or deconstruct any meaning they associate with depression. Depression is not necessarily a state but a process – in flux – and therefore under continual change and creation, no matter how small or subtle. Sometimes clients can gain comfort from gaining insight that their depression is not this fixed and ungiving state but rather can fluctuate and can involve subtle variations. This can help clients to perhaps experience some control over their depressive symptoms, at least for some of the time. The following are some useful exploratory questions that can be used to help clients better understand the depressive/low moods that they experience:

> Can you tell me a little about how you feel when you say you are depressed?
> Are there any images that you can think of that help capture how you feel?
> How does your low mood/depression impact on your daily life?
> Are there times in the day when you feel better/worse?
> Can you remember when you first started to feel like this?
> Are there any strategies – helpful and unhelpful – that you use that help you cope with your low mood/depression?
> Can you think of any strategies that might help you to cope with the depression/low mood?

> Can you tell me about any thoughts you have whilst you are in a depressed mood? Can you identify any patterns of thinking?

The above are just some useful exploratory questions. In drawing on these questions as a therapist it is possible to begin to gain some sense of how knowledgeable the client is about their low mood/depression and also to gain a sense of whether the client is using any helpful coping strategies. Any images of their low mood/depression that a client constructs can be helpfully used in order to help the client to begin to experience their low mood/depression as being separate from them, as something that is not necessarily beyond their control and not something all-encompassing. As the story of the girl with a ghost demonstrates, metaphors can help clients to capture what it is that is affecting them, thereby giving solidity to something as ephemeral as depression. It can be useful to then encourage clients to explore how they might relate to the particular image that they have created that symbolises their low mood/depression – whether they might like to give comfort to this image, or draw a boundary around it or shrink it down in size so that it no longer feels as big to them. This approach is exemplified well by Matthew Johnstone's (2007) book *I Had a Black Dog*, which has received much praise for its ability to provide insight into depression and how to live with this.

Clients experiencing depression and/or low mood can be overwhelmed by feelings of guilt, shame, loss. Guilt may be guilt around not being able to do the things that previously they would have been able to do – housework, going to work, gardening etc. Shame might be the shame that they feel with family, friends, former work colleagues for not being their 'former jovial or sociable selves'. We have seen clients ashamed of the fact that they avoid friends because they do not want their friends to see how much they have changed since experiencing depression. Clients will often talk about not experiencing fun or joy in anything anymore. Person-centred approaches can help clients to explore those aspects to themselves or their lives that have become less pronounced after experiencing low mood/depression. Through 'sustained empathic enquiry' (Stolorow & Atwood, 1992: 33), person-centred therapists enable clients to explore aspects of themselves that they feel have become more pronounced since experiencing depression. It may be that for some clients it is important for them to redefine their values because the things that they used to place a lot of value on – career, socialising, material wealth – may no longer have meaning for them. Loss may be part of this – the loss of a former life, of certain friends and relationships. Thus, depression might be thought of as a personal journey, and we as therapists can help clients raise their own awareness and understanding of their journeying. Some clients find it useful to mark their journey through symbolic representations. For example, one client bought a myriad of yellow tulips and placed these around her house as a marker of her experiencing severe depression for the previous eight months of her life. Another client considered having a tattoo as a marker of having survived a severe depressive episode. These symbolic acts can be a powerful way of lifting any guilt or shame that a client may be experiencing. The symbolic markers can be an important mechanism through which acknowledgement is made of the client's experience and survival. Thus, depression/low mood do not have to be hidden away and silenced, but rather can be brought out into the open. Of course, there are multiple layers of openness and it is for clients to negotiate what extent of openness they wish to have in relation to their depression.

CBT in relation to depression

Whilst person-centred approaches can lay strong foundations for therapeutic work with clients experiencing depression, CBT-based approaches are also often an important strand to approaching depression through an integrative lens. Aaron Beck (1967) discovered that patients experiencing depression had certain thinking styles that were similar. Thus, by being alert to these thinking patterns therapists can help raise awareness within clients of their thinking processes, and can facilitate clients learning and utilising helpful thought. Beck (1967) found the following patterns in thinking amongst depressed patients: thinking negative thoughts about the self (for example, viewing oneself as helpless or inadequate or worthless), negative thoughts about the world (for example, viewing the world that one inhabits as having problems that cannot be overcome), and negative thoughts about the future (for example, seeing the future as hopeless, as something that cannot be improved). Encouraging clients to keep a thought record can help raise their awareness of their thinking, and clients can be encouraged to consider alternative thoughts to those thoughts that might be deemed as unhelpful. Some clients experiencing depression find that keeping a gratitude journal can be helpful, reminding them that there are small and simple things that perhaps they can be grateful for. We often encourage our clients to keep a record of three small things every day that they feel they can be grateful for – these being as simple as the sunshine, the sky, clouds, grass etc. For clients experiencing significantly reduced appetite we suggest a food diary. Thus, we encourage clients to schedule in what they will be eating and at what time each day. Some clients find that by scheduling in food that they really like this can be motivational for them to eat even though they may not necessarily be experiencing hunger.

As discussed previously in this book, CBT approaches have a strong behavioural component, and so clients with depression and/or low mood can be encouraged to consider activities that they can do on a daily and/or weekly basis. Some clients can find it helpful to actually write down in their diaries or on their mobile phone apps the actual activities that they will try and undertake as a way of motivating themselves. Activities not only get clients physically moving – rather than simply lying in bed or sitting on a chair all day – but can make them feel better. Clients often talk about how outdoor activities help lift their moods, how physical exercise can also improve their mood. At the same time, simply completing one task can be an important confidence builder for clients whose depression has led them to be fearful and/or full of self-doubt. One client spoke about how even just emptying the dishwasher can be a significant activity when he is experiencing severe depression. Sometimes it can be too overwhelming for clients to do more than one thing, but even completing one task can be hugely significant. Some clients experience rumination as part of their depression. They may spend hours a day going over past events, unable to let go of these psychologically and emotionally. By encouraging clients to undertake activities and tasks this can be a helpful distraction for them, interrupting their ruminating minds, forcing their minds to focus on something else, and this can be extremely helpful. As a therapist it is important to acknowledge the effort that clients with depression have had to make in order to complete even the most simple of tasks. When experiencing severe depressive symptoms, even emptying the dishwasher can feel like rowing across the Atlantic Ocean! Thus, giving positive feedback and encouragement in a non-patronising way, from an empathic position, can be extremely motivational for clients, positively reinforcing their actions.

Relational therapeutic modalities and depression

So far we have explored person-centred and CBT modalities that we might integrate when working with clients who are experiencing depression and/or low mood. Another important therapeutic modality that can help shed further light on depression, and that also potentially provides useful tools when supporting clients, is, broadly speaking, relational therapy. As the term implies, here the focus is on relationships – the client's relationships with key caregivers when they were children, and the client's current significant relationships. It is important to explore with a client their current and historical family dynamics in order to get a sense of how supportive their relationships were with their main caregivers as they were growing up, and how supportive their relationships are now. Working with clients who are experiencing depression does not necessarily involve deeply exploring their childhoods, but it is important that as therapists we have a sense of the client's attachment styles and the kind of attachment styles their caregivers demonstrated with them. This is because a client with a family history of secure attachment is likely to be more resilient to managing their depressive symptoms than a client with other kinds of attachment styles. At the same time, a client with a predominantly secure attachment base is likely to be able to maintain supportive relationships as an adult and is thereby perhaps more likely to be able to draw upon a wider circle of family and friends for support. A client with a secure attachment style is also perhaps more likely to be able to demonstrate meta-thinking – thinking about thinking – and thus is more naturally inclined to explore their depressive symptoms and episodes without being emotionally overwhelmed. For example, one client who one of the authors of this book was seeing arrived for their assessment and spoke about a number of symptoms linked commonly to depression. During the assessment the therapist explored their childhood background and discovered that this client's father had died when she was aged 15. The death itself, however, was not unexpected as her father had been of ill-health for a long time. At the same time, this client spoke about her mum, with whom she got on with well and had found supportive and the client said that she had had a happy childhood. It may be the case that the death of the client's father was part of a number of factors causing her depression, but at the same time, knowing that this client had experienced a positive childhood and currently had a supportive network of family and friends around her, influenced the therapeutic work that was undertaken with this client. Relational aspects really matter and as therapists it is important for us to be able to tune into these with our clients very quickly (see Gilbert and Orlans, 2011 for an integrative aspect to developmental/relational issues).

A client who has experienced a less supportive, and even traumatic, childhood background with their main caregivers will have attachment-related challenges in addition to any depressive symptoms that they may be experiencing. For example, a client with depression whose childhood was experienced through the lens of rejection by her caregivers, is likely to bring this sense of rejection into therapeutic sessions when working with their depression. It is important for a therapist to be aware of dynamics between themselves and their clients, dynamics that might be linked to historical relational dynamics, on both the part of the client and the therapist. Life themes (indeed schemas if seen through the lens of CBT) around rejection that the client has might be helping to feed their depression. It is important for the therapist to have a sense of these dynamics as these will influence the nature and process of any therapeutic encounters. It is also important to consider how depression can affect relationships – see for example books by Johnstone (2009) and Kulakowski (2014).

Sometimes depression can play an important bonding role between family members within any family system. A client may be terrified of changing – reducing their depressive symptoms – as in their minds this could change and even jeopardise current relationships that they have with family members and even friends. This may create significant resistance within clients to actually manage their depression and/or low mood. The following short story about a boy who cried himself a river reflects the family dynamics that can be associated with depression, something that therapists need to be aware of.

The boy who cried himself a river

The first time ever the boy cried was standing by the side of the ditch into which his mother's coffin was slowly being lowered. The boy had unusual tears, like a sudden and heavy shower of raindrops hitting the ground, the teardrops then weaving their way down the hillside upon which the cemetery stood. The next time the boy cried was as his father and step mother began shouting at him and striking him with a bicycle pump. This time the boy's tears were like torrential rain, soaking the ground below and racing down, down, down into the abyss. Another time the boy cried was after escaping from his home for good and having to sleep on his own in a derelict outhouse far away from anywhere. The boy was cold and hungry and missing his beloved mum, and at that point he could not hold his tears in anymore, and so a monsoon broke out of the boy's piercing blue eyes, and it took three days for the flooding to subside, the water slowly trickling away. The boy was so entranced by the sound of the trickling water that he followed its course, and discovered a deep, gushing river some ten miles away. The boy decided that this is where he would build a new home and life for himself, and during the next few years he grew up, married and had children. But this young man was unable to spend time with his wife and children because he was so emotionally drawn to the deep blue river that lay next to his house. The young man would go there every day and he would sit by the water alone, imagining what it might be like to jump into the river and be completely submersed, his existence becoming one with the river of his tears. As his two children became older they too ventured down to this river, a river familiar to them, for the river was created by their father's deep losses and emotional pain, and they understood these well. All three of them would hang out by the river, their senses intoxicated by the sound and smell of the water, leaving them no space in their lives to connect with, and experience, different sensations, terrains and relationships. Over the course of time, the three of them lay down their roots on the river banks, and that is where they stolidly remained for the rest of their lives.

Hypnotherapy and depression

Although the feelings and experiences that depressed clients bring with them into therapy can feel like we are dealing with the barren eroded *badlands* of Nebraska, there nevertheless exist opportunities for cultivating the seemingly uncultivable through the application of hypnotherapy in the treatment of depression. Michael Yapko's (2001) strategies for treating depression with hypnosis build expectancy through metaphors that focus upon future possibilities and identifying resources that promote motivation and action towards setting and achieving specific goals. Yapko argues that 'cognitive skills can be learned more easily with hypnosis as a vehicle of experiential learning' (Yapko, 2001: 46). Through improved cognitive functioning clients can learn to step outside of their beliefs, becoming the observer as it were, and in this way are better able to learn which beliefs within their internal representation of the world are destructive and which are useful for enhancing factors in life such as relationships and physical wellbeing. Yapko bases his therapy upon goal orientation and skill building, identifying and highlighting through hypnosis the steps that a client can take to lift themselves above the hopelessness and doubt. This opens up a world of possibility and opportunity, otherwise untapped.

Earlier in this chapter a metaphor of a bird remembering that it could fly was presented to the reader. Everything was there for the bird in order to lift itself beyond the skyscraper; all it had to do was *remember*. Utilising the phenomena of age regression and age progression within hypnosis we can take our clients back to moments in their lives before depression while subsequently *soaring* into the future to a point beyond their suffering. According to Spiegel and Spiegel (2004), the process of age regression and the 'strength' of hypnosis – relating to the level of trance that an individual experiences – can be so immersive that the individual relives these moments as though at that age. Often depressed clients are so embedded within a past orientation that taking them *before* these memories and experiences can prove surprisingly useful. In the same way, age progression offers an opportunity for building expectancy for change along the lines of Yapko's metaphoric approach. In short, making up a bright future creates a positive metaphor.

Challenging chronic negative thinking patterns can reframe, challenge and convert the belief of a present (and concept of past) set in stone into something more malleable and flexible. The integration of hypnotherapy and cognitive-behavioural therapy (cognitive-behavioural hypnotherapy) offers the scope for positive change through enhanced imagery and greater unconscious thinking provided by the state of hypnosis (Kirsch, Montgomery & Sapirstein, 1995). Alladin and Alibhai (2007) found that hypnosis combined with cognitive behavioural therapy (CBT) reduced depression, anxiety and hopelessness in individuals to a greater extent compared with those undergoing CBT alone. Central to this approach is the integration of skills based around mood monitoring, thought awareness and creative visualisations as proposed by Chapman (2014). Through hypnosis, clients can be taught to recognise and challenge distorted and destructive thoughts as soon as they arise, offering the potential to disarm their power through non-attachment while shifting focus upon positive experiences such as past accomplishments or future goals. Patterns of rumination can be disrupted, and as a semblance of a future starts to form, opportunities for goals and metaphoric concepts can be introduced in order to foster motivation from beyond the shadows of the skyscraper.

Anything that draws the client outside of themselves, such as reflective journals and self-care diaries can prove useful as an adjunct to hypnotherapeutic modalities addressing depressive states. It is good to talk, but in times of solitude and suffering, it is useful to write thoughts down, to challenge and reframe negative thinking habits and destructive self-labelling. Utilizing hypnosis a client can be taken along a journey where they experience themselves expressing a future based upon any positive thoughts, feelings and emotions that they have outlined in a journal, diary or any other vehicle for self-expression. A future can be created and reinforced through the deeply relaxed states that hypnosis fosters. Reinforcement of positive states can be provided through audio recordings of the hypnosis sessions that clients can listen to at home while post-hypnotic suggestions can be included as triggers for eliciting positive mental and physical states.

Case studies of working integratively with depression

Case study 1: Dzintra

Dzintra is a 50-year-old, married Asian woman, with three grown up children. When Dzintra was 25 years old her husband had an affair and separated from Dzintra, leaving her alone to bring up her three children. For Dzintra, her husband having an affair and leaving her is a culturally shameful event that she has never got over. She has spent the last 25 years ruminating over that day that her husband left her for another woman. Whenever she thinks about what happened to her, she begins to cry, as though the incident happened only yesterday. Ever since she separated from her husband Dzintra has experienced severe depression. On bad days she struggles to leave her bed and she can lie there crying to herself all day as she ruminates over having been abandoned by her husband. During these times she has no appetite and no motivation to do anything. Dzintra feels very grateful that one of her daughters has chosen to stay with her, to continue living with her rather than getting married and moving out of the house. This particular daughter will cook for Dzintra and will clean the house and will take Dzintra to any appointments that she has with her GP or psychiatrist. Dzintra has accessed counselling from within a community centre close to her house because part of her wants to feel better, less depressed. During her initial counselling sessions Dzintra talks about how she feels that she does nothing of any worth during the day, and the guilt that she feels over her daughter staying at home with her to look after her. Dzintra also talks about the shame that she feels as a result of having been abandoned by her husband. Dzintra also talks about how she doesn't feel any joy or pleasure in any activities that she does do, even on those better days when she is able to go to the local shops to buy food.

When working integratively with Dzintra, the therapist in this case drew upon the five integrative concepts outlined previously in this book – *presence, emotional processing, attachment, thinking,* and our *conscious/unconscious* minds. The following is a summarised account of the therapist's work with Dzintra, focussing on these integrative concepts. As mentioned in Chapter 7, it is important to note that whilst these concepts will be discussed chronologically, in practice they are not linear, rather, the therapist will focus on different concepts at different times within therapy, and will often focus on more than one concept during every therapy session.

Presence can be an important aspect to therapeutic work with clients who are experiencing depression. As Dzintra's case demonstrates, clients with depression may talk about the lack of pleasure that they gain from everyday life. Working with *presence* can enable a therapist to empower a client – step by step, often very slowly – to begin to gain some enjoyment no matter how small. In Dzintra's case, the therapist brought a small box of raisins to a session. The therapist explored what it might be like to eat a raisin mindfully, focussing on the sensations on a moment by moment basis. Dzintra agreed that she would like to try eating a raisin mindfully. Dzintra was encouraged to slowly chew each raisin and to focus on any sensations she might be feeling. Dzintra found that she actually could feel the sweetness of each raisin on the tip of her tongue. This was quite an epiphany for Dzintra – the realisation that she could enjoy a pleasure, no matter how small that pleasure might be. Dzintra was also encouraged to practise deep breathing activities and safe space imagery as a way of cultivating presence through self-soothing activities. This would also help Dzintra to learn to be able to ground herself if feeling overwhelmed by her emotions. Coming to the next integrative concept – *emotional processing* – Dzintra was encouraged to write a letter to her younger self, what she would now like to say to her younger self, that young woman who felt she had been abandoned by her husband. It took many weeks for Dzintra to summon the courage to write this letter because she was afraid of the emotions that this might trigger in her. Dzintra brought the letter to her counselling session and she talked about how upset she had got when writing this letter. Dzintra was then encouraged to read the letter out to the counsellor, and the counsellor then related back to Dzintra some of the key emotions and thoughts and challenges that were contained in the letter. Dzintra spoke about how writing the letter and then exploring the letter during a counselling session was cathartic for her, helping her process intense and complex feelings. The therapist explored with Dzintra what she would like to do with this letter, and Dzintra decided that she would place it in a special and pretty envelope and that she would keep this letter as testimony to her life story.

In relation to working with the integrative concept of *attachment*, the therapist explored with Dzintra her relationship with her mother and father as a child, and then her relationship with her husband, before then focussing on her relationship now with her three daughters. Dzintra spoke about how her parents' marriage had been arranged and how they had not got on and had argued throughout her childhood. This had made Dzintra feel unsafe and had helped her to develop a preoccupied attachment style. Dzintra discovered that she had relied too heavily on her husband for her identity and self-worth, and she gained a deeper understanding of the pain she felt when they separated. Dzintra also spoke about her community and how separation and divorce were culturally stigmatised, and the impact that this had had on her. Dzintra also came to realise that she was fearful of letting go of her depression because although she felt guilty of her youngest daughter staying with her to look after her, deep down she did not want her daughter leaving her as this would trigger in her similar feelings of abandonment which had been generated by her husband leaving her. Dzintra was encouraged to reflect upon what healthy adult mode might look like to her, and to distinguish between her child self, that part of her that feels she needs other people and cannot be on her own, and her adult self – what a sense of independence might look and feel like.

In relation to *thinking*, Dzintra was encouraged to keep a thought record during those times when she ruminated. Through the use of a thought record Dzintra was able to see how her thoughts had certain patterns, and links between her thoughts and feelings. Dzintra was encouraged to explore distraction techniques as a way of distracting her mind from her rumination. She found the following distraction techniques helpful: to think about a favourite meal and the steps involved to be able to cook it; taking a shower and imagining her thoughts being washed away; doing some housework. Gradually Dzintra found that she was ruminating less, and gradually she began feeling that she had some control of her rumination. Regarding the conscious and unconscious mind, Dzintra was encouraged to practise safe space imagery as a way of working with her subconscious – by guided imagery Dzintra was essentially subconsciously giving herself reassurance that it was okay for her to be on her own; that she didn't need people to be with her all the time; that she could feel safe when alone. Over the course of two years of therapy, Dzintra's depressive symptoms gradually reduced; Dzintra also began embarking on activities that she normally would have avoided, like joining a local crafts group, and she began to depend less on her daughters.

Case study questions

> How, and in what ways, are person-centred, CBT and relational modalities relevant in this case study ?
>
> In what ways do you think that an integrative approach can be helpful when working with depression ?
>
> What interventions would you use with Dzintra and can you link these with the integrative concepts of presence, emotional processing, attachment, thinking, and our conscious/ unconscious minds?

Case study 2: Bill

Bill, a former teacher and keen amateur actor in his early sixties, came to therapy with the presenting problem of stage fright. The anxiety had started some three years prior to his consultation and had progressively worsened to such an extent that Bill found himself vomiting before each performance at his local theatre. On stage his body would shake as his heart palpitated, and Bill would find himself checking to see where the exits were in the theatre. Hypnotherapy and CBT were utilised in order to help Bill overcome his anxiety and after two sessions he was able to perform on stage with little or no discomfort. A follow-up session was arranged in order to monitor Bill's anxiety. A day before the session Bill telephoned the therapist. Crying on the other end of the phone, Bill explained that he had been suffering from depression for a long time and that he often found it difficult to get up in the mornings. He had forced himself through the last few drama productions, only performing because his wife was also in the group and he didn't want to let her down. His appetite had gone and he had lost his purpose in life. When he arrived in the office the next day Bill looked a broken man, his face alabaster white and his posture that of a man much older in years. Bill referred to his depression as 'like a surfer stuck on an ocean forever waiting for the next big wave'. Bill had been a keen surfer in his younger days when he had lived in America.

Helping Bill through his depression utilised the key principles of *presence, emotional processing, attachment, thinking and the conscious/unconscious mind*. In order to gain a rich picture of Bill's depression it was necessary to integrate *presence* in order to open up to his world. *Presence* allowed the therapist to gain an intimate sense of Bill's suffering and to present to him the possibility of change in a natural and instinctive way. Bill felt that his depression was somehow linked to his anxiety, and utilising age regression within hypnosis, Bill was taken back to the source of his anxiety. Bill remembered that it was during a visit back to America, at the funeral of his best friend, that the anxiety had started. He was delivering a speech about his friend in front of the congregation in church when he suffered his first panic attack. Probing the memories around this episode and earlier memories surrounding his friend, Bill determined that the depressive thoughts had started when he found out that his friend was suffering from terminal illness. Bill had often enjoyed surfing with his friend, in younger days, and the focus of subsequent sessions was to engender a state of deep *presence* within Bill based around the positive memories and associations that he had experienced on the surfboard and with his friend.

Bill was able to imagine himself on a movie screen around the time that he found out about his friend's illness and, through his re-experiencing of these events from a birds' eye perspective, was able to reframe the powerful emotions and feelings held within him. The concept of *emotional processing* was integrated within his treatment plan and Bill, who enjoyed writing, was instructed to compose a scene where he played himself dealing with his friend's announcement of his illness in a manner that introduced a degree of light-heartedness. Bill enjoyed the work of Monty Python and returned with a short script filled with quirky observations and an element of dark humour. Together with the therapist, Bill acted out the scene and returning the next week, reported that he was feeling a bit better and that his friend's passing did not feel 'so gruelling anymore'. There was still the regret that he hadn't been there for his friend. The focus of *attachment* was brought into play, and Bill explored his difficult relationships with a mother who drank and a father that was absent for long periods of time. Bill was able to understand that these early relationships may have fostered the obsessive need to care for his friend during his isolation with illness. With this in mind he was able to reframe this need within the context of the powerful emotions that he was feeling, getting rid of the guilt and regret of his friend's passing.

Surrounding his friend's illness were thoughts of death and the fact that Bill was not getting any younger. Bill found himself ruminating about the futility of life and what there was after death. In order to break the pattern of destructive thinking that held him within the confines of depression, the concept of *thinking* was explored and Bill began to challenge his thoughts cognitively with the use of a diary. Several sessions were spent with Bill, under hypnosis, rehearsing positive thoughts and experiences referred to in the diary that he brought to each session. Metaphors built around surfing, the sea, and progression of existence, the ebb and flow of life and changeability, were introduced hypnotically by the therapist in order to address the *conscious/unconscious* strands of the mind. Consciously Bill was experiencing his depression lifting; he began to feel motivated to act while his appetite had improved. He began to think about life rather than death. Unconsciously his mind was processing the metaphors. At the end of therapy, a now focussed and fully present Bill invited the therapist to a one-man show that he was performing in the local community.

Case study questions

Using Bill's interest in surfing, create a metaphor that focusses upon letting go of the past and planning for a positive future instead. What suggestions could you include in this metaphor that would allow Bill to unconsciously find the answers?

What elements in a treatment plan focussed upon Bill's depression could benefit from being delivered utilising hypnosis?

What interventions based around the core concepts of presence, emotional processing, attachment, thinking, and our conscious/unconscious minds could you develop that would be helpful to Bill?

Conclusion

In this chapter we have explored working integratively with depression. We have singled out person-centred, CBT, relational and hypnotherapeutic modalities and explored them regarding how we work with depression, before then presenting a couple of case studies of how we integrate these modalities to work with the following integrative concepts: presence, emotional processing, attachment, thinking, and our conscious/unconscious minds. We hope that this chapter has conveyed some of the complexities and sensitivities when working with clients who are experiencing depression, and we hope that we have also discussed some of the challenges for therapists supporting clients. We have also made good use of stories in order to explain our understanding of depression, as an educational tool. The next chapter explores working with relationships from an integrative perspective.

References

Alladin, A. & Alibhai, A. (2007) 'Cognitive hypnotherapy for depression: An empirical investigation', *International Journal of Clinical and Experimental Hypnosis*, vol. 55, no. 2, pp. 147–166.

Beck, A. T. (1967) *Depression: Causes and Treatment*. Philadelphia, PA: University of Pennsylvania Press.

Chapman, R. (2014) *Integrating Clinical Hypnosis and CBT*. New York: Springer.

Carrey, J. (2017) 'Jim Carrey – What it all means – One of the most eye opening speeches'. [video] Available at: https://www.youtube.com/watch?v=wTblbYqQQag (accessed 24 March 2018).

Gilbert, M. & Orlans, V. (2011) *Integrative Therapy: 100 Key Points and Techniques* London: Routledge.

Johnstone, M. (2007) *I Had a Black Dog*. London: Robinson.

Johnstone, M. (2009) *Living with a Black Dog*. London: Constable and Robinson.

Kirsch, I., Montgomery, G. & Sapirstein, G. (1995). 'Hypnosis as an adjunct to cognitive behavioral psychotherapy: A meta-analysis', *Journal of Consulting and Clinical Psychology*, vol. 63, no. 2, pp. 214–220.

Kulakowski, S. (2014) *When Depression Hurts Your Relationships.* New York: New Harbinger Publications.

Mearns, D. & Thorne, B. (1988) *Person-Centred Counselling in Action.* London: Sage.

Shakespeare, W. (2008). *The Oxford Shakespeare: Macbeth.* Edited by Nicholas Brooke. Oxford: OUP.

Spiegel, H. & Spiegel, D. (2004) *Trance and Treatment.* Washington, DC: American Psychiatric Publishing.

Stolorow, R. & Atwood, G. (1992) *Contexts of Being.* New Jersey: Analytic Press.

Yapko, M. (2001) *Treating Depression with Hypnosis.* Philadelphia, PA: Brunner-Routledge.

Chapter 9

Working integratively with relationships

> There is always some madness in love. But there is also always some reason in madness.
> Friedrich Nietzsche, 'On Reading and Writing',
> *Thus Spake Zarathustra* (1883–1885)

Introduction

As counsellors we often find ourselves working with clients regarding relationship issues. Being human means being involved in many different kinds of relationships, and we can often struggle to figure out the dynamics of our relationships, our feelings, our thoughts and behaviours within relationships. There are often significant relationship aspects to the different mental health and wellbeing issues that clients present with, and so we consider it important to include a full chapter in this book dedicated to how we work integratively with relationships. This chapter is not about couples counselling, which is a specialist field in its own right, rather, this chapter explores some of the challenges of including a focus upon relationships in the client work that we do. Relationship issues directly and indirectly affect our clients' lives, and so to miss out this key aspect of people's experiences would be unprofessional.

Whilst the previous chapters in this book have explored relational modalities within psychotherapy, this chapter looks at relationship issues that clients bring and how person-centred, relational, CBT and hypnotherapeutic modalities can be integrated to help people. We also provide a couple of in-depth case studies that show how we integrate, through a focus on presence, emotional processing, attachment, thinking, and our conscious/unconscious minds. It is also important to realise that the most important relationship that we and our clients are ever going to have is the relationship that we/they have with our/themselves, hence this chapter also looks at this dimension to relationships, beginning with a short story to illustrate this important point.

The grown woman with a troll, in a little girl's body

'Big nose, big nose, look at her with the big nose'
'You're a swot, you're so boring'
'I'm gonna beat you up because you're so tall and ugly – giraffe head'
'You fucking bitch'

Lucy listened to these harmful, abusive, words almost on a daily basis when at school. This was supposed to be a good school, her parents had moved house just so that she could attend Meridian Academy, and yet Lucy felt completely out of place here – the other girls seemed so brutal and cruel and they enjoyed picking on her. In the space of six months of attending Meridian Academy, Lucy had withdrawn into herself, spending her time at and outside of school alone, feeling that there was something inherently wrong with her. Then one-day a troll appeared on her right shoulder, green, slimy-looking with a big salivating gob and pointed ears, saying to her constantly, 'You are so pathetic; you are a nobody; nobody likes you; you are ugly.' Somehow this troll had an even greater impact on Lucy's wellbeing than the school bullies. Lucy began feeling that she was this tall, fat, ugly troll, and from that point onwards she began to eat less and to exercise more.

By the time she was 28 years old, Lucy was attending an eating disorder clinic because she was deemed unhealthily thin and was controlling her food intake. However, because Lucy was not putting on enough weight quickly enough the therapist Matthew told her that she would have to leave the programme, which Lucy did, the troll on her shoulder saying to her, 'See, not even a specialist clinic thinks you are worth receiving treatment; remember I am your only friend.' Lucy walked for the next six hours to try to shake the troll off from her shoulder, but he clung on and Lucy collapsed out of exhaustion. At this point, there was a ser-endipitous occurrence. 'Can I help ?' a friendly voice enquired, and Lucy saw a young woman standing next to her. 'I'm Barbara and I work here.' The woman gestured to the beautiful old Victorian building standing behind her. 'This is a new counselling centre.' Lucy followed her inside and immediately signed up for therapy.

Counsellor Barbara was not at all like Matthew because she was genuinely interested in getting to know Lucy's troll, what motivated him, how he made Lucy feel, when this troll had first appeared to Lucy. Gradually Lucy began to understand that the bullying that she had expe-rienced at school had traumatised her, that because she had internalised the bullies' critical voices in the form of a troll, she had been terrified of becoming herself, and she had restricted her diet to prevent her from becoming the person that she was destined to become. Lucy worked hard in and between counselling sessions with Barbara to start to experience herself in more healthy and positive ways, to develop a safe and supportive relationship with herself. In doing so, the troll on top of Lucy's shoulder shrank in size and intensity. Gradually, Lucy began eating more and she began to gain some weight and Lucy discovered that she could feel happy being herself. Lucy was able to become a full grown-up with a grown-up body as she came to value who she was and she came to experience a positive relationship with herself.

The above story captures well the importance of humans developing healthy relationships with themselves. The story also captures the significance of abusive relationships with oth-ers, how these can be internalised thereby creating a dysfunctional relationship with oneself. Thus, external relationships with others are inherently linked to the internal relationship that we develop and have with ourselves. This can take some time to realise, and it can take clients a long time to begin to experience themselves as safe and supportive people – where there are trolls perched on people's shoulders forever criticising them there can be distress, uncertainty, toxicity, unhappiness, alongside fear and even terror of being alone and fully becoming one-self. In Lucy's case it was important for counsellor Barbara to allow Lucy to explore what might be underpinning her eating disorder, thereby viewing the eating disorder as a symptom rather than a cause of Lucy's distress. Through therapy sessions Lucy came to the realisa-tion that she was restricting her food intake as a way of preventing herself from becoming a grown-up, because she felt that she was a bad person who did not deserve to grow up. Lucy

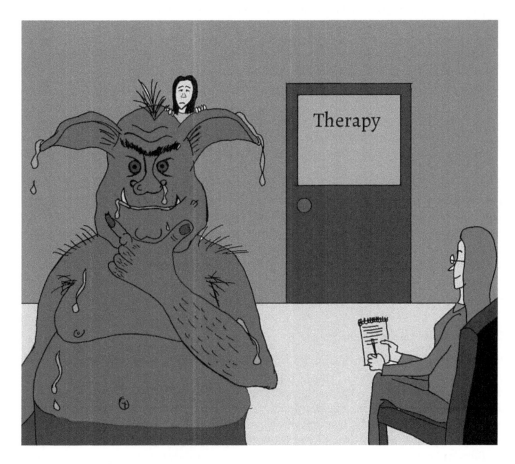

also showed courage in that she began to try out experiencing herself in more positive and supportive ways – for example, thinking about what she might value about herself, challenging herself to respond to her hunger pangs by eating something rather than ignoring her body's needs. Lucy also created her own relationship with food – one where she saw food as fuel for her mind and her body rather than seeing food as number of calories. Lucy came to discover that she valued herself as being strong, and eating properly was part of that. Lucy came to see that what was most important of all was her relationship to herself, and in this way was able to tackle her eating disorder.

Ten honest questions to ask yourself

If being in a supportive relationship with yourself is key to being an effective mental health practitioner, alongside a grounded human being, then it might be worthwhile spending a few moments reflecting upon the following set of questions being used here to explore your own relationship with yourself:

- How challenging do you find being by yourself?
- When you become emotionally distressed, what do you do?

- How often do you engage in activities that make you feel good?
- How regularly do you prioritise others over yourself?
- How regularly do you check in with yourself to note how you are feeling at any particular time?
- How often do you try to process any distressing thoughts or emotions?
- Are you aware of your own inner critic voicing opinions and if so what do you do about this?
- How regularly do you engage in positive self-talk?
- How regularly do you reflect upon what your values are?
- How able are you to tolerate aspects of yourself that you dislike?

It is important to spend some time reflecting upon the above because if we as practitioners have a good sense of the kind of relationship that we have with ourselves then this can help us to help clients explore the kinds of relationships that they have with themselves.

Relationships also go beyond the self to include family, friend, sexual/intimate, peer, workplace and other connections. The next section explores some of the issues that we have found that clients bring regarding this broader group of relationships before we then look at person-centred, relational, CBT and hypnotherapeutic modalities and how we work with these to consider relationship issues for clients.

Clients and relationships

Presence within ourselves as therapists, and that of our clients, is central to illuminating, understanding and ultimately treating relationship issues. As stated earlier in this chapter, there are a broad range of relationships that clients present with: the relationship with self; the relationship with others; relationships with drugs, alcohol, food and sex; relationships with habits such as gambling; relationships with the past, present and future; imaginary relationships. A presenting problem such as gambling or an eating disorder can have underlying conflicts and experiences that may be associated with our clients suffering. Often relapses into gambling, drugs or unhealthy eating habits illuminate deeper issues that need to be specifically treated.

As our awareness and listening skills develop with *presence* so we can focus in on the story of our client, the metaphors and hidden meanings and messages that are described in the therapy room. For example, the relationship that a client may have with alcohol may mask underlying causes such as anxiety, fear of new situations or the unknown, a lack of confidence, low self-esteem, depression, trauma, relationship problems at home. Relationships with drugs can provide dissociation and temporary succour from past traumas, current relationship issues, future worries and concerns. A relationship with sugar through, for example, comfort eating may be a physical expression of the metaphor that something sweet is missing in our clients' lives: an absence of love or security, a lack of purpose or focus. This connection can also soothe the experience of loneliness and boredom, desperation and low self-esteem. The client may have the need to carry chocolate bars with her wherever she goes and the relationship may be so firmly ingrained, and linked to states such as anxiety and fear, that chocolates can be kept next to the bed at night for comfort. Relationships with food can be 'trance-like', where the person dissociates so completely from the action of eating that they do not realise that the food is going into their mouth.

We have found this dissociative trance-like behaviour to be common in gambling too: the relationship that the client forms with the slot machine or online app can be so utterly engrossing that they feel part of the machine, part of the game. This particular type of relationship fosters a sense of control: press a button and there is a sound or a flashing light, an immediate reward for effort. Playing with the machine or app can be an elaborate experience not always based on wanting to win lots of money. A client once described their relationship with gambling as 'being with God', all-consuming and in similar ways, the sort of feeling an athlete may experience when they are 'in the zone.' Helping the client rediscover a relationship with themselves outside of the stimulus and attraction of a slot machine can be complex and time-consuming. Often there are relapses due to difficult relationships or situations at work and/or at home. For example, a client who struggled with gambling experienced a relationship with his father that was based around bullying. The client worked for his father's business and would regularly find himself the victim of his father's uncontrolled outbursts. The client felt that his father treated him like a slave instead of a vital part of the business. Coupled with the 14-hour shifts that he was forced to work, the client escaped his suffering through an addiction to gambling, a relationship that allowed him to relax, release pressure and forget about his father during certain periods of the day. It took many months of therapy for the client to change the relationship that he had with himself as a victim, to foster a healthier relationship with his father until eventually they became equal partners in the business and to let go of the alluring relationship with betting apps where he could dissociate from the world and dream about winning a million.

Intimate associations such as a marital relationship can influence presenting issues in positive and negative ways. A client with the presenting problem of chronic headaches and IBS reported that symptoms were exacerbated whenever her husband was present in the house. The couple had experienced a volatile relationship over many years; due to international business commitments her husband would spend large periods of time away from home. During these absences the client reported that her headaches and IBS were both less severe. When the husband returned they would often bicker and quarrel; the longer her husband stayed at home the worse the headaches and symptoms of IBS. As well as focussing upon relief from physical symptomatology through muscle relaxation and mental exercises that included dissociation from pain, the therapist helped the client build a more equal relationship with her husband. This proved to be challenging because the husband was not present during the sessions. However, he agreed to undertake cognitive exercises with his wife that helped nurture a more balanced marriage where the two of them would have equal input on decision making. Other homework focussed on teaching the couple to problem-solve instead of dealing with things through argument. Eventually the situation at home improved and the client no longer felt unhappy in her marriage. The headaches and occurrences of IBS became much less frequent.

As well as mental and emotional aspects, relationships can also include a physical dimension. Earlier in the chapter, 'The Grown Woman with a Troll' story illustrated the relationship between body image distortions and eating disorders. Clients can bring to the table many such distortions, both general and localised. For example, a client once came into therapy with the presenting problem of a pronounced limp. Yet when instructed to walk across the room the therapist could detect no sign of a limp within the client's footsteps or body posture. In order to correct the perceived body distortion the therapist explored the underlying issues surrounding the relationship that the client had with himself and the 'phantom' limp and this led to some very interesting discoveries. In the five months prior to his consultation, the client had gained employment within an educational establishment, a position that afforded prestige and responsibility. The perception of the limp had started during the first few days in his new job, when the client had begun to think that he wasn't capable or worthy of being in his elevated position. As his responsibilities increased, the 'phantom' limp became more pronounced; eventually the client would obsess about the limp constantly, becoming very self-conscious of his posture, the slope of his shoulders, the shuffle of his feet, whenever he was in a classroom with other members of staff, or walking along a corridor at work. He associated his imagined limp with himself 'limping along' in the job and he attributed this relationship to his low self-esteem, a result of demanding parents forcing him into studying and excelling in education when he would have preferred to do something with his hands.

Once the relationship between the physical distortion and low self-esteem had been established, a treatment plan was developed to deal with the client's relationships between himself, his parents and his self-esteem. As a result of controlling and highly anxious parents the client had built a submissive bond with his mother and father whereby he would agree to do the things they wanted him to do without any questioning, even though he felt resentment and anger within. The thoughts, feelings and behaviours as a result of his upbringing were addressed and modified through a combination of cognitive exercises and guided imagery that focussed on giving the control back to the client. He began to feel better about himself and became more confident at work. As a result, his obsession regarding a limp that wasn't there lessened as he worked on building a positive relationship with his physical presence. After several sessions over three months the client reported that he no longer felt as though he limped and was much more confident and happier in his job. He had started a painting course and was looking forward to a future filled with more creativity and inner purpose.

Relationships and unconscious influence

The man who dug and dug and dug

There was once a teenager who, after leaving school, didn't know what to do with his life. 'Become a builder', instructed his father, a strong-minded character that had often bullied his son when he was young. Following in his father's footsteps wasn't something that the teenager had contemplated. Nevertheless he felt compelled to carry on with the family business and become a ground worker. There was a need within him to prove to his father that, just like his father, he could become successful within building. And so, armed with a shovel and a box of sandwiches that his mother had made, he went to work with his father, who drove a big white van, for the very first time. The day was spent digging foundations for new houses that were being built next to a large hospital and at the end of it the 16-year-old was exhausted. The next day he did the same, and the day after, and the day after that. The teenager grew into a young man and then a middle-aged man, and still he dug ditches and foundations, trenches and sewers. Some twenty years on from leaving school, the man felt unfulfilled and stuck in his life. He began to hate digging and his body had started to argue with the amount of physical work he was doing.

Then one day his body broke down and he could dig no more. The man thought about his options. He would have to find something else in his life to replace the digging. He would create a new chapter in his story, a fresh start. As he convalesced, the man who had dug for years began to explore his options. He had always been interested in physiotherapy and so he decided to study a foundation course and then a degree in physiotherapy. Although nervous at returning to education after an absence of 25 years, the man applied himself and several years later qualified as a physiotherapist. His world had opened up: for the first time in many years he had choice. There was a freedom in his life that he had never experienced before. He could choose to set up a physiotherapy business; he could choose to work for a clinic or health centre. He could choose to do both! He could develop a career with genuine prospects that would fulfill his ambitions. The thought of this caused something to stir within him but he couldn't be sure exactly what this feeling was; it was almost like a shadow in the corner of a room.

The man spent a great deal of time thinking about which path to take in his new career and the more he thought about this, the more he worried that he would make the right choice. Instead of committing himself fully to setting up a physiotherapy practice or getting a job in a clinic, he dabbled with his practice, not spending the hours required to building up a successful business. He felt that he was doing the right thing: putting in just enough hours but not committing too much time as there were other things in his life that got in the way. Although he saw vacancies for physiotherapists within the National Health Service, he convinced himself that he didn't have the necessary level of experience in order to apply. Other recently qualified physiotherapists from his university filled these roles instead. When he found this out, again something uncomfortable stirred within him.

Several months after leaving university, the man came across the old shovel that had gathered dust in the garden shed. He picked it up and started digging once more. He put more effort into his digging than ever before and at first he felt exhilarated. His father was very happy. Gradually he spent less and less time at his physiotherapy practice and eventually the business folded. Then one day when he was tidying his house, he came across his degree certificate amongst a pile of study books. He lifted it up to the light and sure enough there was his name next to the *BSc. in Physiotherapy (Hons)*. Again something shifted within him, a feeling that he couldn't quite pinpoint. It was like a moth caught momentarily in the headlights of a car before melting into the inky night. He stared at the certificate for a few more seconds before placing it in a cardboard box along with the books and some old photographs. There was some relief by doing this, although there was also the feeling of loss. He stored the box in the attic, where it gathered dust with the other discarded items in his life: vinyl records, toys and books.

Every day is now spent with a shovel, digging a trench or a ditch or a sewer. Every day is back-breaking and exhausting. The man works with his father, who, although physically incapable of building anymore, instructs his son in relation to the tasks that need to be accomplished each day. As the days go by, the man experiences a constant nagging thought: will things ever happen for me?

Although simplified, the above story illustrates the complex, often unconscious conflicts that accompany a life's worth of relationships with someone important to us. If one were to analyze the man's story at the surface level it would not be dissimilar to many others who have tried something different in their lives only to fail and return to a familiar path. However, what is interesting from a therapeutic analysis of the man's story is his relationship with his father and how this relationship influences the uncomfortable feelings and thoughts accompanying his new-found freedom and choice within a career change.

It is natural to experience fear during any period of significant transition, especially when the threat to self is apparent. Yet the thoughts and feelings that are felt, but not quite experienced within the conscious mind of this man, mask a much deeper anxiety. The man worries about which path to take in terms of his career, but underlying this conscious objectivated *fear*

of choice and fear of the application of choice, is an anxiety that as May (1994:110) suggests 'strikes at the central core of his self-esteem and his sense of value as a self which is the most important aspect of experience of himself as a being'. The man's values and sense of himself are part of a complex relationship he shares with his father, whom he respects but feels anger towards whenever he remembers the bullying. Any threat to these values and sense of being, any threat to his self-esteem caused by breaking free of his father's influence and finding a job as a physiotherapist, produces inner conflict.

The man's way of dealing with his inner angst is to evade it through the conscious worry surrounding the choice of whether to set up a business or whether to get a job at a clinic. As long as he focusses on this worry he does not need to jeopardise the status quo of his being and his relationship with his father. He evades the opportunity of finding a job at a clinic by rationalizing that he has a lack of experience, yet he sees other graduates find work. Within him there is a desire for new experiences but the possibility that this brings is a threat to inner security, and this is a threat that cannot be breached. Another dissociative tactic is to set up his practice but not to be fully present with it. Ultimately, by not facing his anxiety and the attachment schema based upon the past relationship with his father, the man limits himself and any potentialities for growth. This in turn leads to guilt that manifests as the persistent thought that somehow things could be better and that he is waiting for the day for this to happen.

Person-centred approaches and relationships

> 'The number one thing I would suggest people do is not separate and buy their own houses straightaway but to wait at least a year before they decide if they want to fully separate.'
> 'I think we were supposed to spend this time on our own to fully appreciate our relationship.'
> 'I wish that I had had the strength to end the relationship sooner – it took me 20 years before I had the courage to leave.'
> 'I relied on him for everything.'

The above are some of the things that clients have said to us concerning the intimate relationships in their lives. These quotes illustrate the diversity of experiences and unique insights that people have and struggle with. This suggests the importance and relevance of person-centred approaches to dealing with relationships, because there are no general rules for people to follow in terms of the relationships that they have – relationships are complex, in constant fluctuation and can present unique challenges. Therefore, having the core conditions that are found within person-centred approaches can help therapists to understand each client's individual experiences of the different relationships in their lives (Mearns & Thorne, 2012). We cannot be prescriptive with our clients, rather as therapists it is our role to be open and empathic and alive to perspectives and experiences on relationships that perhaps challenge our own views regarding what relationships should involve. It is important, however, to consider the issue of abuse within relationships. Sometimes clients may not see what they have been experiencing as abusive; their process may involve blaming themselves. In these situations it is important for us as therapists to name the abuse and to challenge the client to consider what they have experienced as abuse. Sometimes it can take a long time for a client to accept that their relationship has been abusive.

As the case of Lucy in the story about the grown woman in a little girl's body shows, the relationships that we have with others may lead us to developing a toxic, negative self-concept. This is where we internalise the labels and associations that others have made of us. A person-centred aspect to working with clients regarding relationships is therefore considering the self and self-concept. Exploring with a client how others perceive them, how this impacts on their life, the extent to which they agree with the labels that other people have attached to them – this all helps the client to better understand their self-concept and how this has been formed. We can then also explore with the client how the client would like to see themselves, to provide an open and non-judgemental space within therapy for the client to start to experience their true self, and for us as therapists to provide encouragement for clients to begin to approach their life outside of therapy through their self rather than self-concept. This can also involve desensitising a client from how others view them. Clients will often be highly sensitive to the opinions, judgements, statements and actions of other people in their lives. Through open and exploratory questions, through presence and unconditional positive regard, we can facilitate clients increasingly questioning the views and actions of other people, so that our clients begin to see that other people have their own processes and issues to deal with, and that how they behave doesn't necessarily need to be internalised by us, and we don't have to hold ourselves responsible, or internalise, the things that people do to us or say to us. This can be highly liberating for a client, and helps them to self-actualise (Rogers, 1961).

CBT and relationships

It is important to consider the content and pattern of clients' thinking when exploring relationships with them, and to also consider behavioural interventions. As previously discussed in Chapter 4 on thinking, individuals may have dysfunctional thinking, which involves negative automatic thoughts (NATS), underpinned by underlying assumptions/rule for living, which are underpinned by core beliefs (Joseph, 2009; Greenberger & Padesky, 2015). Thus, any relationships that our clients have will feature these thinking patterns, the content of which may be dysfunctional, causing them suffering. It can be helpful for clients to keep a thought record in relation to certain people that they find trigger uncomfortable, unhelpful, emotions. Through a thought record a client can document the situation that triggered their discomfort – involving their relative, work colleague, manager, friend, etc. – their NATS, feelings and behaviours. Therapy sessions can then involve exploring the thinking content that a particular person/relationship stimulates in a client, the historical context to this, identifying patterns of thinking with a client, and facilitating their exploration of more healthy, helpful, thinking content and patterns.

Boundaries between the client and the individuals that they regularly come into contact with can also be explored. For example, it may be that an uncle triggers within a client a feeling of anxiety. When asked to keep a thought record, the client shows that their NATS in relation to their uncle include 'He is scary', 'He is powerful'. We can explore these NATS with a client for there is likely to be a wider historical context to them – for example, is this how the uncle made the client feel when they were younger and relatively powerless? How might the client create more positive thinking for themselves now that they are an adult – for example, 'I am powerful, my uncle is no longer in control of what I say or do.' We can also explore with a client how they might boundary their interaction with an uncle who has in the past been verbally abusive to them – shouting at them, saying unhelpful comments. A client may decide that they will choose to have very little contact with their uncle in the future, or to challenge any toxic comments that the uncle makes. A client may decide that if they do encounter their uncle they may choose to only spend a couple of minutes talking to them before saying that they have to be somewhere else. By illuminating some of the thinking that underpins interactions with other people, this can be very helpful in terms of recreating new, more helpful relational dynamics for clients. We might also encourage a client to view this uncle figure that generates anxiety in them as a cartoon character, as a way of reframing the uncle for the client so that the client no longer perceives them as this powerful figure, but rather as Mickey Mouse or Donald Duck. Some clients find this extremely useful.

Attachment within relationships

This section focusses upon attachment and its significance when working with clients and the relationships that they have with themselves and with others. We have already written at length about attachment in Chapters 1 and 3, so this section highlights the relevance of attachment for relationships and any interventions that might apply. To reiterate, there are predominantly five attachment styles: secure, preoccupied, anxious ambivalent, avoidant and disorganised. A secure attachment style within adults involves adults who can form and maintain trusting relationships, adults who have a healthy relationship also with themselves, believing that ultimately 'everything will be okay'. A preoccupied attachment style in adulthood involves a person experiencing relationships as anxiety-provoking and individuals with a preoccupied attachment style can be overly concerned by what others think, feel and how they behave. Adults with an anxious ambivalent attachment style may also become angry when they believe that they have not had the response from a person that they should have. Adults with an avoidant attachment style tend to rely on themselves for their emotional needs and they tend to avoid becoming attached to other people, very fearful of being rejected (Holmes, 2001). Adults with a disorganised attachment style are likely to be highly inconsistent in their relationships – overly intrusive at times and totally avoidant at other times. When working with clients with a disorganised attachment style this can be extremely challenging. It is important to note that attachment styles can perhaps be viewed as fluid, so that our clients may have more than one attachment style, perhaps having different attachment styles with different people, and also experiencing a different attachment style with themselves.

Clearly, attachment styles will influence the relationships that our clients will be experiencing. Sometimes, psychoeducation is an important intervention in itself – raising awareness with our clients the different types of attachment styles that there are and exploring which attachment styles the client feels that they have with themselves and with others (Young & Klosko, 1994). It can also be beneficial to do some stone work with clients whereby we give a client a range of different stones (with differing colours, weights, shapes) and ask them to identify themselves with one particular stone, then asking them to arrange the other stones around their stone as a way of capturing the different people in their life. We can use the layout of the stones as a way of exploring different attachment styles. Clients may come to see that they exhibit particular kinds of attachment styles with particular people and they can explore whether or not they would like to change this. For example, it may be that a client with a preoccupied attachment style in relation to her boyfriend may find this feeding rather than reducing her anxiety levels, because she feels that she needs her boyfriend's approval for what she does and says. By exploring this aspect to her relationship with her boyfriend, it may help the client to re-evaluate her relationship. By experiencing a secure base from the therapist, this client may also begin to experience what it might be like to have a secure attachment style (Wallin, 2007).

Hypnotherapy and relationships

Hypnotherapy offers a broad range of techniques for working with relationship issues that encompass both psychodynamic and cognitive-behavioural methods (Túry, Wildmann and Szentes, 2011). Within the context of a psychodynamic approach, age regression and analysis utilising hypnosis can uncover underlying issues surrounding, for example, eating disorders (Cheek and LeCron, 1968). By re-experiencing elements of the past, a client can discover the cause of destructive relationships; the realisation and understandings that this fosters allows possibility for change and can be integrated within the treatment plan. Cognitive-behavioural approaches such as relaxation, positive self-esteem reinforcement and healthy self- image projection challenge the sense of rejection and distorted body image that Brusch (1973) suggests is a result of past dysfunctional family relationships and their effect on eating problems. Using hypnosis, clients can desensitise their experiences within traumatic relationships; repressed emotions can be expressed and released through abreaction (Morison and Philips, 2001). Age progression offers the opportunity to experience a future where past relationships have been reframed and put into context in order to correct unhealthy attachments and belief systems. Building *presence* and self-awareness within a hypnotherapeutic framework can allow clients to become conscious of the unconscious metaphors that resonate within their lives, facilitating self-understanding and scope for change. Integrating metaphors and stories can be useful for re-connecting or building a client's relationship with their own inner resources, illuminating meaning and understanding of experiences. In this way, a client can start to make use of a lifetime's worth of learning and experience that will help them deal with relationship issues, be it with people, drugs, alcohol, food, gambling or anything else. Metaphors and stories presented under hypnosis can be designed to reframe relationships, to give relationships an identity or form that externalises them for reframing purposes. Clients can search through memories of past experiences of power and control, or imagined power and control, and can then age-progress to future situations where they can elicit this power and control in order to refrain from bingeing, gambling or arguing with loved ones. This can prove useful in situations where a client's powerlessness with a habit is because of powerlessness within a relationship (Citrenbaum, King and Cohen, 1985). As Citrenbaum et al. (1985, p. 54) suggest, a client with a drink problem as a result of the need to assert himself in his relationship with his wife, where he is otherwise 'passive and powerless', can be taught to express assertiveness through remembered experiences of power and control instead of relying upon alcohol to elicit this behaviour. Post-hypnotic suggestions can be included for ego-strengthening purposes as well as boosting self-esteem and confidence for building healthier relationships.

Case studies in working integratively with relationships

Case study 1: Jonathan

Jonathan is a 50-year-old married man who has been referred to a counselling service as a result of visiting his GP. Jonathan's presenting symptoms are that he is finding it increasingly difficult to get out of bed and be motivated to go to work; he is finding it hard to feel any pleasure in daily activities and he is finding himself increasingly irritated with his young child and with his wife. Jonathan also struggles to get to sleep at night and finds himself dreaming about his ex-wife. In his dreams his ex-wife is criticising him. Jonathan would like to feel more positive about his life and he would like to be able to sleep better, and this is why he has come to counselling. Jonathan feels guilty because he feels that he has a good relationship with his current wife and with his young son, and so he believes that he should not be struggling with a low mood.

When working integratively with Jonathan, the therapist in this case drew upon the five integrative concepts outlined previously in this book – *presence, emotional processing, attachment, thinking,* and our *conscious/unconscious* minds. The following is a summarised account of the therapist's work with Jonathan, focussing on these core integrative concepts.

Sessions one to three with Jonathan involved the therapist building a strong therapeutic relationship with him. The therapist found that Jonathan seemed to be exhibiting an avoidant attachment style and so took his time to build a relationship with him, focussing the sessions mainly on exploration and psychoeducating and facilitating Jonathan in the notion of *presence.* Jonathan expressed an interest in learning and practising activities that would enable him to experience *presence,* because Jonathan felt that this would help lift his mood and also would help him cope with any distress that he might be feeling, particularly when trying to fall asleep. Within and between the counselling sessions Jonathan practised deep breathing and mindfulness techniques and he found that these really helped when trying to get to sleep at night. Jonathan also found that cultivating *presence* helped him in his interactions with his wife and young son, allowing him to take a few moments rather than automatically responding to them in an irritated way. Jonathan found that through developing *presence* he was less agitated generally, and was more calm with his young son and with his wife.

Sessions four, five and six focussed on *emotional processing.* As already stated, the therapist picked up on Jonathan's avoidant attachment style and so explored his family history. Jonathan's father had died when he was young, and his mother had avoided any conversation with him about the grief that this involved, out of a fear of experiencing emotional pain. Jonathan had learnt to deal with things on his own, not to share his feelings with others. The therapist also explored Jonathan's relationship with his first wife and Jonathan came to see that he had avoided any conflict with his wife, and in doing so had built up many years of resentment towards her because she had always put her needs before Jonathan's. The therapist found that Jonathan had not really processed his feelings towards his first wife, nor had he processed the distress that he had felt when ending his 15-year marriage with her. Jonathan was therefore encouraged to write himself a letter where he could explain what he had gone through during the fifteen years of his marriage and then ending it. Jonathan brought the letter to session six and gave it to the therapist to read. The therapist picked out key sentences that Jonathan had written and he helped Jonathan to explore painful emotions, emotions that Jonathan had avoided for a very long time.

Sessions seven and eight included an exploration of Jonathan's thinking in relation to his first marriage. Jonathan discovered that he had often blamed himself for the state of this relationship; Jonathan had believed that he had not been a good enough husband. Upon rationally exploring these thoughts, with the help of the therapist, Jonathan began to view himself as a victim of domestic abuse because Jonathan's first wife had been emotionally abusive to him, which is why he always placed her needs first and avoided any conflict. Jonathan also began thinking about his own needs and rights as a human being, and began to see that he deserved to feel safe in that relationship, he deserved to feel heard. The therapist encouraged Jonathan to explore how he could reach closure on the first marriage, and Jonathan decided that a ritual would help him

reach closure. Thus, Jonathan burnt the letter that he had written to himself as a way of symbolically communicating with his *unconscious* mind that he was no longer in that toxic relationship,
that he had moved on and had found happiness. Jonathan ended therapy after ten sessions. He
found that his low mood had lifted, that he had begun experiencing joy in his life and that the
dreams of his ex-wife had stopped being as frequent and intense. Jonathan also felt that he was
better able to identify and communicate his own emotional needs to his current wife, thereby
approaching relationships through a secure attachment style.

Case study questions

How, and in what ways, are person-centred, CBT and relational modalities relevant in this
case study ?

In what ways do you think that relationship issues underpinned Jonathan's low mood and
his irritability ?

What interventions would you use with Jonathan and can you link these with the integrative concepts of presence, emotional processing, attachment, thinking, and our con-
scious/unconscious minds?

Case study 2: Tony

Tony, a 55-year-old man with a history of depression, came into therapy with the presenting
problem of obesity as a result of uncontrolled bingeing on unhealthy foods, including chocolates, crisps, takeaways and biscuits. The following is an account of the treatment strategies
within sessions developed upon the principles of *presence, emotional processing, attachment,
thinking* and the *conscious/unconscious* concepts of mind.

During the first two sessions, Tony was introduced to the concept of *presence* in order to
gain a sense of self-awareness so that he could recognise triggers for his bingeing and take
back some control in terms of his eating. The therapist began with cognitive exercises that
included simple breathing techniques as well as muscle relaxation. Tony focussed upon the
rate and depth of his breathing, the difference between the temperature of inhaled air compared
to exhaled air, areas of his body where he could feel tension and that needed relaxation. Tony
was able to imagine his thoughts like clouds, distant and mobile, and in this way began to
foster the idea that he could choose which thoughts to attach to and which to let go. Utilising
presence in this way, Tony was able to centre himself in situations where in the past he would
have exhibited trance-like eating symptoms: a pattern of eating that meant he could eat a whole
packet of biscuits in front of the television in a dissociative state without realising that he was
actually eating. Other situations where he had experienced dissociation during eating included
lunchtimes at work and periods where he felt stressed in his job.

After the first two sessions Tony reported that he was better able to recognise, assess and
deal with triggers for bingeing on food by relaxing his mind and body through focussed breathing. He felt confident that he could let go of the need to binge and the therapist began to work
on the relationship that Tony had with his food, himself and his parents. During the initial
consultation Tony had mentioned a stern father and an 'invisible' mother who would leave the
room whenever his father began to bully Tony. Periods of depression were common during
his teenage years and Tony felt that his uncontrolled eating was symptomatic of a deeper pain
he described as a 'weight around his chest'. At the time that Tony came to therapy he had lost
a lot of mobility in his legs, due to his weight, and needed a walking stick in order to walk.

The next three sessions focussed upon *emotional processing* and *attachment*. Through the use of hypnotic techniques oriented to psychodynamic interactions, Tony was able to age regress back to memories where his father had shouted at him and made derogatory comments about his image. During these moments his mother would leave the living room and go upstairs. When the scolding had ended Tony would go up to his bedroom and find a chocolate bar on his pillow, left there by his mother. Tony would then cry and eat the chocolate afterwards in order to comfort himself. Tony was able to recognise the attachment that he had to sugary foods and how this was associated with a sense of rejection from his mother and anger towards the tyranny of his father. He also understood how he was fulfilling his father's prophecy of Tony being 'a fat lump of lard who wouldn't amount to anything'.

Reintroducing Tony to these memories allowed him to experience the difficult emotions of rejection, anger and distorted body image through the lens of an adult. The concept of *thinking* was introduced into the treatment plan and Tony was able to begin to recognise how his destructive thoughts, for example, 'I'm useless and fat' resulted in diminishing self-esteem and ultimately led to excessive snacking. His father's outbursts were reframed under hypnosis to foster the notion that Tony was an important person otherwise his father would not have demonstrated these aggressive outbursts, however misguided. Tony began to realise that inside his father's anger was a seed of care, that the perceived rejection by his mother was actually her trying to make things better for Tony. He recognised that his food binges were a way of dissociating from difficult situations such as an argument with his wife or a stressful period at work. This allowed him to build an adult relationship with himself as opposed to escaping to his childhood bedroom and chocolate bars. Tony imagined himself forgiving his mother and standing up to his father, utilising age regression under hypnosis in order to facilitate a pseudo-orientation in time where his past experiences could be re-evaluated and altered.

Tony had mentioned that he used to walk a lot and had enjoyed exploring his local park when he was more mobile. The therapist suggested that he should take short walks in the park and build on this. Tony agreed and began to walk, aided with his walking stick, along the paths under the trees as much as he could. By simply getting Tony to agree to walking, post-hypnotic suggestions were unconsciously created within him: *I can exercise, I can become mobile again.* This was achieved because Tony had previous positive experiences of walking and could unconsciously age regress to past experiences of himself in the park. By the sixth session, Tony's walks had lengthened in distance considerably and he reported feeling better physically.

Utilising Tony's positive experience of walking in the park, the therapist was able to introduce powerful metaphors surrounding letting go of the anger and resentment towards his father. Tony was instructed to notice bees as they went about their business, collecting nectar from one flower and moving onto the next, and then the next, pollinating the plants as they did so. He noticed that no bee was attached to one flower for too long, that a continual flux of feeding was required in order for nature to occur. He found this process of observation cathartic, recognising that he no longer had to burden himself with anger and resentment but instead could search out happiness and love for himself. He could be a bee. Tony started hugging trees and felt their power; by forming relationships with the trees in the park Tony began to imagine himself being very powerful and solid and this in turn provided therapeutic opportunities for the interplay between the *conscious/unconscious* mind: physically he felt the tree trunk around his arms – this provided the conscious ballast for change – while unconsciously he could experience learning how to manifest his own power, utilising metaphors such as the trees roots forming a *powerful* underground network that provided the *strength and stability* in order to *withstand any storms.*

The final four sessions were focussed heavily on natural metaphors for letting go of destructive thoughts as well as fostering power and control in order to help Tony deal with future triggers for bingeing. Tony was able to imagine himself in these situations without bingeing on food, drinking water instead, and feeling good about himself. Ego-strengthening was included within the hypnosis parts of the session to build Tony's self-esteem and confidence. By session twelve Tony had lost two stone, had regained most of the mobility in his legs, and reported that the bingeing and his past were behind him. He felt happier and more in control than he had ever felt in his life.

Case study questions

What metaphors could you create in order to boost Tony's motivation to exercise ?

In terms of person-centred, CBT, relational and hypnotherapeutic modalities, what intervention strategies could you design linked to the concepts of *presence, emotional processing, attachment, thinking* and the *conscious/unconscious* mind?

What exercises could you employ in order to enhance Tony's conscious awareness of his eating as well as facilitating the power and control to stop?

References

Brusch, H. (1973) *Eating Disorders: Obesity, Anorexia Nervosa and the Person Within.* New York: Basic Books.

Cheek, D. and LeCron, L. (1968) *Clinical Hypnotherapy.* New York: Grune & Stratton.

Citrenbaum, C., King, M. & Cohen, W. (1985) *Modern Clinical Hypnosis for Habit Control.* New York: Norton.

Greenberger, D. & Padesky, C. (2015) *Mind Over Mood,* 2nd edition. New York: The Guilford Press.

Holmes, J. (2001) *The Search for the Secure Base.* London: Routledge.

Joseph, A. (2009) *Cognitive Behaviour Therapy.* Chichester: Capstone Publishing Ltd.

May, R. (1994) *The Discovery of Being.* New York: Norton.

Mearns, D. & Thorne, B. (2012) *Person-Centred Counselling in Action,* 3rd edition. London: Sage.

Morison, J. & Philips, G. (2001) *Analytical Hypnotherapy Vol. 1: Theoretical Principles.* Carmarthen: Crown House Publishing.

Nietzsche, F. (1883–1885) 'On Reading and Writing', in *Thus Spake Zarathustra,* http://quotesfor intellectuals.tumblr.com/post/148307542389/there-is-always-some-madness-in-love-but-there-is (accessed 12 June 2018).

Rogers, C. (1961) *On Becoming a Person.* London: Constable.

Túry, F., Wildmann, M. & Szentes, A. (2011) 'Tandem hypnosis with identical bulimic twins: Case report', *American Journal of Clinical Hypnosis,* no. 53, vol. 4, pp. 265–275.

Wallin, D. (2007) *Attachment in Psychotherapy.* London: The Guilford Press.

Young, J. & Klosko, J. (1994) *Reinventing Your Life.* London: Penguin Books.

Chapter 10

Working integratively with shame and guilt

> Guilt and shame often go hand in hand when entering the client's world. Each plays a key role in creating a new reality of self-hate and loathing. This new reality can be so entrenched that the client is unable to see beyond this. The feelings are so strongly internalised that clients can even fear anyone seeing them because they see themselves as truly unlovable individuals.
>
> Robina Zafar, Integrative Psychotherapist

Introduction

Shame and guilt are rather nebulous concepts, unseen, hard to prove, and yet manifesting within clients in numerous and complex ways. Alongside working with clients to support them with their mental health and life issues – as demonstrated in the previous chapters on bereavement and loss, anxiety, depression and relationships – as therapists we have found that it is important to consider and include a focus on shame and guilt that clients can experience. Nonetheless, how to work integratively with clients experiencing shame and/or guilt is rarely addressed within training materials and books for counsellors. Hence our motivation to include a chapter in this book on working with shame and guilt, through person-centred, relational, CBT and hypnotherapeutic modalities and their integration.

This chapter explores what shame and guilt are, how these can impact upon individuals, and how we as therapists can work integratively with shame and guilt. We use stories and case studies to illustrate key points and we also draw on a broader body of research. Again, as in previous chapters, our aim is to also have a self-development aspect in this chapter so that trainee counsellors and those working in mental health contexts can use this material for some self-exploration. Being human inevitably means experiencing shame and guilt; as such, to be an effective practitioner it is important to understand one's own triggers for shame and guilt, what feelings and behaviours shame and guilt can provoke in us, and how we look to processing our own shame and guilt so that we are able to work with clients by being present to their challenges. Firstly, we begin with a short story that perhaps demonstrates the nebulous nature of shame and guilt.

The boy, the dark ink, the sorceress, and the man who killed his wife

Although Tim was told by his teachers at school not to suck on his pen because ink can poison you, Tim was unafraid of the poison and so he would continue to indulge his fascination for the dark, sticky, liquid. The only problem was that Tim would have to spend up to 15 minutes in the bathroom at the end of every school day washing the ink off his fingers with liquid soap, otherwise SHE would reprimand him. 'Tim, don't come near me until you have washed that shit off your hands' is what the sorceress would say to him unless his hands were clean. Tim always thought this a strange thing for the sorceress to say, given that she intoxicated him with a dark sticky substance herself, a substance that he could feel in his brain, oozing out through the synapses, making him feel deeply ashamed and guilty for submitting to her will, especially given that the sorceress, Jean, was Tim's mother's best friend.

Tim was only 13 years old and yet Jean would often come and see him in his bedroom, touching him, encouraging him to make sexual contact that he didn't really want, and then Jean would make him ashamed and guilty for what he had done. 'This can't be normal,' Tim thought to himself, 'I must be inherently bad because of what I do with Jean. What would my mum think?' and he hung his head low, drooping his shoulders, as the toxin within called shame and guilt spread from his mind into his body.

Over time the toxicity inside Tim built up, even though he was no longer subjected to Jean's insidious control. Now an adult, the toxin within Tim was beginning to spread outside of his body, affecting his relationship with his new wife, Amy. Tim was so overwhelmed by the shame that he felt for defiling his mum's house when he was a boy, and by the guilt he had of actually physically enjoying some of his experiences with Jean, that he would provoke Amy into having arguments with him, just so that he could prove to himself that he was not worth the love of any woman. One day, as Tim was arguing with Amy, the dark liquid in his mind overtook any rationality that he had, weaponising Tim, giving him super-human strength. Tim observed himself strangling Amy until nothing was left of her, her last breath spent, and at that point he let go of Amy's throat and he escaped from his house. The police found Tim later that day confused, and riddled with shame and guilt. Tim was ashamed of himself for having behaved aggressively towards his wife, for having committed an unforgiveable act, for having broken a number of social taboos. Tim felt guilty for taking his wife's life, for being the reason why she was no longer alive. Tim stood trial for murder and was found guilty by a jury and given a life sentence for murder.

The above story demonstrates a number of interesting aspects to shame and guilt. The origins of shame and of guilt can be deeply rooted, from within childhood. There may be aspects of a person's childhood that have created shame and/or guilt within them, and many of these aspects may lie beyond the control of the person. Furthermore, a child who has no-one to turn to for support when experiencing distress or challenging situations may learn to internalise their feelings, and these feelings may be that of shame and/or guilt. Child abuse victims often do talk about the shame and guilt they feel, partly because they feel they enjoyed some of the abuse that they experienced, or that they then enjoyed abusing others. Child abuse victims will also often talk about how they felt alone in the abuse, how they had nobody supporting them; indeed, any allegations they might make to carers are likely to have been dismissed. The story above also illustrates how shame and/or guilt might be thought of as toxins that invade a person's mind and body and how these toxins can have a very real and significant impact upon that person's life or on the lives of those they know or love. Tim was so riddled with shame and with guilt that he was unable to experience a supportive and loving relationship with his wife – he acted in ways to sabotage that relationship. Furthermore, as a result of his shame and guilt remaining unprocessed and inside his mind and body, this led to him being overcome with rage and to his killing his wife. It is likely that Tim would then spend his entire stay in prison holding on to his shame and guilt, unless he was able and willing to access therapeutic support within a prison setting.

What is shame? What is guilt?

It is important to stress that this chapter is focussing on toxic shame and toxic guilt. This is because shame and guilt can play important, regulatory, roles within society. Thus, it may be that individuals follow ethical codes and social norms partly as a result of wanting to avoid the distressing feelings associated with shame and guilt. Shame and guilt become toxic when they become overwhelming for individuals, paralysing them from taking action and responsibility over their lives. Shame and guilt can be toxic when they become a significant aspect of any mental health problem that a person may be experiencing. Shame and guilt can also have a toxic effect upon how mental health issues are experienced in terms of symptoms, ability to disclose upsetting and personal information, and in finding help. Toxic shame and guilt, if triggered in clients or within therapists themselves, can impact negatively upon the therapeutic relationship, leading to therapeutic ruptures (Gilbert & Procter, 2006).

In order to distinguish between shame and guilt, shame might be viewed as evaluating one's self negatively, whereas guilt might be seen as evaluating one's actions negatively. Thus, shame might involve thinking 'I am a bad person' whereas guilt might instead be thinking, 'I did some bad things' (Lewis, 1971; Beck et al., 2011). According to Gilbert and Procter (2006), shame can be viewed as consisting of two key aspects. There is external shame, which involves emotions and thinking patterns regarding how a person exists in the minds of others; there is also internal shame which involves the development of self-awareness, involving negative self-evaluations. The former aspect to shame can involve seeing oneself as unattractive and rejectable in the minds of others so that the person develops a range of defences such as hiding, concealing oneself, not wanting to be seen. The latter aspect to shame can involve the individual focussing upon themselves, developing for themselves feelings and evaluations of self as inadequate. It is important to note, however, that internal and external shame can be experienced concurrently, so that the outside world can be experienced as rejecting alongside an individual's own internal rejection of themselves (Gilbert & Procter, 2006).

Shame and guilt have attracted a lot of research attention in relation to trauma (Beck et al., 2011). For example, there is quite a considerable amount of research looking at combat veterans and their experiences of trauma, guilt and shame. This is because combat veterans are likely to have experienced action or inaction that can generate feelings of shame and guilt in them, as part of any trauma that they experience in combat (Norman et al., 2014). Guilt has also generated quite a lot of research interest in relation to obsessive compulsive disorder (OCD). Sometimes individuals with OCD may have obsessive illicit thoughts that generate in them significant guilt. Individuals with OCD may also have an exaggerated sense of responsibility, hence therapeutic work that seeks to facilitate clients re-evaluating their actual as opposed to perceived responsibility for things, together with a focus on developing an acceptance of any guilty feelings, can reduce OCD (Mancini & Gangemi, 2015).

There are multiple manifestations of shame and guilt as experienced in clients that we see in therapy. Lindenfield (2017) classifies guilt into ten different categories; below is a summary of each of these classifications:

Positive guilt – can provide the wrongdoer with the motivation to correct wrongdoings; includes anticipated guilt, for example, charity advertising on shop counters encouraging donations.

Suppressed guilt – consciously felt but not expressed; can foster mental health issues including low self-esteem and anxiety.

Buried/disguised guilt – unconscious guilt that is unprocessed; can be connected with mental health issues such as OCD, anxiety, addictions and depression.

Childhood guilt – usually originates from relationships with parents and significant others; involves the values of others as opposed to our own present values; often associated with behavioural issues, shame and low self-esteem.

Parental guilt – manifests through the desire for parental perfectionism in bringing up children; there is often a strong link between self-worth and the success of the child; parents can blame themselves for child misdemeanours.

Survivor guilt – common in people who have suffered major traumas, for example, in situations such as war where others have met a worse fate; symptoms can include being stuck in the past.

Affluence guilt – for example, through advertising that highlights people and countries that are less well off; can also be linked to influences from childhood.

Carer's guilt – involves the guilt of wanting to care better for someone.

Shameful guilt – includes both guilt and shame: not only do we think that we have done something wrong but our actions also prove that we are bad people; erodes self-confidence.

Religious guilt – can remain even after someone has given up a religion; multiculturalism in modern society can manifest guilt in living a life that conflicts with religious beliefs.

The above classifications can be useful in gaining an overview of our client's suffering but in many cases, the presenting problem masks issues of guilt and shame. Looking back through case studies for this book, it is surprising how often guilt and/or shame arise after several sessions of therapy, when the bond of trust between therapist and client is firmly established and the client feels that they can open up to the therapist. Clients can sometimes release a flood of emotions: anger, fear, resentment, loss – as they begin to discover more about the guilt and shame that they have held inside for so long.

A woman in her sixties came into therapy with the presenting problem of becoming over-emotional in specific situations; she felt as though her naturally empathic nature meant that she was too open to other people's suffering and emotional turmoil. This in turn made her tearful and stressed, particularly when dealing with her daughter and people involved in her business. As she discovered ways of calming her mind and distancing herself in emotional provoking situations, through techniques that worked upon establishing and maintaining strong boundaries with others, the guilt and shame that she had carried for decades appeared into her conscious awareness. She began to remember the abuse she and her sisters had suffered under their father; the guilt surrounding this abuse was coupled with shame that originated from her ex-husband's physical abuse of their *own* daughter. She blamed herself for not recognising and dealing with the abuse that was occurring at the time. Suddenly it all made sense to her: why she found it difficult to let go, why she couldn't detach emotionally, why she felt negative much of the time. At the tip of this vortex of turmoil sat guilt and shame. Through working on the parts within her responsible for guilt and shame, lifting the emotions and feelings of traumatic memories that she wanted to let go of and instilling forgiveness and compassion within herself, the client was eventually able to let go of guilt and shame. In her case forgiveness was the key that unlocked the door to wellbeing and peace.

Fear of the witching hour

The above example illustrates a progressive realisation of guilt and shame by the client. In some cases guilt and shame can appear very consciously and at specific times or due to specific situations and behaviours that are often repeated. A man in his thirties came into therapy with a fear of being awake at twelve o'clock and an issue with gambling; every evening he would go to bed at ten o'clock and find himself frantically trying to fall asleep before the alarm clock read twelve o'clock. On many occasions he found himself awake at twelve o'clock at night and he would then leave his house, drive to the casino in town and gamble. The issues surrounding this behaviour were complex; the man lived with his mother whom he cared for as a result of a debilitating condition that she endured. Trapped in a confined world, the man sought escape and excitement through illicit gambling, precipitating guilt that would make him feel low and unmotivated during much of the day. Because the gambling had spiralled out of control, a fear of being awake at twelve o'clock had developed as well as a sense of shame for leaving his mother unattended without her knowledge. His self-esteem had dipped to the point of considering some very dark options.

Instead of directly focussing on the fear of being awake at twelve o'clock, therapeutic interventions were utilised in order to release the shame that the client carried within him. Concepts such as *presence, emotional attachment and thinking* were used intergratively and the client was eventually able to let go of his shame. This allowed him to process the guilt that had occurred as a result of the gambling, priming the release of the addiction and ultimately alleviating the fear of being awake. Eventually the client was able to get a part-time job, organise help for his mother and lead a more fulfilling life.

Guilt and shame and the unconscious

Barnett (1989) suggests that the unconscious internal conflict between our ego states as a result of traumatic relationships from the past can manifest into feelings of guilt and shame. The following story illustrates this process:

The castaway

It was a hot suffocating night on board the good ship Venus when the perfect storm struck, casting one of the passengers, a man called Robinson, from the highest deck into the icy swagger of an ocean that broiled and bounced under the blistering rain and bullying gale. Robinson did not experience much of the storm for everything turned black as soon as he hit the water. The next thing he could feel, smell, touch was the damp sand beneath him and the wreaths of seaweed coiled about his ankles. The island was quiet and behind the tranquillity Robinson felt something imposing; unseen darting eyes directed upon him as he explored the beach, the wet sand folding under his feet. The feeling made him feel anxious and there was also the troubling, lingering thought that through his exile on the island, he was somehow being punished for his past life.

After a few days, the feeling of being watched subsided and Robinson began to consider the possibility of being stuck on the island forever. This could simply not happen! He would have to find a way of building some sort of raft. Fragments of the shattered ship had washed up on the beach and Robinson, in a moment of panic, had found a wine bottle and upon emptying the wine into his belly in a single swift draught, took up the notion of writing a message to no one in particular. One of the wooden boxes from the ship's cargo held some paper, ink and a quill. Robinson frantically scribbled *Help! I'm stuck on an island I know not where and wish to be saved! Robinson x.* He folded the paper into the empty wine bottle and cast it off to sea.

For several days he sat on a large rock looking out to sea but no one came. Then one day, when he had lost all hope of ever being found, he noticed a bottle floating in the sea. Surely it couldn't be the message he had written returning back to him! He dived into the water and returned with the bottle. But the message inside was different. *Don't bother trying to escape because you're no good! R x.* What was going on! Robinson cast the bottle behind him and heard it smash against the rock.

The next day he found another message in a bottle. *Stay where you are forever you wicked man! R x.* Once more Robinson threw the bottle at the rock. The next day another message: *You should never have acted in the way that you did! R x.* Every day now a new message would arrive, and each time it was more negative than the previous. Robinson began to feel guilty – had he done something in the past to warrant his status as a castaway? How could this person know so much about him? These thoughts filled him with anxiety and shame and he would spend his days wallowing in self-pity under the shade of a palm tree, waiting for the next message to arrive.

Then one day, he noticed a small mass of land in the distance. Another island! He dived into the water and swam towards it. Sure enough, there was another island. He walked up the beach a short distance to a hammock that swung gently in the breeze. There he found a young boy, frantically scribbling on some paper before placing it in a wine bottle. The boy's eyes widened as he noticed Robinson. A tear moistened the boy's cheek. 'So you found me then', the boy blurted out in between his sobbing. 'I thought I would have to write these messages forever.'

Robinson smiled and gently grabbed the boy under his armpits and lifted him off the hammock. They stared at each other. The older Robinson hugged the younger Robinson. 'I'm sorry that I wasn't there for you when you found out that mother had gone away.'

'I felt angry and I blamed you! Mother said you . . . me . . . were wicked and that was why she was leaving!' The younger Robinson pointed towards the older Robinson. 'But now that you're here I feel different, not so angry and ashamed.'

'There was nothing that you could have done,' the older Robinson said. 'She met someone else you see. . . .'

The younger Robinson nodded his head. 'I know. It was mother . . . not me . . . not you. I understand now.'

'Then let's swim back to my island and build a raft,' the older Robinson said.

'Yes, let's.' Holding hands, the two of them turned to the sea.

The above story illustrates the link between the often complex, acute feelings of guilt and shame that we carry in our lives and the unconscious conflict between Parent and Child ego states defined by Berne (1961). In the above example Robinson has been dealt a harsh blow but it is not the shipwreck that we are referring to; it is the controlling critical voice of his mother that has caused Robinson pain throughout his life. Robinson has carried his mother's admonishing remarks since childhood, illustrated by the messages sent to him by the younger version of himself. Labels such as 'not being good enough' or 'being wicked' have over the course of his life created an unconscious conflict within Robinson as he tries to break free of his mother's influence but at the same time is fearful of abandonment, punishing himself by aligning with his mother's worldview. In the story, Robinson's mother has an affair and eventually leaves but Robinson is not able to process this trauma. Instead the internal conflict within him, the guilt of being abandoned, makes him feel anxious and shameful about himself. In order to break free of the island and, in his mind, punishment for his past actions, he discovers that a meeting with his younger self allows the opportunity of reframing the emotions, thoughts and feelings surrounding past events. Once processed through the adult lens, any guilt and shame can be lifted and the two Robinsons escape the island for good.

Person-centred approaches and shame and guilt

Person-centred approaches can theoretically be linked to shame and guilt through the self and self-concept. As discussed previously in this book, person-centred modalities distinguish between the self and the self-concept, with the self-concept viewed as comprising of how other people perceive and value us whereas the self is that part of who we really are, our attributes and qualities (Rogers, 1951). The self-concept develops out of conditions of worth.

Conditions of worth comprise the wider environment in terms of the key relationships that we have and the messages that we get from these relationships as to what is valued in us by others. As humans we have an inherent need to be regarded positively by others, and so therefore we will often strive to be the kind of person that fits in with our self-concept, which is shaped by the conditions of worth that people attach to us (Mearns & Thorne, 2005). Where there is a disconnect between the self and self-concept there is internal conflict and strain. The disconnect between the self and self-concept can be experienced as shame and guilt. Thus, we can be ashamed of ourselves when we believe that who we really are (the self) doesn't match up to how we should be (the self-concept). We can feel guilt over actions that perhaps come from the self rather than the self- concept, believing that we have failed to act according to the values associated with the self-concept. Therapeutic work with clients can involve an exploration of the self and self-concept, so that clients gain a better understanding of any disconnection and how this might link to any shame and/or guilt that they may be feeling. Therapeutic work can also look towards empowering clients to accept their true selves rather than be judging themselves negatively through their self-concept, empowering clients to be able to forgive themselves, to be compassionate towards themselves. Acceptance of self can be a huge undertaking and so can take a large amount of time; indeed it might be argued that self-acceptance is a lifelong journey, especially given that humans are social beings for whom social comparison is innate (Gilbert & Procter, 2006). In constantly comparing ourselves to other people, and in caring about gaining acceptance from others, it can be a constant challenge for us to be free of toxic shame and guilt. Sometimes therapy can simply involve giving clients permission to be free of shame and guilt, to give them the space to be able to talk about what they feel ashamed and guilty of, for the therapist to validate their feelings whilst at the same time challenging any toxic shame and guilt that detrimentally impacts upon clients' mental health and wellbeing.

CBT in relation to shame and guilt

CBT approaches to shame and guilt distinguish between rational, or 'productive', shame and guilt and that of irrational shame and guilt. As previously argued in this chapter, shame and guilt can play an important role in ensuring that human beings follow wider ethical and social norms. Naturally, if a person breaks a moral code then shame and guilt are normal and if a person were not to feel shame and guilt then this might be because they are socio- or psychopaths! So it is unjustified shame and guilt that CBT practitioners focus on, whereby clients are overwhelmed by toxic, self-critical, shame and guilt, creating emotional distress for themselves and self-loathing. CBT approaches can involve helping clients to make a list of everything that they feel ashamed and guilty of, to then explore how rational or productive these feelings are and the extent to which the shame and guilt involves high levels of self-criticism. A thought diary can help a client to log triggers to their feelings of shame and/or guilt, to write down any automatic thoughts that they have, to then encourage clients to consider more helpful and less self-critical thoughts regarding themselves. CBT approaches look towards identifying and challenging distorted thinking in relation to shame and guilt. This links to the CBT based idea that maladaptive cognitions are learned and so therefore can be unlearned (Kuyken, Padesky & Dudley, 2011).

Distorted thinking in relation to shame and guilt may involve self-criticism, self-blame and also taking on too much responsibility for events that occur. A 'blame pie' can be a helpful intervention. This involves creating a pie chart with the client filling in people and other factors that they can attribute blame and responsibility towards, including blame towards themselves. The pie chart can then be used to explore and challenge any distorted sense of responsibility, self-blame and self-criticism. The exercise below is an example of a blame pie chart exercise.

1. Identify the issue that is causing you to feel ashamed or guilty.
    No room for mother-in-law at local hotel.
2. Make a list of the people and things that you think caused the issue.
    Husband, myself, mother-in-law, road closure, hotel.
3. Fill out the pie chart in terms of how much percentage blame you assign to each person and thing.

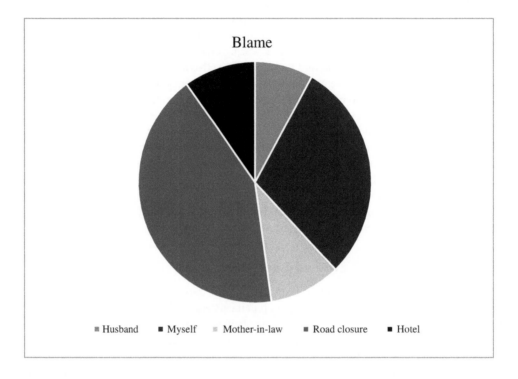

4. In terms of the pie chart, how much blame have you assigned yourself? How realistic is this?

Having a visual representation of blame can be really helpful for clients to see how much they blame themselves, other people and factors for any particular event. The client can also be encouraged to re-draw the pie chart so that it portrays a more accurate picture of blame. In this way clients may start to feel less shame and guilt once they have a more cognitively accurate sense of who and what is to blame for any given issue or situation.

Relational modalities and shame and guilt

It is important to consider different attachment styles and any possible connections here with shame and guilt. As previously discussed in this book, adults with a preoccupied attachment style can be overly bothered by what others think, feel and how they behave, experiencing relationships through the lens of anxiety (Holmes, 2014). It is likely that a client with a preoccupied attachment style has experienced the feelings of significant others as based upon certain conditions of worth. As a result, a client with a preoccupied attachment style is likely to blame themselves for things that happen in their lives, and to be highly self-critical. This means that shame and guilt are likely to be common feelings that such a client will experience. Clients with an anxious ambivalent attachment style are likely to experience relationships with significant others through anxiety and also through anger, and as such may overly blame themselves or others and may also be highly self-critical and/or highly critical of others. These dynamics will influence how clients with an anxious ambivalent attachment style experience shame and guilt. Clients with an avoidant style of attachment are likely to rely on themselves for their emotional needs and they tend to avoid becoming attached to other people, very fearful of being rejected (Holmes, 2014). It may therefore be the case that self-criticism and self-blame are high for such clients because they isolate themselves from others and so experiencing shame and guilt can be part of their experiencing isolation. Attachment-informed therapy when working with shame and guilt can involve the therapist presenting a secure base for the client through which they can explore their feelings of shame and guilt. It can be important to explore how a client experienced shame and guilt in their childhood, and any connections here with significant attachments that they formed. In this way clients can come to see that their current feelings of shame and guilt have histories, which is why these feelings can seem so overwhelming. In gaining a better understanding of the childhood origins of their shame and guilt, and in experiencing a secure base through the therapeutic relationship, this can be an effective way through which to process and alleviate toxic shame and guilt. Toxic shame and guilt can impact profoundly on clients' relationships with others and can be part of a dynamic of intimate abuse. As such, it is important to explore with clients how shame and guilt can influence the relationships that they have with others.

A community of resistance and sabotage

They lived in the darkest corner of the forest, in the shadows, so that they would be unseen and unheard. They made sure that they built their wooden houses in the densest part of the forest, so as not to attract attention, for attracting any kind of attention was collectively viewed by the community as sinful, as transgressing the fundamental community moral and ethical code of silence. There was no music or laughter or venturing out beyond the community perimeter, for shame and guilt were the only emotional experiences that this community knew and valued. Life was not about pleasure but about atonement. Any experiences that came from beyond the community perimeter, as smells or sounds, were resisted and even sabotaged. For example, once when a large music festival was taking place a few miles away the community members filled their ears with moss so that they would not hear the sound of live bands and merriment. Pleasure, joy, laughter, these were things to be ashamed of and to feel guilty about experiencing.

Into this community a young kitten called Cosmo arrived, as if magically from the cosmos. He was a ginger cat, tall and proud with huge paws. Cosmo knew how to enjoy himself: he would climb trees and leap around the grass, he would hunt mice and blissfully stretch out in any sunlight that had managed to squeeze its way through the dense foliage. The community shunned Cosmo, except for Ben, a teenager who was starting to question his community and its resistance to and sabotage of all things nice. Ben spent every hour of every day with Cosmo, and came to appreciate and see just how lovely life could be through the eyes, ears and paws of Cosmo. Eventually the community elders discovered what was happening and they grabbed hold of Cosmo and locked him in a shed so that there would be no more pleasure experienced by anyone or any sentient thing in this community. Ben spent every day and every night lying outside the place where Cosmo was being held captive, and he would talk to Cosmo and try to reassure him that he was not alone.

Then the angel of the forest revealed herself to Ben. Ben could not believe his eyes. He had heard talk of there being an angel in this dark and desperate place but he had never believed this. The angel was so bright that Ben could not look at her directly. The angel smiled at Ben and said,

> 'You must leave this place Ben, taking Cosmo with you. Follow the path that leads all the way to the outside of the community and keep walking along that path and you will find your new home, a space unburdened by resistance and sabotage of all things joyful. There you must stay and build a new life.'

Ben was shocked to see that the door to the shed had come open and that Cosmo had come running out, and had jumped onto his lap. Ben wanted to ask the angel some questions but she had disappeared and in her place a pathway had become visible. Ben did what the angel had told him to do, and he managed to leave this community of resistance and sabotage. Nonetheless, it took many years of playing with Cosmo for Ben to truly leave behind any lingering feelings of shame and of guilt.

The story above demonstrates the collective nature of shame and guilt. It can be important to explore a client's wider environment in terms of their shame and guilt. It may be that sometimes a client lives within, or comes from, a community that has experienced conflict and trauma. As a result, there may be social taboos around experiencing positive emotions, and so a client may experience shame and/or guilt simply for experiencing emotions that are stigmatised within their wider communities. Clients may also experience survivor shame and guilt where they have survived a particular event whereas others have died or continue to suffer. The social dimensions to shame and guilt can be huge.

Hypnotherapeutic modalities and guilt and shame

Hypnotherapy provides a wide range of modalities for treating guilt and shame; the process of getting a client to relax into hypnosis and use their imagination under the guidance of the therapist establishes a natural bond between therapist and client as they share the clients' experiences together. This unique relationship allows the client, over time, to convey his guilt and shame without fear of being judged. *Presence* within the therapist allows him to recognise, not only the mental aspects of shame, but also the physical manifestation of this condition in his client through, for example, a withdrawn posture with the head directed downwards. Recognising the unconscious 'physical' manifestation of shame may prove valuable in situations where the client is not directly aware of his/her shame or does not wish to talk about it.

Since guilt and shame may be rooted from childhood, *age regression* can be utilised for exploring past experiences in order to process emotions and feelings surrounding the guilt and shame. *Age progression* can allow the client to experience themselves without guilt and shame, or to imagine themselves dealing with future situations in ways that are more in line with their values, facilitating the concept of dissociation from these states as well as promoting feelings of freedom and release. Reframing through direct and indirect suggestions can affect the experience of guilt and shame; as Kashdan & Biswas-Diener (2015) suggest, guilt can provide the motivating factor to improve behaviours – itself an example of a reframe that can be introduced as a suggestion. Erickson, Rossi and Ryan (1998: 207) provide an example of a paradoxical suggestion within the indirect treatment of guilt that allows the client to draw upon the multiple meanings within a seemingly direct instruction. For example, Erickson may suggest to a client experiencing guilt over extra-marital affairs that he 'ought to have less guilt about his affairs', understanding that the client will reduce his guilt by *reducing the number of affairs* that he has. Suggestions for releasing guilt and shame can be embedded within metaphors and stories; Hammond (1990: 312–313) provides examples of guilt relieving suggestions that involve the imagination of the client, for example, a hallway with a 'Doorway of Forgiveness' at the end. The client can access this doorway after they have passed through other doors that lead into rooms where the client can experience whatever they see in the room, leading to a resolution of a past experience or relationship involving guilt. Often this type of experience is accompanied with an *abreaction*, allowing the release of suppressed emotions, while suggestive techniques such as these can be employed over several sessions of therapy.

Case studies in working integratively with shame and guilt

Case study 1: Emily

Emily is a 19-year-old student in her second year at university. Emily has accessed counselling because she has been experiencing insomnia and has been finding it hard to eat. Emily is also finding it difficult to revise for her exams because she finds herself easily distracted. She is unable to focus and finds that she ruminates a lot about the past. Emily cheated on her long-term boyfriend. Whilst at university she has been intimate with other men behind her boyfriend's back. Emily feels ashamed of herself and feels guilty about her behaviour. Emily would like to feel less ashamed and less guilty because she is overwhelmed by too much shame and guilt than she can handle. Emily has not yet told her boyfriend about what she has been doing and so feels very conflicted – guilty for not telling him but very afraid of losing him.

When working integratively with Emily, the therapist in this case drew upon the five integrative concepts outlined previously in this book – *presence, emotional processing, attachment, thinking,* and our *conscious/unconscious* minds. The following is a summarised account of the therapist's work with Emily, focussing on these core integrative concepts.

The therapist noticed that when Emily arrived for her first counselling session she would not look him in the eye, instead looking down on the ground. Emily also was stooped and the therapist gained a sense that Emily was trying to minimise her *presence*, that she did not want to be seen or noticed by anybody, including the therapist. The first three sessions with Emily were spent building a strong therapeutic relationship and this meant the therapist taking his time with Emily, not rushing in to doing any deep therapeutic work with her. Emily needed to feel that she was safe with her therapist and that she would not be judged by him. The therapist showed Emily Maslow's hierarchy of needs and explored this with her, as a way of increasing Emily's understanding that she has various physical and emotional needs as a human being and that meeting those needs can be a challenge. Maslow's hierarchy of needs also demonstrated to Emily that she can have *unconscious* needs that influence her behaviours, thereby encouraging some self-compassion in Emily. This focus helped Emily to start to see that she might not be the bad person she thought she was, that she was simply struggling with being human. In order to help Emily tolerate any distressing thoughts and emotions in relation to shame, guilt or any other feelings, the therapist introduced Emily to relaxed breathing and mindfulness techniques as a way of developing *presence*. Emily began to see that she could tolerate better her shame and guilt and that she could let go of thoughts better.

Sessions four to seven were spent focussing on *emotional processing* and *attachment*. Emily was encouraged to write a letter to her boyfriend expressing what she had done and how she felt about this. Emily brought this letter to a counselling session and read it out to the therapist. Emily found this session emotionally intense but also cathartic in that she could process some of her powerful emotions regarding the shame and guilt she felt. The therapist explored with Emily what she would like to do in relation to her boyfriend and Emily was encouraged to make a list of all the positives and negatives to telling her boyfriend what she had done. Emily committed herself to telling her boyfriend whatever the consequences were as a way of facing up to her deceit. Emily also now felt better able to cope with her boyfriend ending the relationship with her through the mindfulness and presence related techniques that she was practising regularly. The therapist also explored Emily's childhood and her relationships with her parents and grandparents. Emily developed a deeper understanding of herself, the impact that her father cheating on her mother had made on her. The therapist explored healthy and unhealthy attachments with Emily, and through exploring a secure base with the therapist, and in exploring her secure attachment with her grandfather, Emily was better able to see the kind of relationships that she wanted to create in her future.

Sessions eight to thirteen were used to document, explore and help Emily to challenge some of her unhelpful and distorted *thinking* about herself, using a thought log. Emily began to develop positive self-talk and she also made a list of her positive qualities as a way of taking attention away from her weaknesses.

By session fourteen Emily talked about feeling less ashamed and guilty of her actions. Emily had built the courage to tell her boyfriend about what she had been doing and although her boyfriend broke up with her Emily felt able to deal with a future without him. Emily also talked about understanding herself better and how her unconscious need for love and acceptance and how her insecure attachment style had led her down a pathway of cheating. Emily reported feeling less ashamed of herself and less guilt.

Case study questions

How, and in what ways, are person-centred, CBT and relational modalities relevant in this case study ?

What might be some of the challenges for a therapist when working with a client who has been deceitful?

What interventions might you use when working with Emily's self-criticism ?

Case study 2: Sarah

Sarah, a 35-year-old woman, came into therapy with the presenting problem of guilt and shame over a relationship with her partner that had broken down. During the consultation Sarah talked openly about her problems, admitting that the source of her guilt was her self-perceived 'stalker' behaviour towards her ex-partner. During the last few months of their relationship, Sarah would check her partner's digital footprint, logging onto social media websites to check whether he was communicating with females. Sarah would wait for her ex-partner to fall asleep and then take his mobile phone. On some occasions she would encourage him to drink and smoke marijuana, wait until he became incapacitated, and then reach for his phone once more. This repetitive cycle of behaviour fed Sarah's jealousy, particularly when she had found her ex-partner had been communicating with previous girlfriends on sites such as Facebook and Instagram. During these periods her own relationship with herself had broken down to a point where she found herself hating everything about her behaviour.

Tied in with her overwhelming guilt was an ingrained shame about her own existence. Sarah believed that this shame was due to the belief that she was, just like her father, a bad person who relied upon bullying and controlling behaviour in order to manipulate relationships. She wished that she could have stood up to him more when he was alive. The client believed that she had inherited her own negative self-evaluation from her father, who was prone to periods of depression. Her goals for treatment were to stop the obsessive checking – even though the ex-partner had left their home several weeks ago, the client would find herself obsessing over him and checking his social media presence – and to lose the guilt and shame over her 'stalking' and to 'live an honest life', a life that would fulfil and make her happy.

The following is a condensed account of the therapist's sessions with Sarah, working integratively with the five concepts of *presence, emotional processing, attachment, thinking and the conscious/unconscious* mind, presented in previous chapters.

The guilt and shame that Sarah carried within had displaced her from her own identity and sense of self. The first four sessions were focussed upon establishing a strong *presence* within her, a presence and sense of self that she could identify with beyond the walls of guilt and shame built around her current existence. Simple breathing exercises coupled with mental visualisation of pleasant memories of places that she had visited (Sarah was a keen traveller) were introduced. Sarah began to learn how to focus upon any pleasant feelings and sensations manifested within her from thinking positive thoughts. She reported feeling more positive at home; because Sarah was a keen cook, the therapist suggested an exercise where she was instructed to prepare a meal giving it total focus and attention so that she could experience every stage of the cooking process fully present and in the moment. Sarah enjoyed the silent ritual of this exercise and how it fostered within her the scope of looking inwards as well as developing awareness of what was happening around her.

Through mental visualisation in a deeply relaxed state, Sarah was able to understand the concept of building and maintaining strong boundaries with others. While under hypnosis she imagined herself as a large castle surrounded by a moat filled with still water. Her imagination provided her with feelings of power, control and security. By fostering a sense of *presence* and being more focussed upon establishing strong boundaries between self and others, Sarah was able to realise that she had no control over other people and how they behaved. The realisation that she could take responsibility for herself and her actions/reactions facilitated a belief that she could lift the guilt over her past behaviour with her ex.

The next two sessions focussed on lifting the feelings of guilt and shame through *emotional processing*. Age regression was used under hypnosis to take Sarah back to key memories of her relationship with her ex, providing the therapist with opportunities for utilising reframing and metaphors in order to help Sarah process the difficult emotions and feelings that she hadn't dealt with at the time. For example, shame and guilt were reframed through suggestions: 'The fact that you have these negative emotions of guilt and shame means that you are a good person.' Sarah was able to manifest the guilt 'part' within her, which she reported appearing as a 'red fuzzy blob', providing opportunities for reframing this part as well as externalising and dissociating from it. Age progression was utilised through hypnosis in order for Sarah to imagine herself at some point in the future without the guilt and shame. This strategy reinforced the goals that Sarah had set with the therapist during the initial consultation.

During these sessions the client began to experience less guilt, felt less emotional in general and had started to lose the anger that had built within her over the last few months. Since her shame was linked to the relationship with her father, Sarah began to explore this connection with the therapist. Reframing was utilised through suggestions under hypnosis: 'Perhaps if he hadn't cared about you so much then he wouldn't have acted in the way that he did' – while stories with metaphors suggesting the idea of letting go and moving on allowed Sarah to further develop an identity of self that was independent of her father.

Sessions seven to nine focussed on breaking the client's *attachment* with her ex-partner and lifting the obsessive 'stalking', which had started to gradually lessen over time. Utilising hypnosis, the client was able to break the obsessive checking by going through the thought processes and actions that accompanied such events and 'scrambling' them into a different pattern of behaviour. Instead of thinking 'Is he still talking to that woman?' and then following this up with a visit to Facebook, Sarah imagined herself visiting the social media site *before* having the thought. In this way, the pattern of obsessive behaviour began to dissolve.

Sarah wanted to put the relationship behind her, recognising that her ex-partner had liaisons with prostitutes (allowing her 'stalking' to be framed as a perfectly natural response due to his behaviour), was deeply complex and manipulative as well as depressed. Sarah challenged her distorted *thinking* through writing her negative thoughts on postcards and then challenging these with positive statements focussed upon building self-esteem and confidence. She began to change her attitude to her ex-partner, acknowledging that the 'focus was on him all the time', while her emotional needs were not met. Sarah set goals for herself, writing these down on postcards. Her goals included 'to think about me' and to let go of the anger, sadness and guilt. Sarah recognised her partner as a narcissist while she played the role of care-giver in the relationship.

By now Sarah had fewer thoughts about her ex-partner and no longer checked his social media so frequently. She reported feeling as though a weight had lifted from her and felt more at peace, accepting that the relationship had ended. She had returned to work and was more focussed on the future. During the final three sessions, the direction of therapy was aimed towards ego-strengthening, confidence boosting and the *conscious/unconscious* mind. Sarah wrote her goals down in a diary and was instructed to imagine achieving these goals while in a relaxed state, developing her conscious awareness of the future. Metaphors and stories were directed towards the *unconscious* mind during hypnosis in order to reinforce the message that it no longer had to *punish* the client with emotions such as guilt and shame. At her final session, Sarah reported that she no longer felt guilty about the past and her actions, had not checked her ex-partner's presence on the Internet for over a month, and was looking forward to the future and getting a new job.

Case study questions

What interventions could you design in order to help Sarah deal with her perceived 'stalking'?

How could you work integratively with Sarah in order to help her lift her shame and guilt?

What metaphors or stories could you create to reframe Sarah's 'bad person' association with her father?

Conclusion

This chapter has focussed upon two key issues that often underpin clients' concerns: shame and guilt. We have explained what shame and guilt might involve and we have presented case studies of how we work integratively with shame and guilt. We also have demonstrated the subtle nuances of shame and guilt and the complexities of the therapeutic work that is involved here. We have also discussed shame and guilt through the theoretical lenses of CBT, person-centred, relational and hypnotherapeutic modalities. The next chapter is the conclusion to the book, where we summarise the key points of learning within each chapter.

References

Barnett, E. A. (1989) *Analytical Hypnotherapy*. Glendale: Westwood Publishing.

Beck, J., McNiff, J., Clapp, J., Olsen, S., Avery, M. & Hagewood, J. (2011) 'Exploring negative emotion in women experiencing intimate partner violence: Shame, guilt and PTSD', *Behavior Therapy*, vol. 4, no. 42, pp. 740–750.

Berne, E. (1961) *Transactional Analysis in Psychotherapy: A Systematic Individual and Social Psychiatry*. New York: Grove Press.

Erickson, M., Rossi, E. & Ryan, M. (1998) *Life Reframing in Hypnosis*. London: Free Association.

Gilbert, P. & Procter, S. (2006) 'Compassionate mind training for people with high shame and self-criticism: Overview and pilot study of a group therapy approach', *Clinical Psychology and Psychotherapy*, vol. 13, pp. 353–379.

Hammond, D. C. (1990) *Handbook of Hypnotic Suggestions and Metaphors*. New York: Norton.

Holmes, J. (2014) *John Bowlby and Attachment Theory*. London: Routledge.

Kashdan, T. & Biswas-Diener, R. (2015) *The Power of Negative Emotion*. London: Oneworld.

Kuyken, W., Padesky, C. & Dudley, R. (2011) *Collaborative Case Conceptualization* London: The Guilford Press.

Lewis, H. (1971) *Shame and Guilt in Neurosis*. New York: International Universities Press.

Lindenfield, G. (2017) *Skip the Guilt Trap*. London: Thorsons.

Mancini, F. & Gangemi, A. (2016) 'Deontological guilt and obsessive compulsive disorder', *Journal of Behavior Therapy and Experimental Psychiatry*, vol. 49, pp. 157–163.

Mearns, D. & Thorne, B. (2005) *Person Centred Therapy Today: New Frontiers in Theory and Practice*. London: Sage.

Norman, S., Wilkins, K., Myers, U. & Allard, C. (2014) 'Trauma Informed Guilt Reduction therapy with combat veterans', *Cognitive and Behavioural Practice*, vol. 21, no. 1, pp. 78–88.

Rogers, C. R. (1951) *Client-Centered Therapy*. Boston: Houghton-Mifflin.

Stuart, W. (2015) *Understanding Guilt and Shame in Counselling and Psychotherapy*. London: Bishopstoke.

Conclusion

Integrative Counselling and Psychotherapy: A Textbook has presented an integrative approach to counselling and psychotherapy, particularly drawing upon CBT, person-centred, relational and hypnotherapeutic modalities. Chapters 1 to 5 have focussed upon explaining the core integrative concepts of presence, emotional processing, attachment, thinking and the conscious/unconscious. We have argued that a good understanding of these concepts, together with an appreciation of the key interventions that come through working with these concepts with clients, can be critical for effective therapeutic practice. Chapters 6 to 10 have then explored key issues that clients bring: grief and loss, anxiety, depression, relationships, and guilt and shame. We have explained each of these complex issues and have set out ways in which therapists can work with clients integratively, drawing upon CBT, person-centred, relational and hypnotherapeutic modalities. We have also provided many different case studies, together with questions, based on real clients, in order to stimulate discussion and exploration for individuals training to become counsellors and/or therapists. *Integrative Counselling and Psychotherapy: A Textbook* also contains many different therapeutic tools that can be applied to clients, which we think counselling students and practitioners will find useful. We will now summarise each of the separate chapters.

Chapter 1 has explored the integrative concept of *presence*. Through presence, we have drawn together a set of fundamental techniques that can help our clients: relaxation techniques, breathing techniques, mindfulness, body posture, grounding techniques, and pacing and leading. It is perhaps useful to firstly practise these techniques with our peers and in clinical supervision before we then draw upon them when working with clients. Chapter 1 also has a theory section where we have linked the notion of presence to theoretical concepts endemic to cognitive-behavioural (CBT), person-centred, relational and hypnotherapeutic modalities. In chapter 1 we have also argued that presence is key to developing a strong therapeutic relationship with clients, and the therapeutic relationship is a fundamental aspect of effective therapeutic practice.

Chapter 2 has focussed upon ways in which we can help clients to process their emotions. We have argued that within a therapeutic setting, emotions are a key aspect of relating to, and understanding, our clients and, importantly, facilitating our clients to be able to process and manage severe emotions can be a key aspect of therapeutic work. In Chapter 2 we have explored emotional processing through CBT, person-centred, relational and hypnotherapeutic modalities and we have shown how to work integratively with these modalities in relation to emotions. We have provided case studies with questions in order to facilitate learning, and we have presented techniques that can be effective when working with clients and their emotions: guided imagery, visualisation techniques, age regression techniques, the use of a thought diary, mood cards and many other tools.

Chapter 3 has explained attachment as another core integrative concept. Increasingly, attachment is focussed upon through a wide range of different therapeutic schools. In Chapter 3 we have explored attachment through CBT, person-centred, relational and hypnotherapeutic modalities, and we have explored how we might work integratively with attachment in relation to our clients. We have also explored healthy and unhealthy attachments and have provided exercises that can be linked to working integratively with attachment, including mindfulness-based techniques, a focus on interpersonal boundaries, mentalisation, and working with clients' lifetraps. We have also presented case studies based on our integrative therapeutic work with real clients and have presented case study questions to encourage reflection and discussion.

In Chapter 4 we have explored the importance of looking at thinking content and thinking patterns or styles both within our clients and ourselves as therapists, as thoughts are key to therapeutic practice. We have explored thinking through CBT, person-centred, relational and hypnotherapeutic modalities and we have presented case studies based on real clients, where we demonstrate the integration of these modalities when looking at thinking processes. We have also presented a number of interventions that can be used when working with clients, for example, exploring key questions in relation to the thoughts *Who am I really? How can I get in touch with this real self, underlying all my surface behaviour? How can I become myself?*; exploring adult, parent and child modes within our clients and implications for thinking content and patterns, and methods for the identification of negative automatic thoughts, underlying assumptions and core beliefs. We have also presented stories and case studies as a way of helping students and practitioners to develop their therapeutic work with thoughts further.

Chapter 5 has focussed on working integratively with both conscious and unconscious processes. We have explored the unconscious and conscious mind and have explored the role, and use, of stories, myths and metaphors in therapy and relate this to the interplay between the conscious and unconscious mind. We have presented the transtheoretical model of change (TTM) as a way of providing structure to integrative practice and have looked at how the TTM can be linked to conscious and unconscious processes. We have presented stories to explore the interplay between the conscious and unconscious mind, and we have also presented a case study that shows integrative practice in relation to working with conscious and unconscious processes.

Chapter 6 has focussed upon the challenges clients and therapists face when dealing with loss and bereavement. We have identified the principles involved within processing loss and bereavement through a combination of storytelling and the dual process model of grief, drawing from the work of key practitioners within this field. We have provided a broad range of interventions when working with loss and bereavement, including letter writing, commemorating anniversaries, discussing the feelings that accompany loss and letting go of obsessive memories and repetitive thoughts during grieving. An integrative approach to loss and bereavement incorporating CBT, person-centred, relational and hypnotherapeutic modalities is presented with practical examples of the use of therapeutic metaphors and use of creative language skills in order to present possibilities for positive change within clients experiencing grief.

In Chapter 7 we have explored the complex phenomena of anxiety, drawing from both theoretical and practical perspectives and presenting an integrative approach incorporating CBT, person-centred, relational and hypnotherapeutic modalities. We have included case studies highlighting the key integrative concepts of presence, emotional processing, attachment, thinking and the conscious/unconscious mind, and how these concepts are utilised when working with clients presenting anxiety and fear. A range of interventions for treating anxiety have been provided that explore metaphors and storytelling for reframing, use of the Transtheoretical

Model of Change (TTM) presented in Chapter 5, Maslow's hierarchy of needs, utilisation of unique characteristics of anxiety and emotional and cognitive processing.

In Chapter 8 we have proposed creative approaches to working integratively with depression, considering person-centred, CBT, relational and hypnotherapeutic modalities. Through stories and examples of working with clients we have illustrated the complex range of experiences associated with depressive states at physical, cognitive, emotional and behavioural levels. Within a person-centred approach we have provided examples of exploratory questions designed to help clients better understand their experience of depressive moods. We have included case studies that explore the integrative concepts of presence, emotional processing, attachment, thinking and the conscious/unconscious mind, providing creative suggestions for interventions when working with depression that include thought records, guided imagery, stories and metaphors, emotional processing and reframing.

In Chapter 9 we have considered the principles and processes involved in working integratively with relationships, taking into account both the relationship issues that clients bring to therapy and also the relationships that we, as therapists, have with ourselves. Through stories we have illustrated the link between a client's relationship with others and the link with the client's own internal relationship with themselves. We have provided a set of key questions for exploring relationships with ourselves, as therapists, within the context of creating a solid platform for becoming an effective mental health practitioner. We have explored the influence of the unconscious mind in relationships through a story, highlighting how our own internal values and belief systems can affect the relationships that we have with others. We have also considered significant relationship aspects in relation to the different health and wellbeing issues presented by clients. We have addressed the relevance of the different types of attachment styles – secure, preoccupied, anxious ambivalent, avoidant and disorganised – and how these affect client relationships. The complexities surrounding harmful relationships have been considered, with examples of eating disorders, gambling addiction and body image distortions. Included within this chapter are case studies that provide examples of integrative interventions for dealing with relationship issues. Interventions such as psychoeducation, activities for building mindfulness and presence, cognitive exercises for emotional processing and therapeutic metaphors have been outlined within the case studies and key case study questions provide opportunities for exploring different interventions based upon the integrative concepts of presence, emotional processing, attachment, thinking and the conscious/unconscious mind.

In Chapter 10 we have focussed on how to work integratively with clients experiencing guilt and shame. We have distinguished between guilt and shame and utilised stories that provide examples of how these states may originate in clients, classifying guilt into ten different categories in order to highlight the broad range of presenting problems involving guilt that a client may bring to therapy. The interplay between guilt and shame and the unconscious mind has been explored through storytelling, and we have provided strategies for working with guilt and shame in relation to CBT, person-centred, relational and hypnotherapeutic modalities. A 'blame chart' has been included for therapists and clients to explore and challenge self-blame and self-criticism. The case studies provided in this chapter have drawn upon the five integrative concepts outlined previously in the book: presence, emotional processing, attachment, thinking and our conscious/unconscious minds. Case study questions have been included for working integratively with clients experiencing guilt and shame.

Index